Twins Talk

TWINS
TALK

WHAT TWINS TELL US ABOUT
PERSON, SELF, AND SOCIETY

Dona Lee Davis

OHIO UNIVERSITY PRESS   ATHENS, OHIO

Ohio University Press, Athens, Ohio 45701
ohioswallow.com
© 2014 by Ohio University Press

To obtain permission to quote, reprint, or otherwise reproduce or distribute material
from Ohio University Press publications, please contact our rights and permissions
department at (740) 593-1154 or (740) 593-4536 (fax).

Printed in the United States of America
Ohio University Press books are printed on acid-free paper ∞ ™

24 23 22 21 20 19 18 17 16 15 14   5 4 3 2 1

Library of Congress Cataloging-in-Publication Data
Davis, Dona Lee, 1948–
Twins talk : what twins tell us about person, self, and society / Dona Lee Davis.
    pages cm
Includes bibliographical references and index.
ISBN 978-0-8214-2111-6 (hardback) — ISBN 978-0-8214-2112-3 (pb) — ISBN 978-0-8214-
4499-3 (pdf)
  1. Twins—United States. 2. Twins—Social aspects—United States. 3. Ethnology. I.
Title.
  GN63.6.D38 2015
  306.8750973—dc23
                            2014029923

CONTENTS

CONTENTS

ILLUSTRATIONS

ACKNOWLEDGMENTS

The idea of studying twins grew out of my experiences in giving a series of lectures on embodiment, self, and society at the University of Tromsø in Norway in the 1990s. During that time there was a considerable controversy among the indigenous Norwegian Sami people and representatives of the Human Genome Diversity Project. The controversies whet my curiosity about the relationships between genes and identity, but in a way that was much closer to home—the home of my own body. A study of twins promised to offer some interesting insights into many intersecting planes of experience and analysis, among which are body/biology, personal/social identity, relatedness/relationality, and culture. The two-day research opportunities offered at the Twinsburg, Ohio, Twins Days Festival made it all seem feasible. After having done fieldwork among fishers in Newfoundland and northern Norway, I found the prospect of conducting a study in an area where I had an insider's perspective based on my own lifetime of firsthand experiences of being a twin—of finally becoming a local expert—very inviting. *Twins Talk* as an exercise in quick ethnography was also developed as a way for my identical twin sister, Dorothy, and me to spend some time together. My intent at its most ambitious was to present some conference papers and perhaps an article or two. I had not anticipated how interesting twins would be to think with, and what started as a short-term project evolved into a much more involved endeavor.

As I became a twin researcher myself and became more and more immersed in the popular and scientific twin literature, I was put off by the predominating biological and genetic essentialism of twin research and the inherent pathologization of twinship or the twin relationship, most prominently in psychology but in other disciplines as well. Identical twins are variously depicted as clones, as a self and almost self inside the same physical package, and as a single unit or closed society of two. These characterizations seem to have minimal relevance to my own more than six decades of being a twin. What did resonate with my anthropological curiosity, however, were the contentions that identical twins are an unsettling presence that undermines a sense of uniqueness or challenges characterizations of selfhood in the wider (Western) society. My goal became twofold: First, to explicate just what those assumptions or characterization of selfhood were. And second, to provide a voice for twins in this process. Thus it is the intent of *Twins Talk* to quite literally address what twins tell us about the experience of being twins in Western society. And in turn, *Twins Talk* becomes a vehicle for comparing twins' own narratives of their being in the world to the narratives of those who have made twins topics of research. In the process, there emerges a very rich and rewarding source for informed anthropological analysis as it intersects with multiple other disciplines.

Many people over the years have helped with this Twins Talk Study. I would like to thank the Department of Social Anthropology at the University of Tromsø in Norway (now the Arctic University of Norway) and the Twins Days Festival Committee for their research grants that helped fund this study. The University of South Dakota (USD) Tuve Fund provided travel funds for Kristi Cody, the projects research assistant, as well as travel funds that enabled Dona to present papers at a number of professional conferences. Kristi Cody, an anthropology major at USD, was an enthusiastic and energetic research assistant. Sandy Miller and the Twins Days Festival Committee provided invaluable help and encouragement during the initial stages of this study. Angela Harrison successfully took on the challenging job of transcribing many hours of taped four-way conversations. Evie Clerx, Danielle Emond, Elizabeth Johnson, and, all USD undergraduate students, have also worked with me on this project. Thanks also go to Jane Nadel-Klein, Gisli Pálsson, Barbara Prainsack, and Elizabeth Stewart for their encouragement and support of the project. Of course, special thanks go to the forty-four twins who participated in the Twinsburg Twins Talk Study, taking the time to sit down and share their lives and experiences of being twins. I hope they enjoyed these conversations. I certainly did. Their stories helped confirm how interesting and wonderful it is to be a twin. Extra special thanks to my twin sister, Dorothy Davis, who played an essential role in the data gathering and attended three festivals with me. It was the first time in our lives that we had the opportunity to talk as twins to twins. Finally, thanks to Richard Whitten, my life partner, whose love and support I will always treasure.

TWINSCAPES

A Sufi teaching story tells of the holy fool Mulla Nasrudin who
ventured to a strange city. Before he left on his journey, his wife
put a sign around his neck with his name on it so that he would
not forget his identity. When he arrived, he spent the first night at a
caravanserai; while he slept, a joker took the sign and put it around
his own neck. When the Mulla awoke, he was appalled to find his
name tag on the joker's chest. "It seems," he cried, "that you are me.
But if you are me, then who am I?"

        —Lindholm 2001

Each individual is biologically unique.

        —Pálsson 2007

What would it be like to have lived one's whole life without ever
having seen your own face?

        —Herdt 1999

LIKE CHARLES LINDHOLM, I BEGIN MY BOOK WITH A FOOL'S TALE.
Lindholm (2001, 3) places the Sufi story at the very beginning of his
book *Culture and Identity*, in chapter 1, titled "Who Am I? The Search
for the Self." He comments that although the Mulla's dilemma is "ridiculous," it nonetheless raises central issues concerning the development of a more culturally sensitive or nuanced understanding of one's

sense of someoneness, or identity. The physical body, perceptions of self in relation to other selves, and self as positioned or situated and acting within a wider cultural milieu are all essential components of one's sense of self (de Munck 2000; Markus et al. 1997). Yet, if you are an identical twin, Mulla's "ridiculous" dilemma becomes a kind of double entendre. In the case of identical twins, the fool's tale becomes real. There actually is someone else who is wearing the visual signs of your identity on their face and body. Twins' physical similarities often result in others confusing, confounding, and conflating their self-identities. Moreover, for twins raised together, their senses of someoneness develop in a dyadic, coexistent mutuality, or sharing of place and space that actually begins before birth. It should come as no surprise that the academic literature, as well as popular imagination, depicts identical twins as living embodiments of two related questions: "What is truly other and what is self?" and "Is it possible to inhabit another person's being?" (Neimark 1997, 3).

SITUATING TWINSCAPES

This is a book about situating twinscapes. *Twinscapes* refers not only to the visual resemblances of the surfaces of twins' bodies, but also to their side-by-side appearance as a pair. This book is about twins who look alike and share space and place. As such, it focuses on twins whose physical likeness is so marked that their identities are easily confused by others.[1] *Twinscapes* as presented in this text also implies not only a view of two look-alike bodies but visions of hundreds or even thousands of twins attending twins festivals and performing their twinship for the gaze of others. Twinscapes as developed in *Twins Talk* also include identification and explanation of the various ways in which twins are subjected to the gaze of academic researchers as they in turn reflect popular or normative cultural ideals related to notions such as identity, autonomy, and mutuality. My aim is to go beyond the observations of researchers who objectify twins and view them as forever silent: frozen side by side in photographs, or reduced to their genes, particular body parts, or a series of testable independent and dependent variables. Many of the deeper questions of twinship, such as the possibilities of inhabiting each other's being, of being betwixt and between, of being simultaneously unique and contingent, are raised in only a symbolically abstract or rhetorical sense (Farmer

1996). There is no voice for twins themselves, as agents of biosocial becoming (cf. Ingold and Pálsson 2013), in this research. How they, as twins, actively construct and negotiate their own twinscapes remains invisible, under the research radar, so to speak. As instruments or objects of research, even anthropologists tend to portray twins in terms of essentialized or generic cultural identities such as Ndembu twins in central Africa or twins in Haiti. Twinscapes, however, are actively situated or positioned within the twin dyad itself. In this view twinscapes illustrate twins' own perspectives on themselves as twins in a "singleton" world. It includes the ways twins see how others view them and also their perceptions of each other. Twins' views on living in and having identical bodies, on their twinship or relational bond, and on daily living with a cultural persona that is both lauded and ridiculed are not always in accord with the vision of twins researchers.

The purpose of this book is to show how identical twins, like the surprised Mulla, challenge commonplace notions of identity. Most books on twins deal with behavioral genetics, the psychology of twins, or how to best raise twins (Piontelli 2008); target audiences are other twins researchers, clinicians, educators, and parents of twins. As in the popular and scientific twin research literature, this book engages the biological/genetic and psychological/relational attributes of twins and twinship. Yet, when it comes to grappling with the "Who am I?" questions raised by twins, this book takes some innovative stances.

First, as the title states, *Twins Talk* seeks to capture the insider's experiences of twinship. This study features and privileges twins' own words about how they actively negotiate lifelong challenges raised by the "Who am I?" question. For identical twins, however, the "Who am I?" (as what is truly self and what is truly other) question hardly ends the story. Self-talk among identical twins also raises issues and questions of "Who are you?" "How are you me?" "How are you not me?" as well as "Who are we?" "How and when should I be me?" and "How and when should I be we?"

Second, I aim to present and analyze the positive as well as negative aspects of the twin experience that go beyond simple platitudes, such as "having a friend for life" or having a "special bond." My focus is on the lived, grounded, day-to-day, and lifetime practical experiences and challenges of being twins. Third, if twins are a mirror of "us all" (cf. Wright 1997), then it is necessary to make the "us all" more explicit. If identical twins undermine our notions of a unique self, then what exactly is this unique self? In *Twins Talk* my aim is to subject Western culture to a critical analysis by comparing and contrasting the selving styles depicted in twins talk to self stylings across a variety of historical and cultural contexts.

TWIN RESEARCH

Scientific perspectives on twins are at best ambivalent. Early nineteenth-century twins researchers (Cool 2007, 7) portrayed twins as both monsters and wonders existing at a tripartite nexus of horror, pleasure, and repugnance. Today, the fields of biology, biomedicine, and psychology dominate the scientific literature on twins. Issues of heredity, although going through a major paradigm shift, continue to dominate biological studies of twins (Charney 2012; Spector 2012). The older school of genetic determinism (Bouchard Jr. and Popling 1993; Galton 1875), viewing nuclear DNA as a blueprint for self, emphasized the genetic identicalness of twins as shared inherited traits rooted in or reducible to biology and little influenced by environmental factors. Emphasis is placed on sameness or being the same. Genetically identical twins in this modeling of genetic inheritance are referred to as clones (Wright 1997) or contemporary clones (Charney 2012; Prainsack and Spector 2006; Spector 2012). In contrast, the more recent emerging field of epigenetics (Charlemaine 2002; Peltonen 2007) focuses on heritable changes not due to structures of DNA but due to cellular mechanisms that turn genes off and on. Stressing genetic flexibility and adaptation, this postgenomic view focuses on inter-twin epigenetic differences—or what Spector (2012) terms twins who are identically different. Rather than differentiate between genes and environment, epigenetics moves away from the older ideas of genetic determinism and introduces news, more interactive ways of thinking about genes and their environment in terms of flexibility and adaptation (Charney 2012). Despite their differences, both paradigms present a gene-centered view aimed at discovering the hidden or subcellular life universes of twins.

If genetics reduces twins to their genes, biomedicine pathologizes twins by focusing on complications of pregnancy and birth for the mothers as well as the twins (Piontelli 2008). The twin relationship or bond is and has been a continual focus of twin research in the field of psychology. While their closely developed emotional ties or intense closeness (Klein 2003) may be celebrated as a unique dyadic capacity to understand and be understood (Bacon 2005; Piontelli 2008; Rosambeau 1987), psychologists tend to describe twins as somehow aberrant or compromised selves and as at risk for a wide range of psychological impairments (Conley 2004; Kamin 1994) and illnesses (Joseph 2004). Twins portrayed as genetically the same and as too close raise an interesting range of sociocultural issues about biological and psychological identity, as well as issues concerning autonomy and mutuality (Battaglia 1995a; Maddox 2006; Prainsack and Spector 2006; Prainsack, Cherkas, and Spector 2007). Like psychologists, sociologists are concerned with the development of a normative independent self and how the closeness and intimacy of twins may complicate identity both within the inter-twin relationship and twins' relationships with the wider social worlds in which they live (Klein 2003). Anthropologists have tended to focus on twins, as a generic category, in terms of exotic attitudes, beliefs, and practices (such as ritual and infanticide) in faraway, non-Western cultures (Dorothy Davis 1971; Diduk 1993; Granzberg 1973; Lester 1986; Lévi-Strauss 1963; Stewart 2003; Turner 1967).

The notion that twins pose and encounter difficulties in the process of identity formation is as pervasive in popular culture as it is in science (Joseph 2004). Twins have been popularly portrayed as objects of wonder, fascination, and fear since the beginning of recorded history (Schave and Ciriello 1983; Klein 2003). Identical twins have been described as seeing double (Wagner 2003), as eerily similar (Neimark 1997), as "unwitting dancers choreographed by genes or fate" (Neimark 1997, 2), as individuality-burdened freaks of nature (Maddox 2006), and as a walking sideshow with four legs (Schave and Ciriello 1983). Twins are disparaged as having mutual or symbiotic identities, as being two halves of the same self (Neimark 1997), as being self and almost self inside the same physical package (Wright 1997), or as being a closed society of two (Kamin 1974).

FAULT LINES AND DEVIANT PERSONA

Whether characterized as an unsettling presence or exceptional exceptions, identical twins may be viewed as what anthropologists have described as a kind of deviant cultural persona (Holland and Leander

2004, 279) or as located on the fault lines (Conklin and Morgan 1996) of identity.[2] These concepts will become central to my analysis in *Twins Talk*. First, the notion of fault lines helps explicate the "us" and "who" as in Wright's (1997) *What Twins Tell Us about Who We Are*, or what exactly is the customary order that twins cause a rift in (Neimark 1997). Identical twins exist on the fault lines to the extent that they challenge, confound, or deviate from normative expectations about self, personhood, and identity. Twins challenge natural assumptions that every individual's body is biologically distinct and unique. For example, Herdt (1999) asks his readers to imagine what a sense of self would be like—as among the mirror-less Sambia he describes—if you have never seen your own face and only see yourself reflected in the faces of others. Yet, for identical twins, there is actually someone else walking around with "your" face and body. In addition, identical twins, in terms of their relationship within the twin dyad, also embody and enact a series of tensions or dialectical qualities of identity held to be characteristic of Western culture. In the spirit of Mulla's question, "If you are me, then who am I?" (Lindholm 2001, 3), identical twins bridge dualisms of same and different, autonomy and mutuality, separate and connected, and self and other, as well as you and me and us and them. Farmer (1996) philosophically refers to this as a kind of symbolic double duality.

From a more practical perspective, twins have to live in a singleton-dominated world where their respective identities can become confused or conflated and their relationship or twinship, rooted in long-term intimate sharing of space and place, is denigrated more than praised. Twins are not only located on the fault lines; they live on the fault lines. In this sense, identical twins constitute a cultural persona as they collaborate to interactively microproduce and perform a twin identity and position their selves as twins (Holland and Leander 2004) both vis-à-vis each other and vis-à-vis the wider singleton-dominated world in which they live. Mol (2003) describes identical twins as embodying a kind of fluid space where boundaries are not always demarcated and bonds between the elements (self/other) are not always stable. But stereotypical portraits of twins, passively embodying fluid space or existing on the fault lines, fail to see or incorporate an insider's perspective. Identical twins are active agents in their own experiential worlds. As twins they interrogate, oftentimes rather militantly, commonsense assumptions of what it means to be a person. In so doing, they advocate and enact alternative models of identity, relation, and selfhood within the wider domains of Western culture. Twins' own twinscapes provide an interesting perspective for consideration of how personhood may be worked through the body in thought and action as well as how images of the body serve as enactments of the social and moral ethos (Conklin and Morgan 1996; Csordas 1994). Identical twins offer an opportunity to examine a multiplicity of constructions and lived experiences of self and other in terms of intracultural diversity as well as in a comparative, cross-cultural context.

In writing this book, I am acutely aware that writing about famous or freaky twins sells books. Audiences and readers want to hear or read stuff about twins that confirms their weirdest stereotypes of them. I am frequently contacted by popular journalists looking for interesting angles on twins. Recently a BBC documentary producer contacted me to ask if I had any "really weird twins in my sample." She gave me an example of two twin women in Holland who had never married and lived together all their lives. The filmmaker was interested in any cases I might know of schizophrenic twins or other twins who were abnormally bonded. When I told her my work was with normal twins and my goal was to normalize twinship, she expressed no further interest in my studies. In the stereotypical view that this particular filmmaker wants to pursue, twins are not straddling the fault lines, they have fallen over the cliff; they are not deviating from an established norm, but are beyond the pale altogether.

At the same time, however, twins are also a more common phenomenon. Globally, today, there are over eleven million identical twins (Spector 2012). Although twins are exoticized in many ways, most of us have firsthand, personal knowledge of twins. A friend, neighbor, schoolmate, or coworker may well be a twin or have twins in the family. Oftentimes, when I lecture about twins, someone in the audience will respond with something to the effect that "My daughter has three sets of twins in her elementary school and really, they have none of the identity issues you describe. All the other kids know who they are and can tell them apart. Really, it's no big deal." During my first in-class lecture on twins, a student raised her hand and said, "I'm a twin and really, I don't find myself or other twins all that scary or creepy." Clearly, day-to-day acquaintances and personal interactions with twins both normalize twinship and elucidate and resolve a series of identity issues for those closely associated with them. What remains unspoken and underanalyzed, and probably is not so obvious unless you are a twin yourself (as my student's comment illustrates), is the active roles that twins take on, individually and together, to "educate or socialize" singletons on how to deal with the identity issues that they raise. Jenna, a participant in this study, makes this patently clear:

> Jenna: There are more differences in twins than what people who are not twins just don't understand. They think we look the same so we are the same. We're not. We're different people. And they don't get that concept. I think it's why twins zero in on the differences, because everyone else sees them as being so similar. We're not. And people get us mixed up and I'm like, Hello!

Twins raised in Western society are like the singleton majority and different from it. *Twins Talk* is about how twins go about normalizing, expressing, and performing their identity and relationship vis-à-vis other sets of twins and how they utilize their twinship to reconfigure "normality" and navigate their own selfways (Neisser 1997), or characteristic ways of being twins in the singleton world. "Like, Hello!" as voiced by Jenna, implies the roles twins must take on as they challenge the stereotypes that singletons may have about twins. All twins do this. To the extent that they are together, they do it pretty much all the time. This I call self work (Goodman 2008) or self styling. Self work is a complex business because it involves both actions as individuals and actions as twins. Poised on or viewed from the fault lines, twins embody selfways that both integrate their selves into wider, normative selfways *and* mark them as deviant. Singletons and the dominant culture hold stereotypes or characterizations of identical twins that identical twins both buy into and challenge with their own counterhegemonic self stylings. In so doing twins also take an active and interactive role in the "process of 'selving'" (Markus, Mullally, and Kitayama 1997, 13). By *self styling* I mean that once having adopted or established their mutual and individual identities, twins act to maintain the integrity of those identities (Neisser 1988, 36). Thus, being located on the fault lines, combating stereotypes, presenting alternative self stylings, while all the time "fitting in," requires a great deal of self work on the part of twins.

Self working is part of the practical experiences of twinship, often noted by researchers, but never (Prainsack et al. 2007) investigated in any detail. Located on the fault lines of society, identical twins' self working both confirms and challenges stereotypes and both bridges and delineates the dualisms of the wider society. Twins self-work as they go about answering Mulla's "Who am I?" question.

TWINSCAPES AND CULTURAL PSYCHOLOGY

Twinscapes are multifaceted, complex, and positioned. The concepts of self work, self styling, and selfways come from the school of cultural psychology. Identical twins, like all other humans, are both natural and social beings. Twins are not monolithic, and it would certainly be misguided to reduce them to their twinship. Their sense of personal and interpersonal identity and experience of twinship is, in turn, embedded in a wider sociocultural context that is also characterized by a great deal of diversity.

A cultural psychology[3] approach works well in the discussion of twinscapes, precisely because it is so multifaceted and recognizes multiple points of view (Chapin 2008; Jopling 1997; Markus et al. 1997; Neisser 1997). Not only does a cultural psychology perspective allow me to integrate what has turned out to be a collage of chapters on twins festivals, bodies, bonds, and life cycles drawn from different research venues, it gives primacy to personal, lived experience (Casey and Edgerton 2005; Holland 2001). First, it recognizes diversity or variation between different cultures and historical periods, as well as variations within them. Selfways and self stylings are emergent. They are situated and participate within particular and multiple, sometimes contradictory, contexts. Twins are not simply a category or a uniform group. Nor can or should they be reduced to their twinship. There are substantive differences to be found among them—biologically, cross-culturally, and intraculturally. For example, when it comes to independence and interdependence, two key features of the twin experience, comparisons within and between cultures demonstrate that there are multiple ways to construct and express interdependence and independence. Additionally, a cultural psychology approach positions insiders' views vis-à-vis outsiders' representations of them. Not only does this book address twins' and singletons' views, it also takes into account twins' views of singletons' views of twins. *Twins Talk* shows how twins are acutely aware that twins researchers have a culture too. Second, cultural psychology recognizes the importance of the embodied, physical, and perceptual self. If a self-system is where the individual as a biological entity becomes a meaningful entity, then "identical" twins, whose very biological individuality is challenged, undermine key assumptions of self-systems. With highly resembling faces and bodies that are confused or conflated by observers or even characterized as clones with the same underlying genetic blueprints, twins' self stylings and self work must start from physical baselines that are hardly familiar to singletons. Third, cultural psychology regards a person as not only situated in time and space but having a variety of interpersonal identities and participating in a variety of interpersonal relationships. Twinship, the twin relationship, or the twin bond is both praised and denigrated for its mutuality and is seen as having profound implications when it comes to nontwin relationships.

A cultural psychology approach also works well as a way of engaging the Twins Talk Study as a multisited study that includes participant observation at three twins festivals and two international twin research conferences, narrative data obtained during conversations with twenty-two sets of twins attending the Twins Days Festival in Twinsburg, Ohio, plus my own lifelong experiences of twinship with my identical twin sister, Dorothy. By collecting data at festivals where twins celebrate their twinship, by gathering narratives from twins themselves, and by positioning myself as an expert, both as a twin and as a researcher, I view twinscapes through the lens of cultural psychology to compare and contrast twins' perspectives on the twin condition to the perspectives of scientists who research twins. Twins are good to think with, but twins themselves never get to do much of the thinking. In *Twins Talk* my focus is on lived experience. Selfways and self work imply a need to get beyond thinking to doing and being (Neisser 1997).[4] A cultural psychology approach gives twins agency as they negotiate their identities, relationships, and lives in ways that simultaneously set them apart from and integrate them into the wider, normative cultural expectations. Twins rebel, adapt, and refine the "Who am I?" questions of twinship that in the twin research literature tend to be hegemonically asked and answered by nontwins. Language plays a critical role, and cultural psychology focuses its efforts on the collection and analysis of narrative. When pairs of twins talk about being twins, they present themselves as multifaceted beings in a wide variety of situations and contexts. They agree and disagree with each other, jump from topic to topic, and punctuate their conversation with caresses, slaps, tears, and laughter. The narrative data in this book invite an analytic framework that engages identities (the "Who am I?" questions) as enacted, imagined, negotiated, and embodied from the ground up (Holland et al. 1998).

Twins Talk is unique in the twin research literature because it seriously, critically, and literally engages the question of what twins tell us about ourselves. In *Twins Talk,* researchers come into an environment dominated by twins, rather than vice versa. When it comes to the twin research literature, twins are only a database; they neither get to determine and ask the questions nor get to provide their responses on or in their own terms. Rather than see twins as voiceless, passive objects of study, or as the carriers of "hidden" genetic codes, or as victims of "underlying" psychodynamic processes, and rather than reduce twins to a series of population-based statistics, a narrative study approaches twins as constructors of and actors in their own dramas. Narrative data from the Twins Talk Study come from sets of twins, in the company of each other, talking about what they feel is important about their experience of being twins. The data have an interactive, dialogic quality about it that is unique in the twin literature. It is the only study I know of that situates analysis in twins' own twinscapes, which include both twins' views of themselves and their reactions to "others'" (whether family's, singletons', the popular culture's, or scientific researchers') views of them.

Charles Lindholm (2001) states that understanding implies an imaginative identification with the position of the other. My advocacy of a behind-the-face, experience-near, everyday-life, and lifecycle approach, however, goes beyond an imaginative identification with the other. I am, so to speak, the other. I am an identical twin and my identical twin sister, Dorothy Davis, worked (and played) with me to collect the narrative data for this book. Rather than informants, we refer to these twenty-three sets of twins as our talking partners. As a twin, I take a culturally and experientially (Throop 2003) informed stance to examine the meaning and experiences of twinship among this sample of twins. My personal and interpersonal twinscapes are voiced in *Twins Talk*. Readers will find a strong auto-ethnographic, reflexive component to this study (Ellis, Adams, and Bochner 2011). To paraphrase Okely (1992, 9), the personal has become theoretical. Through this study I have found myself becoming a "militant twin," one who both champions twins and twinship and resists the more negative or medicalized portrayals of twins and the twin condition in the popular and academic literature.

By comparing twins, the twinscapes of twins, and those who research twins, I further employ a cultural psychology approach to address tensions between self stylings within a cultural system. Culturally dominant forms of selving that are more recognized and explicated by twins than researchers do not occur in a power vacuum; not all identities are equal, and selfways exist within frameworks of social inequality and power relationships based on tradition and history. In the overwhelming majority of twin studies (see Segal [1999] for an excellent review of the literature), twins researchers study from the top down. Twins are approached not as people but as a population of study. Scientific researchers tend to objectify twins and reduce or condense the twin experience to quantitative data or a few variables that conform to highly specific research agendas. Twins, as located on the fault lines, do a great deal to make the cultural assumptions of twins researchers more visible. The often counterhegemonic selfways of twins are of particular interest because they challenge, transcend, and conflate many of the dualisms associated with Western culture. These include mind/body, self/other, nature/culture, normal/deviant, autonomy/mutuality, masculine/feminine, and perhaps most important, same/different. In this volume, I use twins talk to explore the notion that scientific researchers also have a culture (Lock 2005; M'Charek 2005; Pálsson 2007). Past and present hereditarians, biomedicine, psychology, and even anthropology could benefit from a more ethnographically informed analysis of twins and twinship. Western twins researchers admit that their samples come from largely middle-class Western populations, but share with many Western researchers the notion of the West versus the Rest, where others have a culture but we do not. They tend to take their own culture as a given. They view "culturally informed" analyses as suitable for "other cultures" but not their own.

Throughout and within the chapters of this book, I will compare and contrast the voices of twins themselves to those who research them. Except for Stewart's (2003) prolegomenon for a social analysis of twinship, there has been little by way of an informed cultural critique or assessment that challenges as culture-bound many of the so-called objective assumptions of primarily Western twins researchers. This leaves twins researchers blind to the variation in constructions of self and personhood, both across societies and within any specific society, as well as to cultural biases inherent in their models of biological positivism. Moreover, in science and in the public imagination, identical twins have pretty much become the gold standard for understanding what is posited as a dichotomy between nature and culture, and twins studies themselves have come to define the nature/nurture debates (Conley 2004). Despite the alleged interest in nature and culture or heredity and environment, "environment" and "biology" are underanalyzed, as are twins as a biosocial phenomenon that in a variety of ways acts to fill up the spaces between nature and culture. The environmental anthropologist Marshall Sahlins (1976, 105) refers to the "culturalization of nature and the naturalization of culture" as a way of bridging the nature/culture divide. Sometimes twins talk about themselves in ways similar to the ways of those who research them, and sometimes they do not. Unlike researchers who take their own culture for granted, twins reveal a great deal about core assumptions of their culture and are quite self-conscious as they do so. Twins talk does not reduce life experiences to a selection of testable independent and dependent variables. The response of twins to both positive and negative societal stereotypes of twins both bridges the exotic and the mundane and results in a cogent critique of society. It is my intention, in this book, to subject twins researchers, as well as twins, to cultural analysis.

This chapter started with Lindholm's (2001) parable of Mulla's "Who am I?" question. Mulla's dilemma takes on a new meaning in the case of identical twins. What is a lived life like when there is someone who is walking around with your face—the primary identifier of your body self? Clearly, identical twins raise a host of questions about the embodiment of identity, the nature of human relationships, and the dynamic search for self. *Twins Talk* looks to twins to expand on the "Who am I?" someoneness questions posed by twins on the fault lines of person and selfhood. In the process of so doing, it is necessary to recognize multiple aspects of layers of self. Each layer of self carries different kinds of information and different challenges for twins. Jopling (1997), although not referring to twins, describes the layers as somatic, perceptual, motor, interpersonal, cognitive, moral, and cultural. It would be artificial to see these layers as fixed or in any way distinct from each other. As Ingold (2013, 17) notes, "Life is a process of making rather than an expression or realization of the ready-made." Although my chapters do artificially emphasize different aspects of self, such as body, performance, bond, and kin, what integrates them all is a sustained interest in self work and self styling as enacted in the practical, firsthand experiences of twinship. *Twins Talk* will show (cf. Marcus et al. 1997, 15) that while cultural participation is never totalizing or uniform, that while self-concepts are not fully identical to the self they represent, and that although twinship confers a power to shape a twin persona, self and relationship must still be regarded as negotiated and enacted within a particular sociocultural context. *Twins Talk,* through remaining chapters, shows us that twins have a great deal to tell us about ourselves, as Westerners in particular and as bio-psycho-socio-cultural beings in general.

Twins Talk is a book about identical twins (unless otherwise specified, my use of the word *twin* refers to identical twins and not to fraternal twins), but it is also, as in the case of Lindholm's (2003) Mulla, a book about "the relation between self and other and the construction of identity." Situated on the fault lines of identity, twins raise a number of interesting issues about intersections between nature, body, psyche, culture, and society, as well as action and meaning. *Twins Talk* is not a comprehensive opus on twins. It is a kind of opportunistic and positioned collage that represents where the data took me. Chapter 2—"Talk"—focuses on methods and introduces the wide variety of disciplinary perspectives, venues for research, kinds of data, and diverse sample of twins that ground this study. It sets the scene for dealing with insider (twin) and outsider (nontwin or singleton and researcher) viewpoints or perspectives and deals with universals, as well as differences. Chapter 3—"Performance"—features twin festivals as rites of reversal, where twins become the norm and singletons the exotic other. In chapter 4—"Body"—we witness the complex identity stories of living in look-alike bodies that twins tell, and I contrast these stories to the lore of geneticists. In chapter 5—"Bond"—the twin-twin relationship as depicted as unhealthy or dysfunctional by psychologists is contrasted to the very positive evaluation and open-ended views of twins themselves. In chapter 6—"Culture"—we move beyond myth and legend to place twins in a more informed and dynamic cultural context. As twins talk they remind researchers that science is not culture-free. Chapter 8—"Kin"—features twinship not as a static phenomenon fixed in childhood but as a form of kinship embedded within other relational and lifecycle challenges. Chapter 9—"Twindividuals"—sums up by revisiting the "Who am I?" questions of twins and twinship and puts forth the idea of twindividuals as a way of addressing dualisms inherent to Western selfways. Each chapter provides a cultural psychology–informed analysis that interweaves the voices of twins with those who write about them in the name of science.

2

TALK

Discourse is duplex; it both enacts and produces culture.

—*Quinn 2005b*

What do they have to talk about? They are telepathic anyways.

—*Maddox (2006), remarking on the sight of Twinsburg twins in
conversation*

Our best methodology is ourselves.

—*Cohen 1992*

If twins are "like two peas in a pod," this is a view from the pod.

—*Davis and Davis 2005*

TWINS TALK APPROACHES TWINS AS CONSTRUCTORS OF AND
actors in their own dramas. I argue for a person-centered, rather than
a disease- or deficiency-centered, approach to twins and twinship. As
an eclectic and multifaceted text, *Twins Talk* works from the bottom
up as well as from the top down. The predominant practices, agendas, and biomedical positivism of twins researchers are compared to
and contrasted with the subjective and intersubjective experiences as
expressed by twins themselves. The former treats twins from the top
down as a research method for testing specific hypotheses that are

defined and delimited by twins researchers. The latter treats twins from the ground up and views twins as interesting in and of themselves (Cool 2007, 24). The former medicalizes, while the latter normalizes twins and twinship.

Whether I refer to twins researchers or twins themselves, I aim to follow the cultural psychology approach, introduced in chapter 1, to give legitimacy to multiple voices, to emphasize the situated and contextualized natures of knowledge, and to provide space for multiple and sometimes competing twinscapes. The Twins Talk Study represents what Gullestad (1996a) describes as a way of doing ethnography that occupies the interdisciplinary space between the social sciences and the humanities. As a scientific study, *Twins Talk* critically engages the scientific literature. As a humanistic study, it also draws freely on more intuitive and impressionistic modes of analysis. *Twins Talk* is not overly concerned with representative sampling or validity or the discovery of any ultimate or profound truth. Instead, it views knowledge, whether scientific or popular, as positioned and culturally constructed.

Any attempt to compare and contrast what twins say to what has been said about them must be harnessed by some centralizing, or focal, concerns. What integrates or flows through my critique of twins researchers or research, on the one hand, and the lived, experiential worlds of twins, on the other, is a sustained focus on sociocultural constructions of self. This includes self as a bio-psycho-socio-cultural phenomenon. The notions of selfways, self stylings, and self work have already been introduced in chapter 1. The crux of my argument is that in the process of accessing what twins tell us about ourselves, twins researchers leave as unexamined their own culture-bound assumptions of appropriate and healthy selfways. In short, these assumptions privilege a Western ideal of competitive individualism (Lindholm 2001). It is the hegemonic quality of this single selfway that so often places identical twins on the fault lines of identity and selfhood. In response, identical twins, as we shall see, must negotiate or self-work their own self stylings as they set about answering their "Who am I?" questions. Self work, as identities in practice or social action, not only entails how identical twins negotiate individual and collective or connected (as a twin pair) identities in a variety of sociocultural contexts and at different stages of their lives but also compares and contrasts what twins say to what has been said about them. This sustained focus on selfways, self stylings, and self work gives twins talk an engaged, face-to-face, interactive, experiential, and practical quality that is unique in the twin studies literature.

As the title of this volume suggests, this is a study of twins talk. As a study in cultural psychology, it privileges the collection and analysis of narrative data (Neisser and Jopling 1997). The conversational narratives that situate analysis and flow throughout the volume come from twenty-three sets of twins who attended the 2003 Twins Days Festival in Twinsburg, Ohio. My original intent in this study was, with the help of my twin sister, Dorothy Davis, to interview as many sets of twins as possible in the research facilities set up at this particular festival. Yet being surrounded by thousands of twins for one weekend simply whet our appetites to learn more about twins, twins festivals, and our own twinship. Eventually, I would enter the world of twins researchers by participating in two international twin research conferences (Davis and Davis 2004; Davis 2007). All told, the Twins Talk Study is hardly limited to twins talk. It combines elements of multisited (Miller 2006), quick (Handworker 2002), experience-near (Wikan 1991), and reflexive (Behar 1996) ethnography. In what follows, I briefly describe the settings, methods, and populations for *Twins Talk*.

RESEARCH VENUES

Twins Talk is based on anthropological participant observation fieldwork (LeCompte and Schensul 1999; Schensul, Schensul, and LeCompte 1999) at two different types of twin-centered activities or venues. The first type of venue is twins festivals. Dorothy and I attended and participated in three weekend festivals. One was the Twins Days Festival held in Twinsburg, Ohio, in the summer of 2003. Twinsburg is the queen of twins festivals, attracting over four thousand twins per year. At Twinsburg, Dorothy and I sat in a booth at the Twins Days Research Pavilion, surrounded by other researchers who study twins, and interviewed twenty-two sets of twins in two days. Yet participant observation often involves the unanticipated. Restricted to the research areas, Dorothy and I wanted to experience other festival activities. This inspired us to follow up on our Twinsburg experience by attending two additional twins festivals as full-fledged participants.

We chose to attend two annual meetings of the International Twins Association (ITA). Dorothy and I participated in ITAs held in Atlanta, Georgia, in 2003 and in Asheville, North Carolina, in 2007. The ITAs are held every Labor Day weekend at different locations. Compared to Twins Days, the ITAs are much smaller (160 twins), more structured, and more intimate. These three sites of participant observation and research are further described in this chapter.

Besides generating an interest in festivals, the experience of sitting with Dorothy and talking with other sets of twins in the Twins Days Research Pavilion placed us side by side with other twins researchers. Although Dorothy and I were in Twinsburg as researchers collecting narrative data from as large a sample of twins as we could muster during two days, as twins, we could have easily offered ourselves up as data for other researchers (although we did not). The experience of being a twin researcher among twins researchers, as well as the subject of research among other subjects of research, began to tweak my interests in the field of twin research itself. I was able to follow up on this interest when I presented papers (Davis 2007; Davis and Davis 2004) at two international academic twin research conferences. These were the 11th and 12th International Congresses on Twin Studies held in 2004 in Odense, Denmark, and in 2007, in Ghent, Belgium, where I not only attended sessions and presentations but also got to meet and interact with a wide variety of twins researchers. These two conferences allowed for a firsthand, up-to-date, and comprehensive crash course in twin research, and by attending I learned a good deal about the twin research community. I did not anticipate the importance these conferences would have as field sites for the study of culture and for my own developing identity as a militant twin until I started to write this book after the first conference. What had originally been designed as a quick study of a sampling of twins in Twinsburg would evolve into a much more long-term and multifaceted piece of research.

Although they took place over a period of four years, these research events totaled no more than twenty days. Attendance at these large-scale public events, whether they are festivals or research conferences, hardly seems conducive to developing an intimate familiarity with those in the field or acquiring depth of data that is supposed to result from longer periods of "immersion" in the field (Josephides

2010; Schensul et al. 1999). This leads to a third and very important venue of research—me. *Twins Talk* is a view from the pod. As an identical twin, I have maintained a consistent autoethnographic and reflexive approach to my analysis. Dorothy and I were also interviewed in Twinsburg by our research assistant, Kristi Cody. Yet we are more than the twenty-third interview. As Cohen (1992, 225) writes, "Our best methodology is ourselves." In this sense *Twins Talk* has elements of experience-near (Wikan 1991) and reflexive (Behar 1996) ethnography. I have a lifelong intimacy with, or firsthand experience of, twinship and of being an identical twin. My awareness and interest in intersecting and multiple, insider and outsider twinscapes are informed in part by how they form around and affect me as both subject and object of study. I have a firsthand and lifelong experience with the issues raised in this text. Attending festivals and conferences and working side by side with my twin sister, Dorothy, have challenged me to rethink my own twinship and twinship in general. My previous forays into the field of cultural analysis and medical anthropology have also provided me with a background to study twins in various Western cultures. As a medical and psychological anthropologist who has studied Newfoundland and northern Norwegian fishing communities, I am experienced in turning the ethnographic gaze on others (Davis 1998, 1997, 1983). My challenge here is to turn that gaze on a world that is far more familiar to me.[1]

NARRATIVE AND EXPERIENCE:
FINDING CULTURE IN TALK

As a cultural analysis of twins and twinship, this study is eclectic rather than comprehensive. Certainly there are many roads not taken. The book is rooted in narrative analysis and goes where twins talk takes me. Each chapter highlights a particular aspect of a twin's own experience of being a twin. The famous Minnesota twins researcher David Lykken (McGue and Iacono 2007) was noted for his repeated comment that "the plural of anecdote is not data." In twin studies, quantitative data certainly trump qualitative data. Yet within anthropology and cultural psychology we have a much greater respect for the utility of narrative data.

People apprehend experience and tell about the world narratively. Narrative has an interactive, intentional dynamic and is about knowledge as being negotiated, situated and conditional, and positioned (Bruner 1987, 1990; Garro 2000; Nelson 1994; Ochs and Capps 2001; Richardson 1990; Truscott, Paulson, and Everall 1999). Narrative can be viewed as a kind of self-location (Rapport and Overing 2000) and can reveal internalized sides of culture or an individual's understandings of his or her life, motives, and identities (Quinn 2005b). Narrative may take the form of whole stories or dramas involving actors and sequencing of actions, goals, and scenes (Bruner 1990). But narrative may also include everyday, ordinary, interactive, shared and collaborative, conversational activity. Twins talk is a narrative in action and interaction. Our transcriptionist, Angie (whose job it was to record who said what), often cited in text notes that "you are all talking at once," attesting that narrative can be free-ranging, haphazard, messy, and chaotic (Gullestad 1996b; Ochs and Capps 2001; Shweder 1991). Yet stories get told and, in the telling, selves and identities are located.

However chaotic, the rough-draft quality of narrative can air unresolved life events, where a moral stance or disposition toward what is good or valuable, and how one ought to live in the world, may be declared. Narrative is made in terms of preexisting categories or meanings. In *Finding Culture in Talk*, Naomi Quinn (2005b, 2) states that "Discourse is duplex; it both enacts and produces culture." Going beyond generalizations about self and personhood allegedly consistent across all social situations, a discourse-centered approach focuses on specific social events, particular practices, and other types of social arrangements. The psychologist Jerome Bruner (1990) views narrative as a kind of folk psychology that keeps the uncanny at bay and renders the exceptional and idiosyncratic comprehensible. Festival twins as a special population or persona are located on the fault lines, deviating from conventional expectations of identity. They are celebrators of the uncanny. Through their narratives, twins draw on their own experiences as they formulate a sense of self. Yet their self-stories enact both their uniqueness and their shared commonalities with the culture in which they participate. Thus in *Twins Talk* we will see how confronting existing schema and airing doubts (Ochs and Capps 2001) may lead to a recognition of diverse psychologies, as well as explanatory theories or envisaging alternatives that reevaluate and reformulate what culture has to offer, and also how self and culture dynamically constitute each other.

Narrative analysis—as a specialized area of linguistics or cognitive anthropology—can be highly sophisticated and complex (e.g., Nelson 1994; Ochs and Caps 2001). Preferring the term *talk* over *discourse* or *narrative*, Naomi Quinn (2005a, 2005b) advocates the use of eclectic, open-ended, and opportunistic research methods. For Quinn, *talk* entails interviews that capture and record (for transcription) segments of speech or text that are longer than a single word or a sentence and that often tell full stories. In Quinn's view, cultural analysis of talk can be done by anyone with the patience for close, attention-demanding, time-consuming work and an eye for pattern, detail, and nuance. Individual researchers may develop their own personal approaches, finding what works for their own purposes and inventing forms of analysis in the process (Quinn 2005b). Cultural analysis in this sense aims at finding patterns or clues drawn from comparison of multiple samples of discourse. It entails making explicit the largely tacit, taken-for-granted, implicit, and invisible assumptions that people share with others of their group or carry internally. Understanding culture through talk begins with the assumption that people in a given group share, to a greater or lesser extent, largely tacit understandings of the world that they have learned and internalized.

Yet *Twins Talk* departs from Quinn's (2005b) design for talk research methods in a number of important ways. First, talk, according to Quinn, is collected through interviews or conversations between two people, one of whom does not belong to the immediate social world of the other. The narrative data from the Twins Talk Study involve conversations among at least four, and in one case six, people. Data come from a set of twins having conversations about being twins with other sets of twins. Being twins themselves, the researchers do share many key aspects of the relational and social worlds (not to mention embodied worlds) of those with whom they are talking. The data have an interactive quality that is unique not only in the twin studies literature but also in the discourse analysis literature. Second, the Twins Talk Study goes well beyond words transcribed into text. To reduce twin self stylings or self work to verbal abstractions denies the real-world importance of their bodies. I must admit to being amazed that, to the extent a cultural psychology approach assumes an embodied self (Markus et al. 1997, 13), the selfways, self styling, and self work of identical twins have to this point received no attention. For identical twins, the body counts, especially as they sit side by side, enacting, performing, and discussing being twins with another set of twins. Third, the festival context of the twins talk sessions is extremely important. Festivals are celebrations of twinship, and our talking partners come to the Research Pavilion hyped on being twins. Twins festivals are all about simultaneously performing and challenging popular cultural stereotypes of twins as being identical. If only for two or three days, a festival becomes a place where twins dominate, and singletons, with their biological uniqueness, become the exotic other. In the following, I set the scene for the Twins Talk Study by introducing the talking partners and some key features of the contexts of each research venue.

INSIDE THE TWINS DAYS PAVILION

The narratives that flow throughout and structure this book were gathered from a sample of twenty-three sets of twins attending the Twinsburg Twins Days Festival during the summer of 2003. Twins Days is unique among twins festivals in having space on the festival grounds for twins researchers who may recruit volunteer subjects from the masses of twins who attend the festival. Every year the research committee of the Twins Days Festival accepts formal applications from researchers interested in recruiting volunteer subjects. Researchers are vetted and selected through a process of formal proposal writing. If accepted, researchers are given official space on the festival grounds, for which they pay a fee. To an experienced field researcher, the Twins Days Festival is not only an exercise in quick ethnography (Handwerker 2002) but also a kind of ethnographic nirvana for the talk/interview component of a research project. This is exactly the point for all the Twinsburg researchers. Where else could one find, for two long days, large concentrations of twins representing diverse categories in terms of age, twin type, gender, ethnic identity, and so on?

The Twins Days Festival is held annually during the first week of August in the small town of Twinsburg, Ohio. Dating back to 1976 when thirty-six twins attended, the festival now hosts the largest gathering of twins in the world. Twins Days attracts twins—identical and fraternal twins of both sexes—and super twins (multiples of more than two) from all age groups and different walks of life. Since

1989 the number of registered pairs of twins attending the festival has numbered over two thousand. Twins Days is the predominant twins festival in terms of attendance, national and international attention, and press coverage.

Although more permanent facilities have been built since Dorothy and I participated in 2003, the Research Pavilion at the time consisted of a large tent with booth-like table spaces for twelve groups of researchers. Researchers are a formal presence and must follow rules specified by the festival research committee. For example, all tables must have skirts, and researchers are supposed to be in the same place from the opening of the festival to the close. In 2003 we and ten other research groups competed to entice twins to our table as they milled through the pavilion, looked over the research booths, asked questions about the projects, and decided whether to participate in one or more of the various studies. The research groups that year included National Institute for Deafness (hearing and listening abilities), the Evanston Continence Center (incontinence and pelvic floor problems), a university hospital's department of dermatology (skin diseases and hair loss), Burke Pharmaceuticals (hair loss), University of Pennsylvania (sleep patterns), Monell Chemical Senses Center (taste tests), University of California–San Diego Department of Orthopedics (physiological conditioning and space flight), U.S. Secret Service (handwriting), Cornell University (altruism), and Western Reserve Reading Project (reading-related cognitive skills). We were billed in the festival program as the University of South Dakota's qualitative study designed to collect narrative data to identify common themes of twinship. Some groups, composed of cadres of research assistants, processed and tested hundreds of twins. The larger, well-funded research groups come back year after year. We were free to participate in preliminary and evening activities off the festival grounds, but at the festival we were restricted to the Research Pavilion. We conducted interviews in the pavilion for two days from 8:00 a.m. to around 10:00 p.m. In the evenings Dorothy and I were the only researchers left in the pavilion tent. All the others kept a nine-to-five schedule.

A visit to the research tent was a popular activity for many curious and service-minded twins. The day before the festival, when we were setting up our research booth, I had a chat with a man setting up a booth to sell photo buttons to twins. When I mentioned that I was a researcher setting up in the Research Pavilion, he rather sarcastically wished me good luck, stating that twins "in the know" avoided the Research Pavilion like the plague, knowing that once they went in, even though they were promised a quick study, they could actually get stuck there for hours. Fortunately, this proved not to be the case. There was a steady flow of twins through the pavilion during each day of the festival.

Most other researchers in the pavilion had slick booths with big posters, banners, multiple researchers, and flashy technology. The majority offered some form of compensation. Researchers on big teams wore colorful matching T-shirts. Our booth, however, had a homemade or amateurish ambience about it. Dressed somewhat similarly in matching pants (which we had purchased independently) and in different-colored shirts, Dorothy and I sat at a booth we had decorated in red, white, and blue. We had banners strung across the booth that announced us as the Twins Talk Study. Our student research assistant, Kristi Cody, stood at one table, recruiting twins to talk with us, while we conducted our conversations at a table perpendicular to Kristi's. While we interviewed, Kristi explained the study to interested twins, answered all their questions and concerns, and scheduled the interviews. Kristi's outgoing and engaging personality and her public relations skills were instrumental in the success of our study.

Dorothy and I sat side by side across the table from our talking partners. Learning from our fellow researchers during setup time, we rushed off to get cans of soda, bottles of water, and snacks for our project participants. Since it was very warm, we also bought a small fan. We talked with twins through rain and thunderstorms, sunny weather, fireworks, and near one-hundred-degree temperatures. The torrential rains were a blessing because they cooled us off and brought twins into the tent. Large, collective festival activities like a group picture, a parade, and contests hardly affected the flow of twins through the pavilion. During the few lulls, we ate, drank, ran to the facilities, and were interviewed by the media. Apparently, we made good copy because we were twins studying twins. Despite the formalities of the application process, the structured and regimented layout of booths, and the intense recruitment of volunteers, the research setting was informal and relaxed. At times the shared laughter and the antics and stories of the Twins Talk twins would grab others' interest and evoke comments from researchers at neighboring tables. Kristi remarked that other researchers would repeatedly ask her, "Just what are they doing over there?" There was also a marked element of the absurd to the research process. For example, we had adult twins who were waiting for an interview and dressed as bees. It probably was not what Allison Cool (2007, 7) had in mind when she referred to the twin research method as "when scientist and gene meet cute," but it certainly described what happened in the Twins Days Research Pavilion.

Kristi dealt with the rejections from twins who had less enthusiastic views of our study. There were three areas where Kristi encountered difficulty. The first was with men, who were far less interested in the project than were women. The second area of difficulty, voiced most often by men, was that we offered no monetary compensation or gift packages, as did most of the other researchers in the pavilion. Other twins refused because they felt our study offered no solutions to medical problems or served no higher purpose. One set of twins demurred from participating because it looked like the twins being interviewed were having too much fun for a serious research project. After day one, Kristi felt she was becoming quite desensitized to rejection. We also had a problem in scheduling twins for talk sessions later in the day or on the next day because they would fail to show up. This problem was offset by the fact that recruitment was easy and missed slots could easily be filled by twins present in the pavilion. Not only did Kristi deal with rejection; she had to reject others as well. Scheduling an hour for each interview meant we were fully booked. Kristi also found herself having to tell eager parents of twins that their twins were too young for the project, which limited participants to age eighteen and over.

Conversational Interviews

In the Twins Talk booth each conversation lasted from thirty to ninety minutes. Interviews were recorded on tape and later transcribed. In two intense and exhausting days, we interviewed forty-four people and collected as much narrative data (over four hundred pages) as an anthropologist usually gathers in several months of fieldwork. Briggs (1986, 26) distinguishes between formal, structured surveys and more free-flowing and conversational interviews. Our twin interviews were the latter—a kind of interview where control is granted to the interviewee. It is the interviewees' task to communicate what they know to the interviewer, and the explanations of the interviewee shape the interview. Dorothy and I were interested in and open to all responses the informants saw as relevant. Yet, although flexible and open-ended, interviews are not naturally occurring genres of talk (Briggs 1986). Conversational interviews still occur in a specific and structured social context. In our case, the specific context was the Twins Talk Study booth at Twins Days. Conversations or interviews may also be hierarchical or egalitarian. Egalitarian certainly described the interaction styles that developed as we talked to twins.

The talking sessions hardly fit the idea of a question-and-response interview. What is missing from the transcripts is the body talk, which frequently punctuated interchanges. This included twins forcefully touching each other as a prompt not only to say his or her name first but to take her or his turn or to correct or censure each other. These nonverbal exchanges, as we see in chapter 4, would emerge as an important part of the analysis. Language was sometimes colorful. For example, Karen referred to the time when "Mother nailed my ass to the wall." Often it took both twins to make a single statement. This kind of positioned collaboration is illustrated by Donna and Dianne.

> Dianne: In twins,
> Donna: you know,
> Dianne: there's a leader
> Donna: and a leaner.
> Dianne: I was the leader.
> Donna: I was the leaner.
> Dianne: Lean on me.
> Donna: I always did.

Following the lead of the Norwegian anthropologist Marianne Gullestad (1996a), Dorothy and I viewed our informational exchanges as conversations, and the twins we talked to not so much as informants or research subjects but as talking partners. For Dorothy and me, unlike our fellow pavilion researchers, our relative and hierarchical position of being researchers, as opposed to subjects, became secondary to our more egalitarian positioning of twins talking to twins. If there is one thing twins know how to do, it is to interchangeably lead and lean while sharing the stage.

When we sat for our first conversation with Chris and Carla, it was the first time in our lives that Dorothy and I had talked, as twins, to another set of twins. We had a lot to say and so did Chris and Carla. Yet, the Twins Talk sessions were not totally open ended. Although aspiring to a natural conversation, Dorothy and I had a set of guiding questions that we would raise throughout the conversation. Moreover, for the sake of the transcriber, partners were asked to say their names each time they made a comment or entered the conversation. Often this was an occasion of high humor with one twin reminding the talking twin to say her or his name.

The conversations were guided by a set of six key questions printed on flash cards. Revealing one question at a time, we worked our way through the interviews assuring an open-ended context but also steering at least some of the conversation around a preset series of topics, which I, as an anthropologist and a twin, felt would be relevant to anthropology. Topics included notions of embodiment, sociocultural constructions of self and identity, and notions of same and different (Rapport and Overing 2000). In many cases we did not even have to ask our questions. Conversations naturally flowed from one question to another. Sometimes Dorothy or I would interject the next topic when conversation lulled. During our talks, sets of twins frequently informed us that they "were just talking about the same thing last night with another set of twins." Dina, who had recently received her PhD, commented that it was both a conversation and an interview:

> Dina: What I really like about this was how the conversation flowed. It doesn't really feel like an interview. There were questions, I know, but like, one question just blended into the next. And ya'll were really good at keeping us in the subject matter; basically [you are] good interviewers.

When we went to the International Twins Conferences in Atlanta and Asheville, Dorothy and I were delighted to discover that our questions reflected the ways twins meeting twins converse with each other in more unstructured introductions or presentations of self and selves in casual social situations. Questions covered in the conversations were:

1. As twins, how do you see yourselves today as the same or similar?
2. As twins, how do you see yourselves today as different?
3. To what do you attribute these similarities and differences?
4. Have these similarities and differences changed over your lives? How? Why?
5. What, in your own words, does it mean to be a twin? Have these meanings changed or remained constant over your lives?
6. Tell us some of your favorite twin stories.
7. Is there anything missing that we should cover or is there another topic that, as twins, you would like to bring up for discussion?

Responses to our queries certainly illustrate what Luttrell (1997, 8) describes as a "narrative urgency" on the part of informants to define and defend their selves and their identities. The Twinsburg twins were well primed for conversation. That is what festival twins do. They talk, as sets of twins, to other set of twins about being twins. The twins who talked with us were quite positive about the project and certainly engaged in the Twins Talk Study. As an anthropologist who has conducted research in Newfoundland, North Norwegian fishing communities, and South Dakota's Indian reservations, I have never experienced easier interview situations. Newfoundlanders, in particular, I found to be outgoing, witty, and articulate. They can tell great stories, but I feel strongly that the Twinsburg study was enriched by my being "one of them": an identical twin.

During the interview, Tom, one of our talking partners, kept asking us, "How are we doing?" Tom declared that he had only "been rehearsing for this [interview] for forty-nine years." We did not need to establish rapport. It was instantaneous. Our conversation with Tim and Tom started with high fives all around. Conversations were extremely informal. Judy and Janet began their talking session with Judy's announcement that the length of the interview would be determined by the size of her bladder. The conversations were fun and regarded as a positive experience by both researchers and subjects. Our transcriber, Angie, commented that there was often so much laughter that she could not hear what we were saying. She wrote "Ha Ha" to indicate laughter. The manuscripts are peppered with "Ha Has." I have left these out because there was so much laughing and giggling that transcriptions would have been littered with too many Ha Has.

Despite the casual informality and humor of the conversations, the partners also took the occasion to talk seriously. In what follows, Tom assertively takes on the singleton world:

> Tom: From what I said earlier, I just think that when people try to figure out twins, and they're not twins, I'm almost thinking they've got their own bias. You know what I mean? I think it's reasonable for twins to study twins because you have a better understanding of the relationship, OK? Whereas it would be like a man interviewing a woman trying to find out what it is like being a woman. Or the other way around. . . . Because the sexes are so different, a man would never truly understand a woman, and a woman would never really understand a man. All we know is that we [twins] are different. Even though everyone has their own opinion about it, like males and females, single births don't understand the dynamics of multiple births. Obviously!

At several junctures in the interview process, a twin would say something like, "Well, you guys know what we mean, because you're twins too." Usually Dorothy or I would ask for an explanation, but sometimes we were so caught up in the conversation that we would just let some of these loaded statements pass. Toward the end of Pat and Phyllis's interview, Pat told us, "The best thing is you guys are twins, so you understand. As researchers, it's really nice that you are doing this as twins. It's a good idea." Many of the talking partners are interested in the outcome of this project. I have sent them copies of papers I have presented. Response to the papers has been positive, and I remain in touch with a number of the Twinsburg twins. Those who continue to keep in touch are enthusiastic and interested in how the study progresses.

The Talking Partners

The talking partners came from an opportunistic sampling format. Although the sample includes women and men and shows some variation in terms of age and educational, socioeconomic, regional, and ethnic background, it is in no sense a representative sample. Rosambeau (1987) notes that volunteer twin samples almost always end up with a preponderance of identical girls or women. The twins talk sample is overwhelmingly female. We have no way of knowing whether those twins who refused to participate in the study, or those who do not attend twins festivals, would have had significantly different discussions on being twins. Certainly Dorothy and I had never been festival twins and continue to resist the overweening emphasis festivals place on looking alike. Nevertheless, the commonalities of our own experiences of being twins with those of our talking partners, regardless of age, gender, and class, amaze us. The sample, although small, is commensurate with other twin studies that feature twins' narratives (Klein 2003; Rosambeau 1987; Schave and Ciriello 1983; Segal 2005).

Our talking partners could either use their own names or invent ones for the interview. Unfortunately for the reader, a number of twins had the same names. For example, there were four Ginas and two Karens. I have provided alternate spellings, not necessarily for clarity, but so that the twins can recognize themselves in the text. All conversations were two on two, except in one instance when we interviewed two sets of twins (Karan and Kim, and Cindy and Sandy) from the same family. The sample includes 6 men and 38 women who range in age from 22 to 77. Regarding education, the sample included 7 with a high school education, 3 with some technical or college education, 9 with college degrees, and 4 with graduate school degrees. The majority worked in business or sales (21), followed by teaching (8) and nursing (3). There were 2 social workers, 2 housewives, and 2 military personnel. The remaining interviewees were either still in school or retired.

In terms of life cycle stages, the sample seemed to break into 4 age categories. Those twins ages 22 to 26 were just starting out in careers and were not married. The 36- to 46-year-olds were fairly established in their careers, and at least one of the twin pairs had children still at home. The 54- to 58-year-olds had grown children and had begun to enjoy more indulgences, like vacationing and dining out. Those in the 61 to 77 age group were retired or approaching retirement, enjoyed their grandchildren, and spent more time together than they had since they were children. Chapter 7, "Kin," gives the most detailed account of how the Twinsburg twins depicted themselves and what key experiences and challenges they have faced during their lives. The reader may want to read chapter 7 next to become more familiar with the Twinsburg twins.

TABLE 1.			
Age and pseudonyms of talking partners			
22 Chris & Carla	36 Tina & Ginuh	54 Carol & June	61 Janet & Judy
23 Amy & Beth	36 Sandy & Cindy	54 Lucy & Linda	62 Pat & Phyllis
24 Jeana & Dina	39 Karan & Kim	55 Dona & Dorothy	64 Dianne & Donna
25 Gina & Ginger	41 Jenna & Steph	56 Annette & Arnette	69 Jenny & Julie
26 Randi & Dante	45 Tim & Tom	58 Mabel & Bertha	74 Helen & June
	45 Mary & Martha		77 Pete & Emil
	46 Karen & Kristy		

Although this study features the narratives of the Twinsburg sample of twins, Dorothy and I were interviewed at Twinsburg by our research assistant Kristi Cody. Because we are the twenty-third interview, and there is a marked autobiographic or reflexive component woven into the text. Actually, Dorothy and I, with our different-colored shirts and different hairstyles, felt that our talking partners might doubt our identical twin status. We even brought pictures of us looking very alike at various junctures of our lives as proof of our twinship. Although eager to look at pictures and show their own, our talking partners never questioned our being twins. Instead, they said, "When we talk to you we know you are twins." Our conversations with other sets of twins of all ages have led us to reflect on our own twinship. Initially, the Twinsburg study was to be the beginning and end of the Twins Talk Study. Like many ethnographic studies, however, it would develop unforeseen and much longer-term avenues for further research and reflection. These include autoethnography, performance, and twin research conferences, as discussed below.

AUTOETHNOGRAPHIC PERSPECTIVES: A VIEW FROM THE POD

Early in her career as a twin researcher, Nancy Segal (1999), who has a fraternal twin sister, was advised never to mention that she was a twin because it would compromise her objectivity in the eyes of her colleagues. Fortunately, I, in contrast to Segal (1999), come from the intellectual tradition of participant observation anthropology, which not only gives legitimacy to multiple voices and perspectives but sees our best methodology as our experience of ourselves (Cohen 1992, 225). *Twins Talk,* as person-centered (Hollan 2001; LeVine 1982), experience-near (Wikan 1991), or a kind of interpersonal, minimalist ethnography (Jackson 1998; Rosaldo 1986), is certainly up close and personal. As written by a twin studying twins, however, *Twins Talk* also contains elements of what anthropologists call an autoethnographic, autoanthropology or self-reflexive, approach (Behar 1996; Ellis et al. 2011; Strathern 1987; Visweswaran 1994).

Autoethnography, according to Ellis (Ellis et al. 2011, 1), "is an approach to research and writing that seeks to describe and systematically analyze (*graphy*) personal experience (*auto*) in order to understand cultural experience (*ethno*)." Autoethnography is both a process and a product aiming to critique scientific ideas that include what research is and how it should be done. Grounded in personal experience, autoethnography draws on one's self and one's home as ways of bridging artificial divisions among the personal, physical, psychosocial, and phenomenal aspects of living (Rapport and Overing 200, 18). Being multidimensional, autoethnography is also sensitive to identity politics and recognizes that different people make different kinds of assumptions about themselves and the worlds in which they live (Ellis et al. 2011, 1).

For once in my career I am the native. I have firsthand and lifelong personal and interpersonal experience in this field of study. As the "others" in a singleton-dominated world, Dorothy and I have lived our lives in what Hastrup (1995) refers to as the contact zone.[2] If ethnography can be described as the "thickest form of information" (Ortner 2006, 10), in *Twins Talk* I bring my own lifelong, autoethnographic perspectives to the thickening process, filling in holes in the data, giving additional examples, and adding subtext to text. Although the fieldwork portions of this study include little more than two weeks' time, Dorothy and I have over 120 years of living in the field.

As an identical twin, I have had the firsthand physical experiences of living in a twin's body and intimately sharing childhood spaces and places with my identical sister, Dorothy. Hollan (2001, 8) suggests that one of the key problems for those who study the embodied aspects of experience is ascertaining how we can know that the senses, perceptions, and bodily experiences we attribute to our subjects are not actually the researcher's own perceptual projections or preoccupations. Certainly I make no pretense of being Pete and Emil, Donna and Dianne, or Janet and Judy (or even Dorothy), but as an identical twin I have a firsthand experience with the embodiment of twinship that gives me my own perspectives on my body, as well as on what I see as a researcher's own perceptual projections and preoccupations when it comes to me and my own embodied self as a twin. Yet, the Twins Talk Study is not just an exercise in reflexive anthropology or mutual navel gazing. Talking to other sets of twins and attending twins festivals developed my sense of being an anomaly, an "other" in a singleton-dominated world. It also provided me with a kind of stranger status and embodied standpoint with which to view issues of self and identity in the wider cultural milieu that assumes embodied uniqueness and privileges individualism by opposing it to mutuality. Thus, it is important to realize that being twins is but one locus (and a crucially important one) of a set of multiple and fluctuating loci along which we are aligned with or set apart from those whom we study (Narayan 1997).

Although I admit to being an experienced interviewer, at home in my body, and having a longtime, firsthand experience with twinship, none of this mitigated the shock I experienced at my first twins festival and the sight of thousands of look-alike adult twins. Originally thinking of Twins Days only as a way to collect lots of data, I had no inkling of the visual impacts that the festival twinscapes would have on me. My (and Dorothy's and Kristi's) embodied, visceral reaction to perambulating multitudes of identical pairs would eventually figure quite prominently in the Twins Talk Study.

PERFORMANCE

How persons enact culture or act on the world cannot be reduced to language and meaning. Ewing (1990, 253), who contends that the self is grounded in language rather than flesh and blood, has clearly never been to a twins festival. As I have already noted, conversations transcribed into texts or words on paper hardly do justice to the Twinsburg twins' conversations. Talking about twinship as embodied is not the same thing as embodying it. Any analysis of twins in a festival setting must go beyond narrative, or talk, to engage embodied selves in practice and action, in terms not only of how meanings of self are achieved but also of how self or selves are put to use (Bruner 1990). Our interview conversations offered an opportunity to view culture as enacted or produced in moments of interaction that were nonverbal. Twinsburg twins, or our talking partners, sit side by side. They are dressed exactly alike. They link their bodies through held hands and mutual touching, be it stroking, caressing, or poking and hitting the other twin. They have come to Twinsburg to celebrate their twinship. Conversations offered a chance for twins to perform their twinship and put their selves to work. Yet the conversations take place within the purview of the wider festival and are impartible from it. Festival twinscapes are designed to shock and unsettle and festival twins take rebellious joy by collectively performing their twinship in ways that both confirm and challenge their stereotypes. A festival performance approach allows for insights into what "minds and body are doing as they are doing it" (Rosch 1997, 187).

At the beginning of Twins Days, Dorothy and I were standing outside the Research Pavilion with a fellow researcher. We were watching masses of identically dressed twins entering the festival grounds. Our companion, an old hand who had already logged several years at the pavilion, remarked to us on the sight of so many twins, "You never get used to it." Initially, I thought of Twins Days solely as a way of accessing a good sample and collecting a lot of narrative data during a short period of time; I had certainly not anticipated the emotive impact of seeing over a thousand twin pairs. The sight of so many identically dressed twin pairs packs a responsive wallop that is felt in the body. At Twinsburg we witnessed twins being twins by the thousands. I had not anticipated the extent to which the festival would invite its own kind of analysis. The performance of twinship at twins festivals is a key situating context of the Twins Talk Study. For example, chapter 3 offers and situates many of the key arguments detailed in the remaining chapters. At festivals twins perform their embodied likeness and their mutuality or the bond that unites them.

In this participant observation study, not only do Dorothy and I negotiate multiple pathways among selves and others, we traverse boundaries between work and play. At Twinsburg we watched the festival taking place around us and also participated in the nighttime activities that were held off the festival grounds. These included officially sponsored picnics as well as unofficial parties at local hotels.

We booked a room for the weekend in what was advertised online as the "party hotel." Here festivities included socializing, drinking, and dancing until the early hours of the morning. Other party venues included camping sites where twins also could mix and mingle after festival hours. Feeling the need for a more experiential sense of festivals as participants and not just researchers, Dorothy and I decided to attend other twins festivals at public venues where we could be daytime or nighttime participant observers in a less formal setting. Attendance at two annual ITA meetings allowed us to participate in the full range of festival activities.

The ITA meetings are much smaller (160–200 twins, mostly adults), more structured, and more contained than Twins Days. Each year the association meets in a different place with participants sharing the same hotel. Although most of the participants are regular attendees and already know each other, organizers of the two ITAs we attended made sure that new twins were made welcome. The overall ambience was intimate, friendly, and fun. Although they complain about rising costs, most ITA twins participate in the total round of activities that are planned for all. These include dinners, contests, evening parties, and tours of local sights. Middle-aged and older women predominate at the ITAs, and men are few and far between. At the ITAs we discovered how much fun it was to meet other twins, spend time with them, and participate in the planned events. The first ITA meeting Dorothy and I attended was held at the end of summer in Atlanta, Georgia. We enjoyed the experience so much that we decided to return and take part in the association's festivities held in Asheville, North Carolina, in 2007. My analysis of cultural performance and expressive styles (chapter 3) is largely based on observational data collected during public events at the three festivals.

TWIN RESEARCH AND TWINS RESEARCHERS

When I began to conceptualize and plan this study, as in any scholarly endeavor, I set out to review the literature on twins. Since my master's thesis was on biocultural aspects of variation in twinning frequencies (Dona Davis 1971), I had some familiarity with at least the older literature on twins. One of my initial aims in formulating the Twins Talk Study was to first identify anthropologically informed works and then move on to a comparative analysis of anthropological perspectives as compared or contrasted to the perspectives of other disciplines that were also interested in twins. What I discovered was that twin research itself has developed into an area of interdisciplinary specialization, with its own journals, research conferences, and hierarchy of researchers. The more twin research literature I read, the more sensitive I became to its medicalized view of twins and twinship and lack of interest in twins "from the ground up" or in and of themselves.

I am certainly no stranger to a feminist and culturally informed critique of Western biomedical texts and research methods (Davis 1998, 1995, 1983a). My experience in the critical analysis of texts, however, was a far cry from what it felt like to be a twin in the Twins Days Research Pavilion. The pavilion was a warm and welcoming environment where Dorothy and I worked side by side with other twins researchers. Yet, for the hordes of service-minded twins who came through the pavilion, Dorothy and I were the only researchers interested in what our partners had to say about their lifetime personal and interpersonal experiences of being twins. In the pavilion we observed other research groups who were interested in only twins' ears, skin, bladders, hair, taste buds, altruism, handwriting, or sleep patterns, all as they related to their genes. We could hear twins gag as buccal smears were collected from the back of their throats. As the days went on, I became more and more sensitive to being reduced to my genes or even molecules, to being of interest only as an object of research. Like our talking partners, Dorothy and I found ourselves becoming hyped on being twins. At Twinsburg Dorothy and I found ourselves becoming "militant twins," beginning to feel that we needed, "as the native," to strive for a voice in the research process. I complained in a media interview, "We are more than just walking organ banks" (Barrell 2003). It began to seem that the Twinsburg volunteer twins might as well have been zombies or performing monkeys, given the amount of interest researchers displayed toward them as persons or toward their own perspectives on their practical and interpersonal experiences of being twins.

As the biologist Ruth Hubbard (1979, 47) states, "There is no such thing as objective, value-free science." When it comes to issues of women's physical and mental health, I am well aware that what passes for science or truth actually reflects Western cultural, as well as androcentric, ways of thinking (see note 1). A benefit of the cultural psychology perspective is that it recognizes that within and among societies there exist alternative or multiple constructions of self. Hardly benign, these constructions reflect power relations (Lutz 1990; Markus et al. 1997). My first twin research conference was reminiscent of my participation, with other anthropologists, in international menopause research conferences and my work as a consultant on internationalizing diagnostic criteria for mental illnesses. The difference was that this time I, as a twin, was the topic of research, and I was the only anthropologist in attendance. Actually, my original purpose in giving a paper at my first twin research conference, the International Congress of Twin Studies (ICTS), in Odense, Denmark, in 2004, was to be able to attend a Danish twins festival that was to be held at the same time as the conference. The festival, I learned only on arrival at the conference, had been canceled due to lack of funds and interest. My primary purpose for being there thwarted, I had failed to anticipate the extent to which my participation (by presenting a paper) in the Odense conference (and later at the ICTS to be held in Ghent, Belgium, in 2007) would provide a body of data on twin research and those who research twins to be woven throughout this book.

At both meetings of the ICTS a positivist, biomedical, biostatistical approach prevailed. A preference for increasingly larger databases results in the collaborative combining of samples from different studies or data derived from sophisticated twin registries, which already include thousands of twins (Perola et al. 2007), past and present, and vast amounts of potential data. At the conferences twins are seen primarily as a research method rather than as a subject of research. Faceless, depersonalized twins, dead and alive, are reduced to numbers on a form, to a limited series of independent and dependent variables, which are assessed through standardized quantitative methods for purposes of which they had no knowledge when the data were collected. Highly sophisticated, large-scale studies with genotyping laboratories dominate the plenary sessions. More qualitatively oriented approaches such as mine lie at the bottom of the hierarchical heap.

The conferences not only provided opportunities to listen to presentations and be introduced to the current trends in twin research but also, through the lunches, dinners, social occasions, and bus rides to and from the events, allowed me to informally meet and talk with a wide range of twins researchers. Thus the conferences themselves, as public events, provided yet another venue for ethnographic fieldwork and quick ethnography. Additionally, aside from researchers, another major group of participants at these conferences are representatives of international mothers (parents) of twins organizations (such as International Council of Multiple Births Organization [ICOMBO] and Twins and Multiple Births Association [TAMBA]). Both organizations provide symposia on a host of practical issues that affect parents of twin children. Although one meets the occasional researcher who is a twin, twins are not an invited presence at the conferences. As a twin at these conferences, I began to feel like an oddity. Feeling a sense of distance from other researchers inspired me to consider putting twins researchers and twin research under the ethnographic lens. By the time the second conference in Ghent came around, I had a well-developed sense of being a participant observer at this public activity.

Again, to paraphrase Okely (1992, 9), the personal has become theoretical. The ICTS conference organization illustrates what Quinn (2005b, 1) refers to as the "harder sciences' suspicion of anecdotal evidence and a false and unfortunate dichotomy between scientific and humanistic approaches." For example, the abstract proposal guidelines included no category for the social sciences. At both meetings of the ICTS, paper proposals from the social sciences and humanities get routed to posters and, if they actually get to be scheduled in "sessions," are relegated to small rooms and unpopular time periods. Like my analysis of culture in talk with the Twinsburg twins' narratives, my analysis of those who research twins, the papers they present, and the texts they produce has an opportunistic style, rather than a methodologically rigorous style. Rather than see the science of twins researchers and twin research as truly impartial and objective, my goal is to expose and make visible, or more explicit, tacitly held (cf. Hastrup 1995; Quinn 2001b), culture-bound, or biased assumptions that are invisible to the largely hegemonic body of Western twins researchers. Thus I subject twins, as well as those who research them, to a critical cultural analysis.

My challenge to the hegemony of biomedically oriented twins researchers should not imply that I disagree with or dismiss the contributions made through positivist biomedical studies of twins. After all, the Twins Days twins freely presented themselves as research subjects out of a strong sense of service. Yet clearly the agendas and purposes of twin research are set and shaped by the researchers and not by twins. Twins as objects of study seldom have any input into the research process. My point regarding twin studies is that there is room for multiple approaches and points of view. Identical twins are "good to think with," and insider and outsider twinscapes provide the gist for multiple avenues of culturally informed analysis.

After I had spent almost a year doing my first fieldwork research in a Newfoundland fishing village in the 1970s, an eight-year-old girl asked if she could walk with me from one end of the village to the other. As we walked, she told me about each household we passed. She commented on who lived there, what they did for a living, and how they were related to other villagers. This was no small task given the fact that most of the nine hundred villagers shared the same three surnames and that marriage among first cousins was common. Widowhood and remarriage blended families in even more confusing ways. Compared to my young companion, I despaired of my own lack of local knowledge, despite my anthropological training in kinship analysis. When I started fieldwork in Norway, my frustration was even more basic, as it appeared that the family dog understood Norwegian better than I did. Moreover, in my classes at the University of South Dakota, I have to repeatedly engage Lakota, who, often having been the subjects of anthropological study, are wary of anthropology and anthropologists. Although I welcome the challenges these situations offer, when it comes to the Twins Talk Study, I must confess to an unabashed sense of satisfaction that comes from finally being the "native." I feel it incredibly liberating to be a twin and, like my young Newfoundland companion, to have that special insider's knowledge from having been "born there."

Yet *Twins Talk* includes much more than the view from a "pea in the pod." *Twins Talk* provides narrative data that produce and enact culture, as do festivals and twin research conferences. The difference is that as this ethnography brings twins to authorship, it shows how Twinsburg twins, as opposed to those who research twins, seem far more aware of how the "Who am I?" questions intersect with Western culture. Researchers show an overwhelming tendency to take their own or Western culture for granted. Even non-Western researchers and researchers who work in non-Western settings view twins through the lens of hegemonic Western cultural traditions. It also seems that if twins are viewed as more than just a method of research, researchers tend to focus overwhelmingly on twins gone bad. At festivals and in life, twins confront and challenge hegemonic notions of self. They do so by normalizing their twinship and by asserting alternative selfways.

Just as the different field sites—the pavilion, festivals, research conferences, and my own body and twin relationship—offer divergent but overlapping perspectives on identical twins, each of the chapters that follow engages a particular twinscape.[3] Each chapter expresses insider and outsider viewpoints and perspectives. With the exception of performance, the chapters to follow reflect the different disciplinary perspectives that dominate the twin research community. These include biology and genetics, psychology, and the social sciences. Each chapter employs a cultural psychology approach that integrates the chapters and serves to compare and contrast the interest and perspectives of researchers to those voiced by the talking partners. If the purpose of this study is to add to our understanding of how twinship is a standpoint from which life is invested with meaning, the view from the ground up (rather than from the top down) offers a critical reenvisioning of what it means to live in our society.

Doing interviews: twins talk at Twinsburg

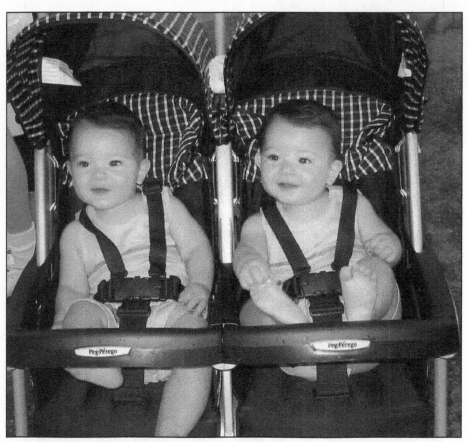

Babies at Twinsburg *(photo by author)*

Young girls at Twinsburg *(photo by author)*

Young women at Twinsburg (*photo by author*)

Midlife at Twinsburg *(photo by author)*

Elders at Twinsburg *(photo by author)*

Look-alike contest, ITA, Asheville, North Carolina *(photo by author)*

Look-alike kings and babies at Twinsburg *(photo by author)*

Two Amelia Peabody's with mummy: anthropologists at Celebrity Night
at the ITA in Asheville, North Carolina

PERFORMANCE

Culture exists in performance.

—*Hastrup 1995a*

The stage is set for you!

—*ITA Brochure for Nashville Tennessee, 2005*

I BEGIN THIS CHAPTER WITH AN INTRODUCTORY SCENARIO.

It had been well over a year since I had last seen my identical twin sister, Dorothy. While on a weeklong visit to celebrate our fifty-fifth birthday, Dorothy took me to her yoga class. As she introduced me to her instructor, the instructor began to catalogue our physical resemblances and differences—just as if we were little kids. Even after years of living separate lives in different parts of the country and after spending very little time together as adults, we enacted what, in retrospect, appears to be a long embodied routine. We moved close to each other and positioned ourselves, at arm's length, in front of the instructor. I put my right shoulder on Dorothy's left shoulder; we tilted towards each other, leaned our heads together and smiled idiotically at the instructor awaiting her assessment. Although neither one of us realized it at the time, we were performing our twinship. Realizing an assessment was at hand, our bodies automatically moved together and our faces smiled widely for our audience of one. Reflecting on the event (and many similar on-the-spot performances to a widening array of Dorothy's friends and colleagues), what I found remarkable was that we just did this without thinking. Our bodies seemed to act independently of any thoughts that this was a stupid way for two middle-aged, professional women to act. We must have done this so many times in our childhood that the act had become automatic. Because Dorothy has a dimple and I do not, our bodies came together to challenge the observer to identify the difference. We simultaneously satirized and performed our twinship by playing the twin game of "can you sort through the same and guess the difference?"

This scenario or depiction of playing or performing the twin game, or acting the part, demonstrates a kind of interpersonal, in-your-face self-styling that is crucial to the practical experience of being identical twins. For us, this moment of identities in practice, expressive styles (Ceronni-Long 2003), or acting the part took place months before we attended our first twins festival. Our impromptu creation of a twinscape, or our enactment of twinship, involved no forethought or conscious planning. Dorothy and I just did it. It happened with grins and laughter but without words. As jest and gesture among mature adult women, it was as idiosyncratic as idiotic. But it typifies a kind of self-work that twins do. In this particular instance, as we subjected ourselves to the gaze of a critical observer, we confounded her prefigured views of nature that assumed every person is unique or distinct. We invited assessment and comparison. Dorothy's yoga instructor knows Dorothy, but she does not know me. As we took center stage, the observer looked for similarities and differences, thus confirming both our mutuality and individuality. Our distinctions became contingent to be assessed. We set the stage, as we performed our twinship for the gaze of the other; we also challenged her to do our self-work for us. As the conversation shifted back and forth between the observer and the observed, Dorothy and I took control of the education process. Our constant and exaggerated smiles and coordinated head movements alerted the observer to

Dorothy's dimple. We listened to the observer's litany of differences until she hit on the dimple as the one that was meaningful to us. Acting the part, our embodied performance of same and different also expressed our connection and mutuality.

We have played this game before. It is part and parcel of the practical experience of twinship. It sets us as twins, the observed, in contrast to the singletons, the observers. As a playful act, the twin game also has a satirical edge that simultaneously mocks and confirms our own society's cultural persona (Holland and Leander 2004) or stereotype of twinship as a deviant, or transgressive, kind of identity. This is true for the observer as well for us. She could easily have said, "One of you is blonde and the other has brown hair." Instead, Dorothy's yoga instructor chose to play the game.[1] The anthropologist Don Handelman (1990) would refer to our twin moment as a *proto-event*—an event that just happens, as opposed to an intentionally designed or organized activity. For Dorothy and me, the performance of twinship probably echoes countless times in our shared, brown-haired childhood when we behaved in a similar fashion. In one sense, it is an old habit of self styling that has lain dormant, buried during all the years we have lived apart. As such, it was a kind of performance that was improvised, created, or recreated in the flow of activity. Like models who pose for the camera, listening to the photographer's constant mantra of "work it, work it, sell it, sell it," Dorothy and I strut our individual and collective selves. This single incident of performing the twin game sets the scene for the analysis that follows. Our seemingly spontaneous and playful performance has an agentive quality in that we refashion ourselves, for the moment, in our own ways according to our own logics (cf. Szerzynski, Heim, and Waterton 2003).

Being repeat performers of the twin game, however, did little to prepare us for the combination of the specula and spectacular twinscapes presented at twins festivals. For twins, acting the part at twins festivals is all about having fun, making fun, and seeing and being seen. Festival twins create themselves as walking, talking, and embodied personifications of a deviant, culturally imagined type of self. As cultural performances and public events, twins festivals are a type of turnabout or rite of reversal where, for a couple of days a kind of full-blown pan-twinness rules. Twins become the norm, and singletons the exotic other.

ACTING THE PART

The dramatic potential of an identical twin pair has not been overlooked in popular culture. Twins sell products, twins can be actors or celebrities, and giving birth to twins has become trendy among Hollywood celebrities. We all probably have firsthand knowledge of at least one or two twin pairs. Yet imagine yourself set down among thousands of twin pairs. Our private proto-event becomes writ large, public and pro forma, at twins festivals where twinscapes are staged to include hundreds or even thousands of twins who gather together to play the twin game. Festivals are not just about one pair of twins working it; they are about twins *en masse* working it. Almost every state in the union has a twins festival that is open to twins and other multiples. Scheduled on weekends and announced on websites, some are held annually and some biannually. They are open to twins of all ages. Some festivals, like those in Nebraska, are attended by only eight to ten sets of twins, while the largest, in Ohio, attracts thousands annually. As organized public events, festivals include games, contests, parties, and parades. The media are always welcome at these events.

PERFORMANCE

"Culture exists in performance" (Hastrup 1995a, 78), and festival twinscapes, where twins self-style as physically identical, pose a kind of in-your-face assault on the Western notion of individualism. Twins festivals as public events have all the trappings of carnival and spectacle. Whether or not you are a twin, twins festivals are a visually stunning and spectacular experience. Yet twins festivals are more than just about seeing and being seen; they are about seeing double. A large part of festival activity consists of a kind of Brownian motion of a seemingly endless number of matched people pairs. Identically dressed twin pairs mill around the festival and participate in contests, games, and parades. Twins festivals provide opportunities to investigate cultures in action (MacAloon 1984a) and are examples of society "cutting out a piece of itself from itself for inspection" (Turner quoted in Stoeltje 1978, 450). The public and an exaggerated performance of twinship at twins festivals offers some interesting insights into the components of a twin's self, as well as twins' selves.

While other chapters focus on biological and psychological dynamics and development of mutuality and identity within or inside of the twin pair, the goal of this chapter is to depict a more public, collective face of twinship. Festival twins become constructors and actors in their own dramas. They act out scripts and codes that directly and indirectly challenge the hierarchies or ideologies of self and personhood that discipline the world in which they live (Szerzsynski et al. 2003). At festivals twins perform multiple selfways, including their deviant personae in both a negative and a positive sense. Festival twins, who assemble at a common location to play with appearances and who celebrate and publicly perform their twinship, both attract and repel outside observers. By emphasizing or parodying their physical resemblance to each other, festival twins deliberately transgress conventional notions about individualism as naturally based in the distinctiveness of each individual's embodied identity. But festival twins also celebrate different or alternative dimensions of human relatedness. They promote togetherness over autonomy. They revel in a sense of mutuality or connection to each other. Twins festivals may thus be viewed not only as statements of personal, interpersonal, and collective relationships and identities but also as embodied rites of resistance or reversal. In this chapter I use the cultural psychology approach (Markus et al. 1997; Neisser 1997; Ortner 2006; Shweder 1991) to examine how self and culture mutually construct each other, as festival twins cultivate a shared dyadic bodily aesthetic and a unique connection to each other.

TWINS FESTIVALS AS PUBLIC EVENTS AND CULTURAL PERFORMANCE

Performance theorists use terms like *cultural performance, social drama, spectacle, carnival, festival, rite of resistance,* and *public ritual* to refer to culturally designed forms of organized, expressive, collective social gatherings, activities, or experiences (MacAloon 1984a). Although I prefer the term *festival,* I will also follow Handelman's (1990) lead by employing the more inclusive term *public event.* Although Twins Days is referred to as a *festival* and the ITAs are referred to as *conventions,* both celebrations of twinship fit the criteria for a public event. Public events involve active and interactive performances that are amenable to direct observation. They are real, discrete, and bounded events that take place at specific times and locations. As dramatic and expressive experiences, public events engage the senses (Handelman 1990).

Twins festivals as public events are times of celebration and satirical high humor that give primacy to sensory, visual codes (Handelman 1990). As public events, mass public performances of twinship may be described as having a paradoxical quality. Festival twins play with appearances. Twins at festivals enact what Laderman and Roseman (1992, 9) refer to as "archetypal personalities." Stereotypes of twins involve more than just being identical. By enjoying a festival's events together, twins also express their sense of connection and mutuality.

Festival twins act not only to become objects of fascination; they aim to elicit shock and wonder. Public events may challenge social order or reconfirm the normative as they present alternatives and new utopian models of social reality or heighten awareness of multiple realities that already exist (Clark 2005; Ehrenreich 2007; Handelman 1990; Kapferer 1984; Laderman and Roseman 1992; MacAloon 1984a; Morris 1994; Rapport and Overing 2000; Stoeltje 1978; Turner 1984). Festival twinscapes offer a kind of identity couvade (Josephides 2010)—a chance to "freak the mundane"—where twins rule and singletons become the exotic other. At festivals, twins can emerge as weird and scary, if not threatening or even dangerous. Adult twins, dressed alike and meandering around festival grounds and venues side by side or even hand in hand perform a version of what Bakhtin (cited in Morris 1994), referring to festivals, calls the grotesque, exaggerated, or transgressive body (or, in this case, body pair). Twins performing twinship represent both structure and antistructure. They mock and they celebrate. They are betwixt and between—a special condition in the world that simultaneously embodies unity and duality (cf. Turner 1985). Twins invert the norms and override or reverse everyday distinctions and categories. The low may be exalted and the mighty abased. Another space is created (Lindholm 2001) in which festival twins not only perform a counterhegemonic act of resistance to outside moldings of their personality but also set forth alternative values and more relational styles of personhood, where twinship becomes desired, if not necessarily normalized, in the process.

TWINSBURG'S TWINS DAYS FESTIVAL AND THE INTERNATIONAL TWINS ASSOCIATION CONVENTIONS

Although both fit Handelman's (1990) criteria for a public event, Twinsburg's Twins Days and the International Twins Association meetings are distinctive types of twins festivals. Twins Days, the largest and best known, draws twins and twins researchers and attracts extensive national and international media attention. Activities at Twins Days take place both on and off the festival grounds, but the main festival is held at the local high school. If not exactly Saturnalia, or a party when "anything goes," off the festival grounds at hotels around Twinsburg, wild parties last till the early hours of the morning, and as our research assistant, Kristi, reported, can become so rowdy that the police get called to intervene and restore order. As one twin remarked to a reporter, "It's not really fun until you're of drinking age." While the Twinsburg festival has the feel of a rather impersonal meeting of strangers or a mass event and media spectacle, the much smaller ITA feels more like an intimate, friendly social club consisting of an annual gathering of about 160 sets of twins.[2] The "wild" element of the ITAs consists of silly games and elaborate costumes. The ITA takes pride in being the oldest festival in the United States and changes its venue every year so that participants can travel to different locations. One participant told us that she preferred the ITA festival because it was "old faces and new places" instead of the "old places and new faces" of Twinsburg.

Although both are well-established twins festivals, each has a distinctive ambience that affects the performance of twinship and the configuration of insider and outsider perspectives. Due to its status as a massive, media-savvy event, the Twinsburg festival may be used to explore a variety of positioned perspectives of insider versus outsider views on twins and "being identical" across a number of dimensions that contrast the strange and familiar. The ITAs, which draw on the same core participants year after year and feature activities that include all attendees, are characterized by a sense of inclusiveness and intimate conviviality lacking at Twinsburg. While Twinsburg is family friendly, the ITA is more like a family itself.

Each festival has a similar mission. The Twins Days' mission is "to provide a vehicle for celebrating the uniqueness of twins and others of multiple births" (Miller 2003, 5). The ITA describes itself as "one of the world's most unique fraternal organizations organized by and for twins to promote the spiritual, intellectual, and social welfare of twins throughout the world." A large part of the differences between the two festivals stems from the backgrounds, agendas, and expectations of those who organize and promote each festival. Twins Days is run by a small, full-time staff of singletons with the assistance of volunteers. Although both are nonprofit organizations, the ITA is a much smaller organization, and its festivals are planned by a member set of twin cochairs who are different each year. Twins Days does bring a substantial amount of tourist dollars into the town of Twinsburg and the surrounding areas, whereas the venues of the ITAs change every year. By and large, Twins Days is a massive event in which participating twins choose from a variety of events and find their own niches for participation, their own accommodations, and transportation to events. Nightlife at Twins Days is focused around nonfestival venues where twins stay, including campgrounds, trailer parks, and hotels. At the much smaller ITA convention, participants stay in a single hotel and eat lunch and dinner together. Twins take rented buses to tour local sites and attend organized dances and games in the evening. Almost all attendees at the ITAs participate in the scheduled activities, which occur from morning to night.

In terms of organized programs, the events are similar, sharing an emphasis on performance of identicalness. This is true even among fraternal twins. Each event has an organized program that includes registration and fees, interdenominational religious services, contests, games, talent shows, and golf tournaments. There is also a 5K race at the Twinsburg festivals and bowling night at the ITAs. Concerts, dances, and group photos are also important events at each venue. The Twins Days' "Double Take Parade" marches through the main streets of Twinsburg. Both organizations elect kings and queens, while Twinsburg also votes for princes and princesses. Both the ITA and Twinsburg festivals have a series of most-alike and least-alike contests in which twins are broken down by age and gender. Few twins participate in the least-alike contests. Although Twinsburg welcomes both identical and fraternal twins at these festivals, it is clear that MZs upstage DZs, and triplets and quads are the biggest stars.

Why do twins come from all over the United States and beyond at considerable personal expense to attend these festivals? Certainly festivals provide an opportunity for twins to act out their twinship. Twin gatherings contain elements of the absurd and a carnivalesque atmosphere (Bakhtin cited in Morris 1994; DaMatta 1984). Both festivals play to the identicalness of twins and celebrate the joyous mood of twinship. Most twins come to Twinsburg or the ITAs with a sense of play and humor. Participants say the festivals are fun, and they look forward to attending all year long. Proud parents of young twins get to show them off while seeking and sharing parenting advice and frustrations with other parents of twins. Older twins get to relive and remember their childhoods together. As Mary and Martha say, "We get to play at being twins like in the old days." Many twins have been going to the festivals since they were small children and now return to renew the long-standing friendships they have formed with other sets of twins. New friendships are also established. The festivals provide opportunities for twins to meet those who share common interests. As Amy and Beth say, "It is an opportunity to stare at other sets of twins instead of always having people stare at you."

Festivals also provide an opportunity for twins now living apart to spend time together. Many festival twins we talked to said they typically see each other infrequently. Festivals provide a chance for twins to socialize, often without partners or children; but, ultimately, the festival experience itself is the big draw. The party atmosphere, especially in Twinsburg, also offers some twins a chance to get away from family obligations and cut loose. Arnette and Annette come to Twinsburg with all their grandchildren in tow. Pete and Emil, Judy and Janet, and Kim and Karan first came to Twins Days to celebrate the recovery of one of the twin pair from a serious illness. Similarly, some twins appreciate the festival as a way to reconnect when children are grown or a spouse has died. Some twins who have lost their brother or sister also find comfort in attending the festivals. Certainly to attend either festival is to capture attention, win prizes, and perhaps to have a photograph appear in a newspaper or magazine. Attendees may even attract the attention of a talent agent or be asked to appear in a documentary film. Attending a festival and being the objects of constant photographing, attention, and the gazes of others can make every twin pair feel like celebrities. Being special for looking or acting the same is what these festivals are all about. When Dorothy and I were on stage participating in contests at the ITAs, there were so many flashbulbs going off that I felt like an A-list Hollywood star posing for the paparazzi. The pleasure of a few moments of being in the spotlight, of working it for the cameras, of being the center of attention, and of sharing the stage should not be underestimated. It is a rush.

In this section, I focus on the public performance of twinship en masse at Twins Days, as well as twins talk. I doing so, I reflect an insider's view. But twins talk also includes a twin's view of the outsider or singleton's view of them as twins. Originally, I had viewed Twins Days solely as an exceptional opportunity to gain access to a large sample of twins during a short period of time. Yet Dorothy and I, sitting in the Research Pavilion where we were surrounded by sets of twins, became as enthusiastic about the festival experience as our talking partners. One of our background questions for our talking partners asked if this was the twins' first Twins Days. Unexpectedly, this question set a tone for talking about the festival experience at the beginning of each conversation. Twins talk in the pavilion was grounded in what was happening around them. What emerged in the Twinsburg conversations was a well-articulated countervoice of twins. In a sense, edgy expressions of twinship are an artifact of the Twinsburg experience. As formerly stated, twins festivals are about seeing and being seen. Even twins report being shocked at the sight of so many identical pairs in one place. As massive as it is, Twins Days positions twin participants against non-twin participants. Non-twins include the media, festival organizers, researchers, and those who provide services, including hotel accommodations and restaurants.

At the Twinsburg festival, Dorothy and I bridged the roles of researchers by day on the festival grounds and participants at night in offsite, unorganized activities. Kristi also supplied us with a constant narrative on a young singleton's perspective of the events. It was very clear to us, moreover, that twenty-something Kristi's experience of the after-hours revelry was very different from our own experience. Also, as twin researchers of twins, we had the opportunity to interact and talk with the media as well as the singleton twins researchers. Additionally, twins talk frequently engaged a multiplicity of perspectives that festival participation and performance of twinship en masse seems to evoke. As the cultural psychology approach views selfways as positioned and multiple, in what follows, I draw on the Twins Days experience to present and discuss a number of overlapping themes regarding the notions of situated or positioned identities and perspectives. When it comes to insider and outsider perspectives, acting the parts of twins can take an interesting series of twists and turns.

My analysis of acting the parts at Twins Days features three distinguishable combinations and permutations of insider and outsider perspectives, as they relate to the festival and to the participant twins. As a twin and as an anthropologist, I have little problem bridging the three different perspectives. The first is an insider perspective that describes how twins view themselves in the festival setting. It focuses on the enactment or performance of twinship from the twin's perspectives and from experiences of the twins themselves. Here, the stress is on "doing" and the more visual, embodied aspects of performance. Doing centers on the existential, experiential enactments of twinship as unique, but paired, identical bodies. A second perspective entails an outsider's view or how festivals and festival twins are depicted by the media, non-twins, and skeptical twins. Although festival twins are portrayed as objects of fascination, twins performing twinship en masse clearly both attract and repulse the outside observer. The third section joins insider and outsider perspectives and looks at how the twins, as they interact with other sets of twins, come to see themselves as insiders *and* outsiders at the festival. This third perspective also addresses how festival twins view the outsiders' views of them. The discussion then moves from the idea of being identical as an embodied counternorm to an emphasis on feelings of mutuality and connectedness as an even more powerful counternorm that twins characterize as lying at the heart of the twin experience. When thousands of twins repeatedly perform the twin game for thousands of observers, an exaggerated version of the experience of being twins becomes enacted. Festivals focus attention on the practical experiences of twinship by serving to heighten awareness of self stylings and self work done by identical twins as located on fault lines or borderlands of identity.

Insider's View: The Actors

At twins festivals, twins play the twin game. They perform or enact the cultural persona of twinship or society's stereotypical caricature of them. "Getting into the festival spirit" entails being identical. Although the phrase "seeing double" seems trite, it captures the essence of twins festivals. Looking as alike as possible is the performance goal of most of the twin pairs at Twins Days. Adult twins—identical and fraternal, young and old, male and female—who were never dressed alike or have not dressed alike for years, make a great effort to present themselves in ways that enact stereotypes about them as identical. It is not just about bodies; it is also about trappings on the body. Dressing identically becomes a kind of body art. It should hold up from first casual glance to a more detailed scrutiny and assessment of how alike a twin pair looks. Many twins pay painstaking attention to detail, matching earrings, pocketbooks, makeup, nail polish, glasses, and hairstyles. The idea here is to celebrate, or relive twinship, and to have fun.

There are plenty of adorable children dressed identically who receive the "oohs" and "aahs" of onlookers. Some children are dressed in identical T-shirts emblazoned with phrases such as "It's a twin thing," "Like two peas in a pod," and "If no two snowflakes are alike, then I'm glad we're not snowflakes." There are also adults who walk around in T-shirts that proclaim their twin status with the word *twin* written across their chests. Their identical T-shirts bear messages such as "Double Trouble," "Born Together," "Look out, there's two of me," "Clones," "I'm the evil twin," "It must have been my evil twin," and the classic "I'm with stupid." Adult T-shirts also reflect relational themes such as "Friends Forever," "It's a twin thing / you wouldn't understand," and "I'm smiling because you're my sister / and I'm laughing because there is nothing you can do about it." A carnivalesque sense of high humor and a sense of challenging, bending, or breaking singleton norms and rules predominate. Twins can even replicate their replicate selves, with each twin wearing a photo button of their twin pair in the same place on their bodies. All this can get confusing, which is exactly the point. Jeana and Dina told us how the photographers coached them on how to look alike for their button pictures. They went through (and paid for) many takes before they got a photograph that suited them both.

The effect of twins festivals is well depicted as "uncanny." Ironically, one's sense of being unique and special as a pair of twins is both enhanced and muted as one is surrounded by twins by the dozens. Some festival twins develop expressive self styling or personae that make them stand out among the thousands of sets of twins that surround them. At Twinsburg Dorothy, Kristi, and I began referring to sets of high-profile twins (those who stood out) with identifying labels like the Fabio twins, the Parrot twins, the Harley twins, the Kings, the Playgirl and Playboy twins, the Cowgirl twins (in Western outfits) and the Cow girl twins (in cow suits), the Doctor twins, and the twins on *The Simpsons*. Talking with ITA twins who had also attended the Twinsburg festival, we found other sets of twins had come up with the same labels. Some twins dress like a famous celebrity. At Twinsburg, twin sisters dressed like Dolly Parton. In their case, my own sense of reality was suspended. Initially, I thought they were over-the-top, rural southern throwbacks to the 1950s, but Dorothy and Kristi convinced me they were in costume.

Although the websites and promotional materials for Twinsburg note that it is not necessary to dress alike, attendees are advised that most twins get into the festival spirit by dressing alike. Jenna and Steph, identical twins in their early forties (who do not look much alike and regard themselves as "complete opposites"), told us that they had arrived for their first time at Twinsburg with no similar clothes. They felt like pariahs on the first day because they felt that no one would talk to them. On day two, they bought identical festival T-shirts and said they fit in then, entering conversations and making friends with other twins. Deciding to dress in similar clothes but in different colors, Dorothy and I also felt like outsiders among the mass of pairs at Twinsburg. We had the impression that our decision to wear essentially the same clothes but in different colors (as our mother often had dressed us in later childhood) was a cop-out. Having different hairstyles and hair color (dyed) also marked us as not in the spirit of the festival. At Twinsburg we were constantly advised that identical baseball caps would be a simple and quick fix to the hair problem.

The appeal of dressing alike and participating in contests, however, can become strangely addictive, as Dina and Jeana explain.

> Dina: I planned this whole vacation. Jeana had no idea.
> I told her we were in the parade. It was fun. I like
> this whole twin fest thing because we've learned so
> much. Next year I want to come back in costumes
> like other people were doing and throw out candy.
> During the parade it was funny because I like waving
> to people; it's like I'm saying, "Thank you for
> supporting us twins."

Jeana: We're going to have to plan next year. We've learned and lived through this one. Next year will be even better. What we've found interesting is how much we desire to look alike now, whereas before it was like, well, OK, we look similar. We went to a restaurant where the waiter said, "I would never have guessed you were twins." I mean that, like, hurt. In high school we tried so hard not to look alike. Now we want to look alike.

After their first time at Twins Days, Jeana and Dina planned to dedicate more planning and effort to dressing exactly alike for the festival. They have become socialized by the festival experience to dress alike "with attitude" for Twins Days. Three years after we first met them, Pete and Emil sent me an article from their local newspaper that announced they had finally won the look-alike award for their age category at Twinsburg. They were also proud to have finally won, at age eighty, recognition for being the third-oldest twins at Twins Days in 2004. Annette and Arnette are two middle-aged women who describe themselves as "Twins Days regulars." They have attended the festival for eight consecutive years. When they competed in their first festival look-alike contest, Arnette was over sixty pounds heavier than Annette. After the first festival, Arnette was inspired to lose the extra weight so they would look more alike for future contests. Twins who attend twins festivals are enthusiastic performers of an envisioned twin persona. At festivals, twins become the norm as look-alike twins of all ages dominate the *peoplescape*. By performing identical or sameness, twins place themselves at odds with Western society's notions of independence, autonomy, and individuality. This becomes clear when we take into account the views of the media and singletons.

Outsider's View: An Audience of Singletons

Because twins dominate the peoplescape in Twinsburg, they provide a dramatic twinscape for outsiders who attend the festival. Outsiders are singletons who include researchers, reporters, spouses, siblings, parents, children, friends of twins, service or sales personnel, and the general public who watch the parades and contests. Reporters, feature writers, filmmakers, and photographers from all over the world descend on the Twins Days Festival. Outsiders' views of festival twins can be ambivalent. Festivals are designed to shock and unsettle and, as public events (Handelman 1990), twins festivals give primacy to sensory visual codes. If a pair of twins can be described as "dramatically visible" and a "fascinating condition of humanity" (Wright 1997, 110), then what effect does the sight of thousands of pairs of twins have? Wright's (1997) depiction of identical twins as an unsettling presence in the world well captures the singleton, outsider's experience of twins festivals. Our research assistant, Kristi Cody (2004, 14), felt visually assaulted by the sight of so many twins. Kristi reports that she was "totally freaked" by Twins Days and claims, "It was like entering an episode of the *X Files*." Journalist Tony Barrell (2003, 22) writes of Twins Days that the casual observer "is at risk of flipping out when they see all these human carbon copies." Like Barrell, reporters have a field day with word play as they describe the impacts of seeing so many twins together. Their prose is peppered by references to "seeing double," "double vision," "double trouble," "double the interest," "two heads are better than one," "freaks with four legs," "queues of twos," "doppelgangers," "seeing double without the penalty of a hangover," and so forth.

Seeing thousands of twins is a kind of assault on the senses and conflicts with the idea that one's face should reflect one's distinctiveness, or personal identity. Twins in this sense are weird and scary to the outsider, if not threatening or even dangerous. But the unsettling effect grows with the age of the twins. The anthropological literature on twins indicates that identical twins lose any of their culturally elaborated distinctiveness after childhood (Dorothy Davis 1971; Stewart 2003). Yet at Twinsburg, over 30 percent of twins registered for the festival are over twenty-one years old (Miller 2003). As Kristi told us, "The little kids are really cute, but for adults it's kind of sick. They [identical adults] need to get a life." Likewise, Bacon (2005) notes that while identically dressed babies are seen as a delight, identically dressed adults are not. In our society identically dressed adults will be stigmatized. Piontelli (2008, 219) has this to say about adult female twins who continue to dress alike.

> Although doppelganger behavior elicits the attention of
> passers-by, it makes adults appear freakish or pathetic, just
> like the fading stars in "Sunset Boulevard" who try uselessly
> to hang on to their withered glory.

For singletons it appears that the face is a sort of label for a distinctiveness that lies within. If identical twins complement their like faces with identical outfits, the singleton observer suspects that the self may somehow be divided, diluted, or duplicated. If personal identities can be conflated, the self, especially at adulthood, is therefore impaired.

At festivals, as twins revel in dressing alike and surrender themselves to the pair, there is certainly a sense of what Bakhtin refers to as the exaggerated or grotesque body (Morris 1994). Although Bakhtin was describing the clowns of early medieval festivals, his depiction of the grotesque body as not individualized, as open, as having a double aspect, and as a kind of co-being that implies self/other interaction, certainly describes the twinscapes at modern-day festivals. Because they subvert normative expectations of unique identity, because the low are exalted, and because the freaks become the norm, twins festivals can be viewed as rites of inversion.

This perspective of the grotesque body and co-being is well verbalized by Maddox (2006, 66), a popular science writer who wrote a negative commentary about the 2005 Twinsburg festival. Portraying the festival, with its "muted horrors of pan-Twinism," as exemplifying the dark side or doomsday scenario of a future world populated by clones, Maddox (2006, 66) refers to the twin participants as "deeply creeping me out with their mutual bodies." He depicts twins as clones "without souls," "without their own identities," who will "never know the quintessential joy of feeling different." Maddox also extends his distaste of what he sees as the biological duplication of one's self to the twin's relationship or what he terms the twin "love factor." Maddox describes the Twinsburg twins who perambulate the festival grounds dressed alike and arm in arm as "existential puzzles," with one twin knowing exactly what the other is going through and with a twin loving the other twin "arguably more than anyone has or ever will love us [singletons]." Maddox refers to the "I heart-heart my twin" T-shirts that depict two side-by-side hearts and that some pairs of twins wore at Twinsburg 2005 as a kind of "quiet ecstasy of platonic love" implying a kind of self-love that would promote cloning. Maddox's equation of twinship—with fears of cloning—demonizes, oppresses, and marginalizes them. His over-the-top text, published in the popular science magazine *Discover*, no less, demonstrates the extent to which outsiders may see Twins Days twins' sense of communion with each other as disintegrating or undermining boundaries between self and other. Twins, thus, undermine Western notions of relationality and an individualism that should maintain a "mystery of mutual distance between individuals" (Ehrenreich 2007, 12).

Maddox, although overwhelmed and spooked by the mass performance of identicalness, appears to have made no effort to talk to twins. Kristi, however, who began referring to the Twins Days Festival as "clone days," repeatedly told us that what kept her grounded was the fact that Dorothy and I (who did not dress alike) were obviously "two separate individuals, two different people, two real people." Although this chapter starts with an example of us performing our identicality, Dorothy and I initially shared Kristi's shock at such calculated and flagrant exhibitions of likeness and what we saw as a denial of individuality. We should have known better, of course, as any twin or anyone who knows twins well understands that twins are individuals. At twins festivals, twins are doing the part of their self-work that addresses their similarities and mutuality. Yet, for us the visual and visceral impact of so many people, particularly adults our own age, looking alike and dressing alike was deeply disconcerting. As we talked to twins, however, we began to see beyond the stereotype and came to better understand the difference between public, festival performance and reality.

Festivals are fun and freaky. They entertain and excite the imagination. The outsiders' perspectives, however, are not all negative. Singleton observers can and do positively identify with the mutuality and connectedness they observe between and among the twin pairs. Kristi reports that on the plane ride back home to South Dakota, she had never felt so alone in all her life. In his feature article on the Twinsburg festival, a British journalist writes, "I hadn't bargained for the emotional consequences of socializing with hordes of twins. After two days I began to feel profoundly lonely, as if I were lacking another half who walked, talked and wrote features exactly like me" (Barrell 2003, 5). In this positive view of twinship, twins are viewed as uniquely close and are envied for having a best friend (Stewart 2003). Twins are assumed to have an ideal companion who understands them (Wright 1997). Kristi told us that after Twins Days she was haunted by wishes that she too had a twin; having a singleton sister was just not enough.

Twins often hear others wish that they too were a twin. Twinship clearly has a positive side that celebrates a mutuality, a friendliness, and a sense of "we-ness" that singletons recognize as absent in their own lives. Obviously, the twin persona, although deviant, has negative and positive aspects. Twins, as we see in chapter 6, often refer to "having a friend for life" or "always having someone there for you." Twins and twinship reflect multiple realities and selfways. Twins talk reflects these multiple realities and ambivalences, but first I need to comment on how twins themselves blur or bridge insider and outsider roles at Twins Days by becoming their own audience.

At all festivals and public events there are performers and audiences, but their roles are often blurred. At festivals the individual feels he is an indissoluble part of the collectivity, or the crowd—a member of the people's mass body. In this scenario the individual body ceases to a certain extent to be itself, and at the same time people become aware of their sensual, material, bodily unity and community (Bakhtin [1965] cited in Morris 1995, 226). This is also true of twins festivals. One particular example is what I call a "twin agglomeration." Twin agglomerations are spontaneous happenings that occur repeatedly throughout the festivals. During the festival, twins and the media are constantly taking pictures. For example, at the Twinsburg opening night picnic, there were twin sisters who wore identical, colorful West African tie-died dresses and elaborate cloth headdresses. As they agreeably posed for photographs, the twins photographing them would then join them as others took their picture. What was originally one set of twins in a photo became a line of twins standing shoulder to shoulder until the crowd got so large that no more twins fit into the picture. This happens repeatedly as festival twins switch from audience to performer with enthusiastic fluidity. Twins thus perform their identicality for the lens of other twins as well as for outside observers in which the press figures prominently. Although fun for twins, agglomerations are frustrating for professional photographers, as revealed to me by a photographer who was shooting pictures for an article in a popular science magazine. His attempts to capture one pair of twins were constantly thwarted by the continued entry of other sets of twins into his shot.

Attending a festival can be too much for some twins who try it once and never again. Yet for twins who are hooked, a large part of the pleasure comes from saving and planning for the Twins Days weekend. Our talking partners told us that when they return home, they no longer make any effort to dress alike (except for Julie and Jenny) and would feel uncomfortable doing so. It is also interesting that despite considerable effort invested in looking alike for two days, every set of twins we talked with remarked that they felt that most other sets of identical twins at the conference looked more alike than they did.

Insider View of Outsider View: What We Think You Think

Being among other sets of twins en masse ironically heightens twins' senses of not only being twins but also of being anomalies. Our conversations with Twins Days twins reveal that they have much to say about the outsiders' views of them as twins. Dorothy and I, before Twins Days, had never used or even heard of the term "singleton." We certainly had a sense of being special because we were twins. We were lifelong actors of the twin game, but we had never developed a sense of "us" as twins versus a "them" of the single born. At Twinsburg, we found ourselves buying into and frequently referring to this new boundary of identity. Like other festival twins, we began to position ourselves as distinct from the singleton other. By performing twinship, Twins Days twins report that one of the attractions of participating in festivals is the sense of resisting or inverting the singleton norm. Twins festivals are a counterhegemonic act of resistance to outside moldings of one's personality (cf. Lindholm 2001, 218) or the very nature of being. Festivals are occasions where, for a few days, a new space is created (Lindholm 2001, 219) in which twins as "us" become the norm and singletons become "them," or the other. At festivals from a twin's perspective, the singleton becomes an exotic other and twins the norm.

As the archetype of "twins as freaks" takes over, twins become normalized in the process. When performing as twins, insiders feel less freakish while at the same time actually confirming their freakishness to the singleton outsider. By reversing the rules, the "freaks" take over and the "mighty" are found wanting. By literally parading around, twins challenge what is seen as the natural order and everyday constructions of being. Many of our talking partners would remark on how good it felt to be surrounded by twins, to be in an environment where twins were the norm rather than the exception. For once they felt free from the question "What is it like to be a twin?" They repeatedly told us that it was liberating to talk to Dorothy and me as researchers who were also twins.

Twins Days has a way of creating militant twins. Tim and Tom had been in the festival parade before coming to us for an interview. When we asked them at the end of our interview if they wanted to add anything, Tom presented the following commentary:

> Tom: Maybe one question [to pursue] is on the way society
> looks at us. Like when we were walking in the parade
> this morning and it was, "Oh, the twins are walking
> down the thing [street]." And I explain to somebody
> during the parade that the twin parade is like a regular
> parade. You have clowns and you have elephants.
> And I said, "We're the elephants." And then I told
> Tim, "There's someone with a shovel in the back."
> We're the normal ones, OK? . . . When people ask
> you, "How do you feel about being a twin? Do you
> feel like you are special or do you feel like you are a
> mistake?" We're what? One percent of the population?
> We're born that way so we're not a mistake. But when
> people ask me what does it feel like to be a twin, I
> answer, "What does it feel like not to be a twin?" I
> don't know what it feels like to be a twin, I am a twin.
> I tell them, "I'm normal; you're the freak."

> Dona: You're [singleton] the one with the imaginary friend;
> mine was real.

My rejoinder to Tom may be an example of "leading the witness," but it also brings out another important theme about the twin self.

Performing twinship is not just about seeing double or being identical. Twins come to Twinsburg (and the ITAs) to celebrate a sense of connectedness and mutuality that lies deep below the mere surface of their bodies. Karan's observation below has an edge to it that was common in our interviews.

> Karan: I keep saying this . . . it's just on the surface but
> everyone keeps asking, "What is it like to be a twin?"
> I'm like, I have no idea what it's not like to be a twin.
> So I have no idea what it's like not to have somebody

> at my side all the time. . . . really I could care less
> about what it means *not* to be a twin.

Side-by-side festival twins perform what they see as a special sense of mutuality or a special kind or condition of self. Elizabeth Stewart (2003) calls this the "we-self." It is a mutuality twins know firsthand and so they come together for a pan-twin celebration of this shared sense of connection. They refer to this as the twin bond; it is a special bond that twins feel yet singletons fail to appreciate or experience. Although this theme is developed in chapter 5, suffice it to say here that at festivals, twins celebrate the we-ness of their twinship. In doing so, they provide a counterpoint to what Wright (1997, 55) rather benignly characterizes as their "uncanny relationship" and what Maddox (2006, 66) refers to as a "quiet ecstasy of platonic love" among "every double one of them." What twins feel the outsider does not understand is that their celebrated sense of connection is rooted not only in the similar faces and bodies but also in the sense of connectedness that comes from shared lives. Twins report a special sense of connectedness, or relatedness, that is unlike the other forms of relatedness they experience in their lives. What it means to be bonded as twins, they say, is something only a twin can know. Twins feel that within the twin dyad, needs for affiliation and autonomy work themselves out differently than for singletons. If culture exists in performance (Hastrup 1995a), then at the Twinsburg festival, identical twins may be seen as negotiating their duality and unity in what McCollum (2002) characterizes as a culture that views autonomy and relationality as opposites and privileges the former. For the adult talking partners, attending Twins Days results in a kind of renewal, or revitalization, of their twin identities and relationship. For two or three days of heightened experience, they relive, rehone and refashion, and share (with other twins) the practical experiences of twinship. Getting in the spirit at Twins Days, certainly among participant twins, fosters a sense of rebellion, of being apart from a singleton-dominated world, and in the case of our talking partners (and ourselves), an emergent identity of being a militant twin.

THE ITA: TOURING TWINS

Being relegated to the Research Pavilion at Twinsburg had isolated us from the daytime festival activities such as the parades, group photos, look-alike contests, and talent shows. After Twins Days, Dorothy and I wanted to have the full experience as participants at a twins festival. We also wanted to see if the twins talk we shared in the more formalized settings of Twinsburg also carried over to less formal settings. After Twins Days we decided to attend the International Twins Association meetings held at the end of summer 2003 in Atlanta, Georgia.

Although organized around similar activities the much smaller ITAs have a far different ambiance from Twins Days. The ITAs lack the funds and media savvy of the numerous Twins Days committees. Attendees at the ITAs know each other and renew their acquaintances every year, while Twins Days twins largely are and will remain strangers to each other. Twinsburg, with its thousands of attendees, is a kind of common interest activity. The ITAs, attended mainly by adult twins, is a common interest group. There are hardly any parents of young twins in attendance, and the media is neither a notable nor active presence. Twins Days, in contrast, treats twins more as a category of paired persons. Twins Days twins mill around a common ground while deciding as a twin pair which activities they will participate in or merely pass by. While evening parties and activities reveal that there are cliques composed of twins who have known each other over the years, the overwhelming majority of Twins Days twins will remain anonymous to each other. The ITAs are organized around formally scheduled activities in which all attendees are expected to participate. Unlike Twins Days, it is impossible to participate without registering. Wearing name tags, all attendees get to know each other. ITA attendees make an effort to introduce themselves to all the participants. While both festivals have an ecumenical Sunday church service, the more intimate and elderly oriented ITAs express a concern with the spirituality and well-being of the members. Unlike Twins Days with its permanent professional or semiprofessional organizers, each ITA meeting is organized by local sets of twins (or triplets) who live near the meeting site and put a great deal of time and effort into ensuring a successful festival. ITA leadership rotates among members, and each year's conference organizers take on visible roles as hosts for all the weekend activities. Unlike the more cosmopolitan Twins Days and its attendant outsiders, there is no sense of "us" against "them." At the Atlanta ITA, Dorothy and I discovered how pleasant it was to make friends with and hang out with other sets of twins. Over the three days we came to feel a mutual sense of affinity with the ITA twins that was strong enough to bring us back to another meeting.

The ITAs lack the wild party atmosphere of offsite events at the hotels in Twinsburg. Although welcoming and extremely sociable, the ITAs are not as much freaky or wild as they are wholesome fun. Even if the overall ambience of the ITAs is a bit different from that of Twins Days, which can be characterized as having an expressive disposition toward rebellion and revelry, the ITAs embody what Barbara Ehrenreich (2007), bemoaning the loss of ecstatic rituals, carnivals, and celebrations in Western tradition, describes in the title of her book as "collective joy." Ehrenreich (2007, 11) is mainly concerned with public events, which she terms "ecstatic rituals," as forms of collective excitement and festivity that place participants as liminal or marginal to the social order and result in a spontaneous sense of communion with one another. Ehrenreich also notes, however, that mind-altering states also may be more secularly understood as collective joy or having fun. While I would not describe ITA events as generating mind-altering experiences, spontaneous moments of joy, happiness, elation, excitement, and exhilaration—in the form of shared and sustained giggling—are certainly part of the communal ITA twin experience.

Maybe it is because I am an academic and we all take ourselves too seriously, but what has been largely absent from my adult life are moments of extreme silliness. I remember them well from adolescence, when Dorothy and I, in the company of friends, would get silly and laugh until we lost our breath, shed tears, or worse. I treasure those few and far between incidents that encourage super silliness. In my fieldwork in remote fishing communities in Newfoundland and northern Norway, I found those moments to occur among groups of adult women with far more frequency than was the case in my own adult life. At the ITA events, unacquainted twins do not remain strangers for long; the personal identities of all participants become eroded by the nightly hilarious, but humiliating and undignified, activities in which they participate. It is these activities, and the conviviality that emerges from them, that I situate my analysis of the ITAs as public events.

ITA organizers and participants take having fun to the point of absurdity, in a way that both is extremely entertaining and creates a sense of collective intimacy among participating twins, who suspend their own sense of dignified individuality or sense of self to join in a playful collective celebration of twinness. The ITA revels in (nonalcoholic) silliness as a kind of high hilarity. At the ITAs already liminal selves—twins—commune and make merry. Every night is dress-up night. Twins dress according to themes chosen by each venue. At Asheville's Hollywood night, triplet Bill Clinton doppelgangers elicited hysterical laughter as they worked the crowd, flirting with all the women. Skits and talent contests performed by acquaintances, who may or may not be all that talented, elicit shared audience laughter, as do more professional shows where a hypnotist amuses the audience with the antics of hypnotized twins. But it is the silly games that lead most participants to hysterically shared laughter. Participants at the ITAs are a rather conservative and sedate group. (For example, no one in our age group dressed as hippies for High School Night.) In addition, religious ceremonies and a nonecstatic spiritual element of camaraderie prevail at the ITAs. Nonetheless, the satirical and sexually suggestive behavior that does exist is more potent precisely because it is perceived as naughty. For example, one game in Atlanta involved two teams. One team consisted of participants holding rolls of toilet paper between their legs; the other team held toilet plungers between their legs. The aim was to put the plunger into the tissue roll hole. Nobody was very good at this and it became most amusing. Not all games are sexual parodies. Trivia games exaggerated personalities as they pitted teams of twins against each other. Although such high jinks and high times may not be the kinds of ecstatic experience that Ehrenreich (2007) attributes to festivals in the Middle Ages, they are certainly shared, high-spirited good times. As such, it is not so much twins at play with twinship (as at Twins Days), as twins at play.

THE PUBLIC FACES OF TWINSHIP

The idea of twinscapes becomes quite literal at festivals where hundreds or even thousands of twins of all ages gather to celebrate their twinship by performing society's stereotype of them. Even very different-looking DZ twins dress alike. As the Twins Days website advises and as Steph and Jenna learned, getting into the festival spirit means dressing alike and looking alike as much as possible. Yet twins, as we have seen, are envisioned differently by the different types of festival participants. These include twins, researchers, festival organizers, the general public, and the media. In this chapter I have described different perspectives on twins festivals that reflect a variety of combinations and permutations of insider (twins) and outsider (singleton) perspectives. Festivals also exhibit a number of discordant attributes that the wider society accords twins. Festival twins as a kind of deviant persona are positively viewed for their companionate, shared identities as well as for their mutual understanding and interpersonal closeness. Yet it is also these same features that characterize twins as a deviant persona in a negative way. While the insider twin's view celebrates the positive, the media tends to express the negative. An extreme example of the negative perspective is illustrated by Maddox's (2006, 66) popular science depiction of Twinsburg as a freak show. He writes, "You can't be an individual and like being twins; you can't be twins and, you know, want to be like the rest of us: all alone and unique and, you know, individual." At Twinsburg and the ITAs, however, for two days twins embrace and celebrate the positive dimensions of their cultural persona as they act out or perform society's stereotypes of identical and paired best friends for life. Certainly festival twins buy into society's stereotypes by going over the top or exaggerating their twinship. But, perhaps more importantly, they also celebrate what Maddox would see as a counternorm: they are not alone, they are not unique, and they are not always individuals. Twins festivals as public events can, thus, be viewed as social heresy. They invert the prevailing Western and singleton view of a distinct, bounded, and separate self, as opposed to a distinct, bounded, and separate other.

I started this chapter with an example of Dorothy and me playfully performing the twin game for Dorothy's yoga instructor. In many ways festivals, as we have seen, are the twin game writ large. They are about sharing a good time. As individuals and as a pair, they tease and challenge the observer to play their same and different identity games. Festivals fit well with the anthropological literature on festivals as rites of reversal or rebellion. Handelman (1990) speaks somewhat metaphorically of festivals as public events amounting to stories people tell themselves about themselves. I take a more literal approach. What twins actually have to say about their festival experiences evolves as a kind of positioned countervoice that challenges, critiques, or satirizes the twin persona in its positive and negative aspects. The Twinsburg talking partners had a great deal to say about their festival experience and, in so doing, reengage issues of biological identity. By embodying and performing "same," Dorothy and I invite observers to discover "different" or to bridge their own dualistic attitudes. A pair of middle-aged festival twins dressed like Dolly Parton are a single Dolly and not a single Dolly. They know it and so do we. In today's Western culture there is both unity in diversity and diversity in unity (Goode 2001). Festival twins revel in playing these notions against each other. Twins at festivals do not negate individuality. When the proud and tired parents of twins return home, they worry about how to develop and nurture their children's twinship and their independence and individuality. When festivals are over, each twin goes back to his or her own life and looks forward to spending more time with her or his twin in the future.

Referring to intergenerational clones rather than identical twins, Deborah Battaglia (1995a) raises two important questions that continue to be central themes in chapters 4 and 5. First, she asks why looking at a copy of oneself should violate some profound sense of individuality. Second, taking the perspective that cloning extends possibilities for connecting to others, she posits that rather than ask "What constrains autonomy?" we should ask "What constrains connectivity?" The answer to these questions moves from a focus on twinship as public performance or twins en masse to a closer look at twins and twinship as acting the parts within the twin dyad.

4

BODY

Isn't it rich? Aren't we a pair? Where are the clones? Send in the clones. There ought to be clones. Well, maybe we're here.

—*Stephen Sondheim's "Send in the Clowns," revised lyrics by dinner tablemates at an ITA event*

Genes have lost their privileged and prominent status particularly as the distinction between nature and nurture disappears.

—*Spector 2012*

If two people do the same thing, then it is not the same thing.

—*Devereux 1978*

AT THE 2007 INTERNATIONAL CONGRESS OF TWIN STUDIES IN Ghent, Belgium, I was frequently corrected by a prominent, single-ton twins researcher for using the term "identical twins" and for re-ferring to myself as "an identical twin." In casual conversation, the researcher repeatedly told me to use the term monozygotic, or MZ, instead of identical. I found her constant corrections to be quite irri-tating. This was her idea of political correctness because, of course, no two individuals are completely identical.[1] My pique lay in the fact that an "outbred individual" (Charlemaine 2002, 18), who made her living studying twins, had taken on the role of defining the parameters of my identity for me. She was appropriating my own "Who am I?" questions and turning them into her own "Who or what are you?" questions. On the one hand, by the researcher's repeated use of the term *monozygotic,* I felt that my identity as an identical twin was being reduced to our "one-egg status" (cf. Casselman 2008) or (in terms of DNA twin type testing) the identical genes I "share" with my twin sister. These sensitivities were certainly heightened by my immersion in a setting where "bio power" ruled (cf. Nichter 2013, 647), where biology and genetics dominated this twin research conference, and where studies that did not have laboratory data confirming genetic twin types were relegated to a second-tier status.[2] On the other hand, the researcher was suggesting that my resemblance to my sister was (to paraphrase Zazzo, cited in Farmer [1996, 93]) "only a superficial" likeness. To me, *monozygotic* not only is a mouthful in the saying but hardly defines my sense of self as a twin, since it roots my "true" identity in an invisible, subcellular level that can be truly assessed only in the laboratory. Moreover, whether *superficial* is used in the sense of surface or shallow, the phrase *only superficial* denies the realities of the daily lived, practical experiences related to the surface of twins' bodies and consequently the embodiment and management of identity among twins who look alike.

If Dorothy had attended this conference and had been sitting beside me, would this researcher, who was so willing to call the tune, have played the twin game? Would she surreptitiously gaze at our conference badges in order to get our identities right? Or would she just avoid using our names, perhaps collapsing our identities because she could not tell us apart? Dorothy and I have always thought of ourselves collectively as identical twins and individually as an identical twin. Although it plays with and against type, *identical* was also the popular or lay term of self-reference used by the Twins Days and ICTS twins. A defining feature of self among our talking partners in Twinsburg was one's existence as and with a twin brother or sister whose body looks very much like one's own.

My pique at the ICTS researcher for co-opting my twin identity is hardly idiosyncratic, as an interesting incidence from Twinsburg illustrates. At Twinsburg, as Dorothy and I were waiting for twins to arrive on the festival grounds, we asked a fellow researcher how his team handled ethical issues when it came to twins supplying body products for his research. The researcher, stating that there were standard procedures for following ethical practices in medical research, was nonplussed by this issue but did mention the ethical uproar over a past project that offered to inform twins of their chromosomal status as MZ or DZ twins. Blinded by their own gene-centrism, the researchers had failed to anticipate that telling a set of twins that they were not identical could be very traumatic to some twins, who, having a lifelong identity of being identical twins, contested or refused to believe the chromosomal assessments.

THE PRAGMATICS OF EMBODIED IDENTITIES

As Stewart (2003) states, twins are a biological and a social fact. Yet *biological* and *social* tend to exist as two separate fields of inquiry. My goal in this chapter is to develop and present a more interactional biosocial perspective, in terms of both theory and data. In this chapter I focus on identity issues raised by twins' bodies as biological and sociocultural phenomena. I compare and contrast the perspectives of those who research twins' bodies with the embodied perspectives of twins themselves. The former draws in large part on the two ICTS conferences I attended, particularly research sessions that privileged the twin research method and genetics. These sessions held center stage throughout both the conferences I attended. The latter draws from twins talk, as voiced by the Twinsburg twins. It privileges the notion of the biosocial as embodied through human activities (Pálsson 2013, 24). Posed side by side, the talking partners reflect on, perform, and embrace the body pragmatics of being same and different. I eschew research paradigms that oppose biology to culture or nature to nurture. Whether phrased as an old-school genetic determinism that emphasizes same or a new-school genetic flexibility that emphasizes difference (Charney 2012; Spector 2013), both schools focus on heritability and reduce real people to subcellular processes identified through the sophisticated, technologically complex practices of molecular biology. Instead, my focus is on how culture shapes and gives meaning, not only to the physical surfaces and relational bodies of twins but also to the methods, agendas, and assumptions of those who research them.

When twins use the term *identical*, it becomes a far more adaptable, flexible, and polytypic term for selving than is the case for the far more rigid or fixed terms like MZ. Genes are hardly the essence of being for twins. Twins' narratives show that subcellular referents or essentializing terms, like *monozygotic, contemporary clones,* or *histone acetylation,* do not allow much leeway for self-determination and identity management. The practical experience of twinship entails the negotiation and practice of multiple, complex, and sometimes contradictory selfways within a particular sociocultural milieu. As we have seen, at the same time that society expects twins to be identical, it also locates twins on the fault lines of identity. Western society carries a lot of moral baggage when it comes to twins—as two people who look "too much" alike. As self work, volunteering for buccal smears (saliva samples) pales in terms of the self working that twins must do, and are skilled at doing, because it is a reality of their lived experience that the surfaces of their bodies are viewed as so identical that others confuse, conflate, deny, or overlook their individual identities.

In this chapter twins talk shows how biology counts but not in ways expected by more biologically oriented twins researchers. As the focus shifts from the scientific perspectives of twins researchers to the subjective experiences of twins themselves, explanatory frameworks that feature the laboratory-based discoveries of hidden codes or acquired heritable characteristics (Charney 2012) give way to more experientially based expressions of talk and action that flesh out the surfaces of twins' bodies. To fill the gaps between professional and lay understandings of twins, new lines of inquiry are proposed that feature and develop notions of body pragmatics and intercorporeality as they shape the practice or practical experiences of twinship. These reflect twins' own takes on being, conterminously, both same and different and on being both separate and together.

GENETICS: DUPLICATES AND CHEMISTRIES OF SELF

Genetics as blueprints, hidden codes, or chemistries of self from the very beginning has dominated the twin research literature. According to Ramirez-Goicoechea (2013, 60) genetic determinism remains the dominant theoretical perspective in both academic and biomedical research settings. In this more linear approach, twins are seen as genetic clones with exactly the same DNA structure, with every body cell containing the same 25,000 genes. In this view genes trump environment and emphasis is placed on sameness. Others, such as Charney

(2012) and Pálsson (2013), argue that we have entered a new genetic era that is marked by a shift to a more complex systems approach that emphasizes genetic variability among identical twins and focuses on molecular processes related to the expression or suppression of genes. In this view environmental conditions may regulate the actions of genes, and the emphasis is placed on what Spector (2012) in the title of his book terms "identically different twins." "Gene talk" (cf. Pálsson 2013, 31) dominates both approaches, and both approaches address the same set of identity issues in Western society, such as who we are and why, and how we explain similarities and differences.

Even before the actual discovery of genes and zygosity, nineteenth-century researchers used photographs of identical twins as a kind of visceral or specula proof of hidden codes that duplicated the inborn natures and identities of identical twins (Cool 2007). As the "century of the gene" (Keller 2000) or the "age of genomics" (Reardon 2005) begins, interests in the visible surfaces of twins' bodies have been replaced by a more singular interest in genes and twin genotypes. As early as 1904, Wilder (1904, 389) critiqued the term *identical* as an untrustworthy, unscientific source of data because it put too much emphasis on appearance. Instead, Wilder (1904) posited that the physical resemblance of identical twins was merely an outward manifestation of invisible loci. Wilder went on to locate twin types on a continuum of individuality. While Wilder described DZ twins as self and other or autonomous individuals, MZ twins were termed duplicates or between self and other.

Recently, twins and the twin method have been described in a positive sense as the "Rosetta Stone of behavioral genetics" (Bouchard 1999, ix) and negatively as the "workhorse of genetic determinism" (Charlemaine 2002, 90). *Twin Research*, the official journal of the International Society for Twin Studies, has recently been renamed *Twin Research and Human Genetics*. According to Parisi (1995), the twin research community draws important distinctions between indirect approach hereditarians and direct approach hereditarians. Others would label the former genetic determinist as "old school era" currently being eclipsed by the new genetics, depicted as the postgenomic or epigenetic era (Charney 2012). The earlier indirect approach is typified by the heydays of Bouchard and the Minnesota Twins Studies (Bouchard 1993; Segal 1999) that employed batteries of mainly psychological questionnaires and interviews designed to assess shared behavioral and personality traits among twins. That which is the same or shared is considered to be indicative of shared and hidden, but unknown, genes. These studies represent a large and influential body of scientific literature that continues to argue that because they are as alike as peas in a pod and because they share the same DNA, identical twins are close to being the same person (Nelkin and Lindee 2004). Identical twins are depicted as "puppets dancing to the music of their shared genes" or as "inhabiting one another's being" (Neimark 1997, 2). Genes, seen as blueprints or codes for identity, continue to raise a series of interesting questions not only of what is truly self and what is truly other but also of what is shared and what is sharing. Currently, in their wane, the indirect hereditarians are being replaced by the direct hereditarians such as Peltonen (2007) and Kaprio (2007), GenomEUtwin researchers, who place their twin studies in the new era of molecular genetics, where new, sophisticated laboratory technologies have allowed for more direct approaches to the study of genes, chromosomes, or even sites on a single DNA base or SNP.[3] These researchers are more interested in what twin studies can reveal about how interactions among genetic, environmental, and behavioral factors influence the epidemiological characteristic of particular diseases.

While the indirect hereditarians are also interested in the discovery of hidden codes, they do work from the outside in, having twins who participate fill out questionnaires, sit for interviews, and answer survey questions that provide the data for studies in behavioral genetics. Because they answer familiar questions about different aspects of their selves, twins who participate in this process say this method has some modicum of meaning for them. They are, after all, even if by marking appropriate places on a Scanatron with number two black pencils, asked to describe themselves in terms that resonate with their own experiential worlds. The new era, direct hereditarians, however, work from the inside out. They abstract DNA matter from twins who have a limited understanding of how these subcellular products of their bodies will be used in the research process. Twins, as subjects of this kind of research, have little understanding of how such molecular data relates to their own personal and interpersonal experiences of being identical. Examples of these two approaches and their implications for the embodiment of twin identities are presented in the sections that follow.

HIDDEN CODES OF SELF AND INDIRECT APPROACH

Indirect studies of the embodiment of identities and personhood among identical twins as encoded in their shared genes may be on the wane, but indirect geneticists remain a significant presence at the ICTS, and their brand of genetic determinism continues to capture the popular imagination.[4] In this subfield of twin research, the "Who am I?" questions of twinship are answered in terms of genes being the root determining factor of one's identity and even one's lifelong destiny or fate. I briefly present and critique two examples of the indirect approach. The first is Thomas Bouchard Jr. and his famous Minnesota Twins Studies. These studies, if not the name Bouchard, were familiar to most of the talking partners. For over a quarter of a century, Bouchard and his consortium of students and scholars (Bouchard et al. 1983, 1990; Lykken 1995; Segal 1999) have characterized identical twins as congenital duplicates or natural and contemporary clones. Shared behavioral and personality traits among identical twins are linked to their shared genes. The second example comes from David Teplica's (2004) photographic portrayals of twins as the lifelong embodied objects of a predetermined genetic destiny. Teplica not only poses twins as eerily similar exact duplicates, but photographically morphs their images to challenge his audience's common-sense assumptions about the uniqueness of each human's identity. Both approaches pride themselves in their objectivity and scientific rigor. Both approaches privilege internal chemistries as doing twins' self work for them.

Bouchard and Behavioral Genetics

For better or for worse, "twin studies" in the popular imagination are defined by the controversial Minnesota Twins Studies (Minnesota Center for Twins and Adoption Research), which began in the 1970s and ended in 2000 (Miller 2013). In Bouchard Jr.'s (Bouchard and Popling 1993, 193) brand of genetic determinism or essentialism, identical twins are as close to being the same person as possible in the human condition. Bouchard attributes everything that is same among twins to genetics, and everything that is different and nongenetic to the environment (Wright 1999). Bouchard argues that much of our identity is formed at conception and genes not only determine physical characteristics among sets of twins but also determine complex aspects of their selves. These include intelligence, or cognitive ability, personality, temperament, behavior patterns (including criminality, alcoholism, and sexual orientation), and even personal quirks and preferences, such as using the same aftershave lotion (Wright 1998). Shared genes have also been linked to social attitudes and values, including art appreciation (Wright 1999) and religious interests, such as attitudes toward Sabbath observance, divine law, and Biblical truth (Waller et al. 1990, 141). Using standardized personality assessment inventories or questionnaires, along with personal interviews, Bouchard (1998, 315) concludes that when twins raised apart are compared to twins raised together "the best estimate of shared environmental impact for most scales is essentially zero" and that the overall family environment component to personality measures is negligible (Tellegen et al. 1987). For hereditarians like Bouchard, environment, as opposed to genes, is held to have a limited influence on behavioral traits (Joseph 2001).

David Teplica: A Dermatologist of Destiny

It is one thing to say that across a series of traits genetic influences outweigh environmental ones and another to say that genes shape one's destiny. Surprisingly, I heard this very question being raised at the plenary lecture at the 11th International Congress on Twin Studies in Odense, Denmark (July 2004). The speaker was David Teplica, a plastic surgeon from Chicago, who is well known for his photographs of identical twins. Teplica was introduced in a large lecture hall to twins researchers with the promise that he would present twins in a way that had never been considered before and that would totally change the way people think about twins. Teplica then proceeded to introduce himself as a "lone twin" or "survivor twin." He had recently been informed by his mother that she had lost his twin early in her pregnancy. Having thus established his "insider status," he used a slick PowerPoint presentation (Teplica 2004) to show numerous and rather unflattering, Dianne Arbus–like photographs of very identical twins. His pictures were taken during a ten-year period at the Twinsburg Twins Days Festivals.[5] The stated purpose of his project was to "capture" similarity of facial form and structure and to record and document genetic-based similarities focusing on skin, especially in terms of visible patterns of damage and aging. First, we were treated to photos of identical twins with matching moles, wrinkles, and skin cancers. Next, we were treated to quick flicks of morphed pictures of twins in which right and left sides of each twin were combined to create a third virtual individual. Whereas Bouchard Jr.'s indirect approach emphasized *same* as opposed to *different*, Teplica is interested only in the same. In Teplica's view, twins with precancerous moles in the same place on their necks at age seventy means their destinies have been fixed by their genes. We saw no photos of different-looking or even differently posed twins. I wonder how many photos he must have taken during the ten years to find his selective examples of remarkable sameness. Teplica's pictures rob twins of any sense of agency as they lock gazes into each other's eyes or stare (like fashion models) vacuously into the camera, frozen forever and silenced for science.

Teplica presents his project, on a whole, as a merging of art (the photos) and science (dermatology), with the caveats that "science must prevail; objectivity must not be compromised." His stated goal is to "combine art and science, but not in a frivolous way" (Teplica 2004). Interestingly, Teplica repeatedly referred to the Twins Days Research Pavilion as a "circus tent." He used the terms "scary" and "frightening" throughout his presentation as he referred to the physical similarities of the twins in his photographs. Having a mole or birthmark in the same place on the body as one's twin does surprise Teplica, who remarks that it's "incredible that one egg and one sperm could determine that." The plenary speech ended with the question "Do we have no control over our destiny?" I cannot resist referring to Teplica's cases as "mole-specula genetics" in which a shared mole shapes one's destiny. One wonders, if Teplica's twin had survived and if the two of them had grown up together, would twins be quite so scary to him or would their destiny remain only skin deep?

Critique of the Indirect Geneticists

The indirect genetic determinism of Bouchard Jr. and Teplica and their ilk, along with their pretexts of scientific objectivity, has critics both within and outside the twin research community (Charlemaine 2002; Joseph 2001, 2004; Kamin 1995; Tucker 2002). Within the twin research community there has been a sustained critique of indirect genetics. The Minnesota Twins Studies have been referred to as "good show biz but uncertain science" (Rose 1982, 960), sloppy science (Joseph 2001), "cockamamie" (Marks 2003, 3), and "just plain bullshit" (Marks 2004, 190). For example, Bouchard et al. have been criticized for their reliance on a "peas in a pod" approach (i.e., if they look alike and are the same sex, then they are probably MZ twins) to determine twin type (Parisi 1995). Bouchard is faulted for not having a representative sampling of twins or a control sample of nontwins (Horwitz et al. 2003; Freese and Powell 2003; Joseph 2004). Bouchard's studies are also critiqued for a bias toward similarities as they posit sameness and find that sameness and selectively focus on random traits that match up as a pair (Joseph 2001). The twin method as a viable way to measure the degree to which a trait in a given population is attributed to genes rather than to environment is also questioned (Charlemaine 2002; Colt and Hollister 1998; Conley 2004; Hay 1999; Horwitz et al. 2003; Joseph 2004). For example, if identical twins, compared to nontwins, are 48 to 61 percent concordant on a trait, it is considered to be genetic. A discordance of 52 to 39 percent is ignored (Joseph 2001). Furthermore, concordance, however measured, does not indicate cause (Joseph 2004). Critics fault Bouchard for constructing the relationship of nature/genes to nurture/social/environment as dichotomous, or oppositional, or a zero-sum phenomenon (Freese and Powell 2003, 134). Perhaps more disheartening are the critics who raise issues concerning the politics of science. Bouchard does not publish or share his raw data (Beckwith, Geller, and Sarkar 1991; Joseph 2001), making it impossible for other scholars to independently scrutinize, replicate, or reanalyze his findings. The political scientist William H. Tucker (2002) has questioned the racist agendas of those who have funded Bouchard's research.[6]

Teplica, who aims to combine art and science with artful posing of his subjects to enhance their visual similarity, also emphasizes sameness. Tamed, hushed, and stilled by his camera, Teplica's twins do not get to play the twin game, to actively and interactively engage in the education of their artful observer, or to negotiate embodied clues of same and different. Bouchard's and Teplica's assumptions of genetic determinism and the primacy of genes over environment not only obscure the complexities of genetics but overlook ways in which biology and culture interact. In a more current view, simple behaviors may actually be related to a multitude of genes and an "infinity" of environmental factors (Piontelli 2008, 8).

Twins researchers tend to limit their criticism of the indirect hereditarians within the frameworks of twin studies rather than engage wider critiques of genetic essentialism or determinism. Across the social sciences and in anthropology, there is a large and vibrant literature that questions, on a more general level, the types of genetic essentialism and purported scientific positivism of the so-called hereditarians. Critics argue that genes have become a kind of a cultural icon and that the "science" of genetics may be a cultural construct (Haraway 1991; Hubbard 1979; Hubbard and Wald 1993; Lock and Nguyen 2010; M'Charek 2005; Nelkin and Lindee 2001; Pálsson 2007; Rabinow 2005) or even an artifact of research techniques (M'Charek 2005). Nelkin and Lindee (2004) note how genes often depend on contexts being ambiguous, multiple, and open to more than one interpretation. Critics fault genetic determinists for their failure to examine their own cultural assumptions about the body as a machine or blueprint. In the Euro-American context, the person has been imagined as a machine or computer that carries basic operating instructions on the inside. A computer controls behavior and functions in the same way, no matter where it is located or what it stores. Genes, in this sense, become a kind of blueprint for the body or hidden codes of self (Lock 2005; Markus et al. 1997) or even a new form of divination (Teplica 2004; Lock 2005). This is what Sahlins (1977, 105) refers to as the "culturalization of nature."

Biologists like Harris (2004) remind us that among all humans, genetic affinity is the rule, not the exception, noting that a mother shares 99.95 percent of genes with her daughter, 99.90 percent with any randomly selected person on the planet, and 40 percent with a banana.[7] Arguments for genes as fate (the mole-specula genetics, as espoused by Teplica), as units of heredity that somehow match up directly to human behaviors (Marks 2003), or as predictors of future health have been challenged by a number of researchers (Lock 2007; Lock and Nguyen 2010). In addition, dichotomies of nature and nurture, heredity and environment, or biology and culture are also questioned. A biocultural, biosocial perspective holds that social and natural worlds cannot be separated (Marks 2003, 2012b; Ingold

2013); instead, they coproduce each other in mutual acts of becoming. Physical anthropologists criticize the essentialists for confusing genes with environment and for viewing genes and environment as oppositional. These oppositional models are faulted for conceptualizing the environment as a kind of default category, for equating nature and genetics with the inside and the sociocultural environment with the outside, and for attributing sameness to genetic factors and difference to environmental. When hereditarians deal with culture, they either dismiss it as irrelevant, gloss over it as that which is not genetic, or use it as a dumping bag for various aspects of nurture.

Yet to their credit, Bouchard Jr. and Teplica still see twins in terms of issues of (albeit compromised) identity and selfhood. Although Bouchard's group (Johnson et al. 2002) may argue that twins are just ordinary folks (with regard to personality) and not systematically different from the rest of singletons, they also see twins as special kinds of self—as a biological, relational, and environmental phenomenon worth investigating. Although viewed primarily as a biological fact, the social lives of twins, in terms of family relationships and attitudes and values, do receive some note. Even if they are reduced to predetermined research variables or creatures of their genes, the Minnesota twins are not just a research category or method. They are of interest, as twins, in and of themselves. Twins were welcomed to the Minnesota study site. Bouchard's student Nancy Segal, now a prominent twins researcher, brings exemplary twins to life through case histories of exceptional twins in two of her books (Segal 2005, 1999). When not morphed, Teplica's photographs are still portraits of two people. His analysis engages the surfaces of the body, asking the observer to play the twin game even if the rules are altered by his camera's lens that is aimed to capture likeness.

Bouchard and Teplica are twins researchers interested in hidden codes of self among twins. They both view twins as a special or interesting kind of being in the world. As such, the old hereditarians can be contrasted to the new genetics or direct genetic approaches of the newly ascendant hereditarians (Parisi 2003), where new technologies raise a host of new issues with which to engage not only the debates over the embodied natures of self and identity among identical twins but the very natures of the relationships between them as embodied biological or physical entities.

DIRECT GENETICS AND THE BIOLOGIZATION OF IDENTITY BY TWOS AND BEYOND

The genetic determinism of the late twentieth century is being replaced by a new genetics that views the expressions of genes or genetic processes as malleable and adaptive and blurs distinctions between genes and environment (Lock and Nguyen 2010; Piontelli 2008, Spector 2012). Whereas Teplica viewed genes in terms of a fixed destiny of two, the new genetics—with sayings like "The genome you are born with is not the one you die with" (Bruder, Piotrowski, and Gijsbers 2008) and questions like "Do we have more control over our destinies than we think?" (Spector 2012)—focuses on what causes genetic difference in twins. The realization that hundreds of genes may influence a single trait (Spector 2012) and the recognition that twins undergo more than three hundred genetic mutations, or copy errors, in utero and will go through a lifetime of epigenetic changes (Brogaard and Marlow 2012) show that twins differ in important ways. In contrast to the determinist, Weiss (2005) even goes so far as to state that genes give us individuality.

Twins researchers in the new era of genetics represent a combination of experts in epidemiology, clinical medicine, molecular genetics, statistics, and biocomputing. A medical model predominates as researchers engage in a kind of genetic prospecting to discover and assess roles that hereditary factors may play across a range of medical issues like asthma, diabetes, stroke, hypertension, smoking, and obesity. Compared to indirect approaches, the direct genetic approach posits a more integrative or interactive modeling of the heredity and environment questions. Miller (2012) contrasts the old genetics as written in ink with the new genetics as written in pencil The emerging field of epigenetics focuses on cellular molecules and dynamic and multiple ways genes are activated or expressed rather than on the actual composition of genes (Lock and Nguyen 2010). The activations take place not in terms of DNA mechanisms but as interplay between the physiochemical environment within the cell and the environment external to the organism (Newman and Muller 2006, 41). External environmental factors of interest in the new era of twin research include the presence of environmental toxins and lifestyle choices, including diet, exercise, tobacco, stress, and drugs.

At the two ICTS conferences I attended, it was obvious that a new era of direct genetic research has arrived and dominates the hierarchy of twins researchers. Large-scale research consortiums, such as the collaborators in the GenomEUtwin Project (Peltonen 2007; Kaprio 2007), are able to pool information from national twin registries, granting access to data of thousands of twin pairs. This new era of genetics for twins researchers also includes access to genotyping facilities that would otherwise be cost prohibitive (Peltonen 2007; Kaprio 2007). Armed with huge international databases and sophisticated, expensive genotyping labs, the direct hereditarians are definitely the stars of the ICTS conference. Not only do they get the plum plenary sessions, but the Ghent conference had actually been scheduled earlier than usual to accommodate the genetic researchers who dominate the organizational hierarchy. Research groups that did not use or have access to DNA or molecular labs (even if they had a fairly large research population or were once prominent researchers) are politely received, but they get the less desirable hours, last sessions, and small rooms for their presentations. In the worst-case scenarios, they have their paper proposals converted into poster sessions. Furthermore, TAMBA and ICOMBO presentations and activities designed for mothers of twins are scheduled at the same time as the more academic, genetically oriented presentations. Despite the fact that a number of mothers of twins are twins researchers, it is assumed that the interests of mothers of twins and twins researcher do not overlap.

In the case of twins studies, the new molecular genetics represents a new kind of biological essentialism. Now even individual difference is rooted in genetic processes. Concerns with individual risk assessment and personalized medicine (Rajan 2005) drive the research agendas of today's twins researchers. Identical twin pairs remain crucial to research, and MZ and DZ statuses are evaluated through body products, like blood and buccal samples that are collected from twins and shipped to genotyping laboratories. Codes are no longer hidden from researchers; they are subject to observation and analysis with sophisticated and expensive forms of laboratory technology. Many of the practitioners of the new genetics focus on difference rather than sameness. The new science of epigenetics aims to explain why identical twins are not always actually identical. Researchers look for samples of identical twins that are discordant for particular traits.

Twin registries exist today that specialize in phenotypically discordant twins (Bruder, Piotrowski, and Gijsbers 2008). Twins can be epigenetically indistinguishable when young, but as they grow older, spend less time together, and lead different lifestyles, they may develop remarkable differences in their patterns of epigenetic modification. Referred to as *epigenetic drift,* these modifications can account for the differential frequencies or onsets of common diseases such as schizophrenia and bipolar disorder; they also have implications for cancer research (Fraga et al. 2005).

In order to find twins discordant for certain diseases, databases must include thousands of identical twin pairs, living and dead. What becomes more important than individual twins are the twins as a research method, population, or tool for bioprospecting. At the ICTS, if identified at all, twins are classified by location or name of database (Finnish twin registry, Australian twin registry, etc.). Twin identification takes the form of statistical tables representing sample size and population characteristics such as gender and age, or graphic representations of chromosomes, supposed genetic markers, and / or SNPs. Although the new genetics appreciates complex interactions among genes, their products, and the environment, the environmental "context" becomes either highly specific, as in biochemistries of the cell or gene, or highly general, as in life style issues as accessed through standardized epidemiological surveys or questionnaires. Although such huge and sophisticated population-based studies (Peltonen 2007) provide statistically significant data, twins and twinship are not topics of interest in and of themselves. Sophisticated and expensive technologies are used by highly trained twins researchers for purposes that the subjects, or twins, neither understand nor find relevant.

Although twin selves, personhood, and twinship as a kind of relationship are not issues of concern when twins are viewed primarily as research subjects—as the title of a multinational research consortium, the GenomEUtwin Project (Peltonen 2007), which dominated most of plenary sessions at the ICTS, suggests—the new genetics also raises questions about the biologies of relatedness among people and populations. The GenomEUtwin Project takes its name from the Human Genome and Human Genome Diversity Projects. (The *EU* refers to data sharing among twins researchers throughout the European Union.) Ancestry, as a form of genetic relatedness, has failed to capture the attention of contemporary twins researchers, but cloning viewed both as a form of collateral genetic relatedness and as a form of sameness has captured the imaginations of contemporary twins researchers. Even the new genetics that focuses on discordance among MZ twins, asserts that MZ twins are far more alike than DZ twins (Charney 2012). The new hereditarians' discourse on identical twins as clones reengages themes of sameness among twins. As cloning becomes feasible for non-human animals, debates over identical twins glossed as human clones, contemporary clones, or genetic duplicates are brought into debates over the ethics of cloning as well as the nature of relatedness (Battaglia 1995a; Piontelli 2008). Identical twins as a kind of natural, contemporary clone are even distinguished from artificial or laboratory-produced generational clones for being the more similar, or identical, kind of clone. This is because an artificial clone comes from two different donor cells, while identical twins originate from the same cell (Segal 1999). As the scientific discourse of embodied relationship moves from an emphasis on shared genes to the very nature or biology of shared being (Battaglia 1995a; Prainsack, Cherkas, and Spector 2007), identical twins, as clones—as was the case for the indirect hereditarians—are posed as violating or challenging expectations that each individual is, or should be, biologically distinct and personally unique.

When twins talk about, present, or represent their embodied selves as biological entities, they do so, as we shall see, not in terms of hidden or underlying codes of self (as do the old and new hereditarians); instead, they feature and negotiate identity on the surfaces of their bodies. Like the hereditarians, though, the talking partners are also interested in parsing out how same and different works on their respective embodied selves. Twins talk about sameness in terms self, personhood, and identity in ways that are certainly reminiscent of Bouchard's cataloging of shared characters of behavioral traits. In twins talk, however, same and different become entangled as the partners draw on shared experiential or anecdotal data to argue their points. When genetics of relatedness as expressed in the notion of clones does enter into twins talk, it takes the form of play.

Bring in the Clones

When twins as clones speak about the implications of genetics for the management or negotiation of identity and relatedness, what is it that they have to say? At this point, the analysis shifts to what Goodman (2013, 360) refers to as "real people and real places." How do twins feel about being reduced to their cellular physiochemical environment or their DNA? How do the interests of twins researchers intersect with twins' firsthand knowledge and lived, practical experience of being twins? When given a voice, how do identical twins enter into the biology of identity discourse? How are relational and embodied notions like identical, duplicate, or shared—whether genes, being, or environment—enacted and expressed in day-to-day practice?

According to Battaglia (1995a), physical likeness can be associated with signs of incomplete individuality. Looking alike on the outside makes one's inner humanness dubious. As clones, twins may be seen as copies or remakes, as a second of the same thing, as two halves of a self or a uniform whole, or even as the same person existing twice (Prainsack and Spector 2006; Prainsack et al. 2007). As "android, soulless Golem-like entities" whose very humanness is suspect (Prainsack et al. 2007, 1), clones and twins as clones have certainly captured the popular and scientific imaginations (Maddox 2006). Biological essentialism, however—or any kind of genetic inheritance mechanisms, in the sense of hidden codes, blueprints, or prime movers—was largely absent from twins' discourse.

When twins' voices are featured, the talk about the essence of the twin experience shifts from inside the body to the surfaces of the body and from shared genes to shared place and space. Viewed from a biosocial perspective, twins talk show us that (cf. Pálsson 2013, 39) "nature and culture have always been one." When analysis shifts to the practical experience of look-alike twins, the scientific laws or principles, identified by geneticists, pale in view of "environment" as the practical exigencies and skills that twins bring to identity assertion and management within an immediate social cultural milieu. When it comes to clones and cloning, festival twins are not, however, altogether silent.

Conversing with Contemporary Clones

Although the Twinsburg twins had little of substance to say about cloning, the word did come up in the contexts of informal joking. When Dorothy and I attended the Atlanta ITA event, at the first evening's dinner we sat down at a table with other sets of twins. As the twins complimented each other on their identical outfits, someone mentioned clones and someone else started to sing Stephen Sondheim's "Send in the Clowns," substituting the word *clones* for *clowns*. After the first line, we all joined in singing. As this irony of clones, all together, joining in song at the dinner table suggests, cloning serves as a good point to enter a discussion of twins as social rather than biological fact. When twins talk about themselves as clones or genetically identical, they do so not in the sense of the hereditarians or of the new genetics but in terms of what they playfully view as outsiders' sociocultural stereotypes of them as twinned clones, or as the ITA twins sang, "Aren't we a pair?"

To say the least, our Twinsburg talking partners appeared to be underwhelmed by their genetic resemblance, shared genes, or status as clones. Annette and Arnette joked about who was the original and who was the copy, or clone. Steph and Jenna mentioned that Steph had gotten the schizophrenia gene, whereas Jenna had not. They asked Dorothy and me why this happens, since they were supposed to be genetically alike. Mabel and Bertha referred to their children as being "half genetic" but stated that "none of them looked alike." Tim and Tom told us that they had always thought they were fraternal twins until they participated in a Research Pavilion study during a previous festival and learned that they were actually identical twins and therefore qualified for our interview. Tim and Tom were delighted to learn that they were identical twins.

Whereas twentieth-century scientists privileged twins' genes as "visible and visceral proof of our immutable and inborn natures" (Cool 2007, 28), the talking partners are more likely to privilege God as the creator of their natures. Twinship as a blessing from God was mentioned by four sets of twins. But interestingly, God, like the new genetics, is associated with difference, not sameness. Tina and Ginuh attribute their differences to God; in Ginuh's words, the differences are "a natural thing that God put within us." Kristy and Karen would agree.

> Kristy: Where did our differences come from? I've done a lot of observing and I did a twin study when I was in high school and in college. It was like a written paper.
>
> Karen: Our difference didn't come from the environment; it was the same.

Kristy: It came from God.

Karen: She thinks too much. I do too much.

Pat and Phyllis also associated their very being with God's, not nature's, design.

Pat: God saw Phyllis and made Phyllis and said, "Now I'll make a spoof and it will be Pat."

Phyllis: How can you improve on perfection?

Pat: She's the good twin and I'm the twin's twin.

The closest we got to any kind of biological essentializing was Donna's statement that their differences came from the notion that "we operate from different sides of our brains. It's like the left-right brain thing." This statement, however, came as a complete surprise to Dianne, who stated, "Well, she never shared this with *me*" and remarks that "this [Donna's] explanation had yet to take root." Dianne would not let the matter rest and a feisty exchange ensued. Donna told Dianne exactly when and where the brain theory was imparted, who was in the room at the time, and what they were doing. Eventually both conclude that the conversation did take place but that Dianne must not have been listening. Their debate illustrates the importance of relationship as context, as shared place and space, agency and negotiation, as well as biology in twins' conceptual worlds. Donna and Dianne's exchange illustrates how "identities are continually produced in our actions and pronouncements" (Ingold 2013, 8). It is biosocial in that twins attribute a difference to underlying biological factors (their brains), but these differences are understood relationally by reference to an event in their life histories.

Even if not directly spoken, clone themes did exist at Twinsburg in the guise of provocative statements on T-shirts as messages to be shared, read by, and reacted to by other twins. This is exactly how Mary and Martha embodied their identities as clones. They came to our interview with matching T-shirts decorated with a picture of identical clowns and the word CLONES boldly printed underneath. Martha and Mary are self-described "creative twins" who design and sell T-shirts at Twins Days. Their shirts are designed to be sold in pairs and to be worn by two people standing side by side; otherwise, they make no sense. Being identical is a pervasive theme in their shirt designs. Their best seller is a shirt that says, "It's a twin thing, like two peas in a pod." The next-best seller has a picture of two babies, one saying to the other, "If no two snowflakes are alike, then I'm glad we are not snowflakes." These shirts sell well in the infant, toddler, and small child sizes. Available in adult sizes only, the clones T-shirts are not one of their best sellers. Mary and Martha attribute the poor sales to a matter of choice.

> Martha: It's really hard to predict what people will like and not like. I was sure everyone was going to like this one. The first two years we didn't sell a single one. People would come up and say, "Clones? Oh, cloning is a horrible thing." I'd say, "It's a joke, people." They would say, "But it's so unethical and immoral to clone." I'd say, "If God did it, it must be okay."

Mary and Martha proudly state that the clown/clone shirt for adults captures their twisted sense of humor. They did think, however, that it would not be appropriate to make clone shirts in infant and child sizes but stated that for older twins, "like us," it was funny because it satirized singletons' and scientific stereotypes of twins. Outside of the Research Pavilion, Mary and Martha were the closest we saw to what could be called the "consumer genomics" (Rajan 2005, 19) at Twinsburg.

While I will contend that the dearth of data we have on twins' attitudes toward cloning or to themselves as clones is limited by our small sample and by lack of direct questions about cloning, Prainsack et al.'s (2007) survey data, collected from a sample of over two thousand identical and fraternal twins in Britain, offers some additional insights and raises some interesting questions about twins as clones. Prainsack et al. (2007) report that although identical twins were upset or frustrated when others viewed of them as clones, they show a greater acceptance of cloning than their fraternal counterparts and expressed a stronger awareness that people's personalities and identities are not exclusively determined by genes. They understand and act as clones in biosocial contexts. For example, I may borrow one of Dorothy's scarves. I may even donate one of my kidneys to her if she ever needed it. We may share a bag of M&M's. We do not, however, share our genes. Each of us has a full complement of genes. If identity and relation lie in your shared genes, then am I also the wife of Dorothy's husband or the mother of her children? When it comes to twins talk, Mary and Martha's T-shirt makes a better metaphor than shared genes, points of connection, or hidden codes—whether directly or indirectly assessed. Like Mary and Martha's clone T-shirts, we, as identical twins, wear our embodied identities not as hidden codes but on the surface of our bodies. Mary and Martha's shirts appear on two real, bounded bodies. Mary and Martha's wash-and-wear commentaries clothe two real people. To paraphrase Devereux (1978), if two people wear two T-shirts, then it's not the same T-shirt.[8] Shared genes, like cloned shirts, do not mean there are two twins crowded or merged into a single big shirt. It does not mean that two shirts are somehow opened or joined at a strategic seam. It does not mean that the shirts are interchangeable or that one stands for the other. Each twin had her own shirt. This seems obvious, yet the shirts only make sense when sold and worn side by side in pairs. As we shall see, it is the complex sociocultural challenges that twins face as a result of their surface similarities and shared lives or co-contemporarity in terms of space and place that take center stage in twins' own narratives.

Marilyn Strathern (1995) has critiqued the privileged representation of an individual as a bundle of individual genes as coming with limited metaphors for a relational view. I would add that so does the representation of two individuals as a single bundle of genes. In the twins and clones study by Prainsack et al. (2007), twins who actually determined the discourse said that what is unique about themselves is their twin bond or special relationship. The term *twin bond* usually refers to the more psychological aspects of twinship and is the subject of chapter 5. It is, however, premature to drop the embodiment of twinship and shared being themes just because genetics is a limited metaphor for a biosocial relational view. The case of the Twinsburg twins looking alike or having highly similar, if not identical, bodies poses a host of identity challenges that do not affect singletons. In the practical experience of twinship, to the extent that two identical bodies share space and place, the physical body still counts. What is called for is an analytic model that mediates the gaps between professional and lay knowledge but also recognizes how twins' biologies shape and are shaped by the everyday sociocultural exigencies of their lives.

When researchers abstract twins to either method or population, they cannot account for the experience or characters of any single pair of twins (Finkler 2000). In the guise of scientific objectivity, twins researchers assume the necessity of a separation or distance between observer and observed.[9] Yet one could say that this sense of distance works both ways. The several sets of Twinsburg twins who came to us complaining of the discomfort (throat irritation) experienced in providing buccal samples could not tell us, despite just having signed informed consent statements, what the study was about. Whether emphasizing sameness or difference, twin research—with its focus on quantification, increasingly larger samples of genotyped MZ and DZ twins, objectivity, and anonymity—reflects the agendas of twins researchers and not the perspectives or experience of twins themselves. In these studies the import of twins is determined by the narrow purposes of the researchers and study at hand. Even narrative data get coded for statistical analysis. Twins have no voice in shaping the research about them. For example, although Teplica judges the surfaces of twins' bodies to be important, Dorothy and I would not be of interest to him because we do not share moles and carcinomas in the same locations. Most likely because of our shared genes, the sun has aged our faces in a similar fashion, but even if Teplica would be interested in assessing our ectodermal similarities, he probably would show little interest in (what is important to us) the facts that, given the different opportunities we have pursued and life choices we have made, my face was exposed to the sun in the Arctic and hers in the tropics. While Ingold (2013) states that life histories, not genes, prefigure us ectodermically, looking alike still matters.

If, for researchers, distance between researcher and subjects of research is depicted as objectivity, for twins the distance is largely one of irrelevance. Researchers in the area of twin genetics pride themselves in methodological sophistication and large population samples. The Bouchard Jr. group's mantras that "anecdote is not science" (McGue and Iacono 2007) and "everything can be quantified" (Finkler 2000; Joseph 2001, 26) tend not only to invalidate the experiences of a single set of twins but also to alienate twins, as the subjects of research, from the lived experience of being twins. Having backgrounds in engineering and accounting, both Tim and Tom described themselves as "numbers men." They engaged the heredity and environment issues at several points during our conversation. They may agree that anecdote is not science, but Tim also states that science is not everything.

> Tim: Twins here [Twinsburg] ask you, "What was it like when you were growing up as kids?" They'd tell us lots of stories. And we would say, "Yeah, we had the same experience." We find that there are a lot of similarities as we were growing up that are extremely common [with other sets of twins]. For example, even in high school and college, we had the same sets of friends all the time; one of us would be talking, and I would take a breath and Tom would pick up the sentence where I left off and keep right on going with the same thought. It would just boggle their [friends'] minds. They would ask, "How did you do that?" The thing is, it is because we grew up together, we already know how [the] other thinks. We've been through the same experiences, so it's really kind of easy to do. So I don't know if that's biology or just environment or a little bit of both. I'd write it down in an equation if I could, but I don't think it really works that way.

Let me tell you a bit more about Tim and Tom that goes back to my example of being corrected for using the term *identical*. Tim and Tom came to our interview qualifying the term *identical* as a label for them. First, they told us that they had always assumed that they were fraternal twins because that is what family members had told them. At their first Twinsburg festival, they volunteered for a study where they could get an actual report on their zygosity. The report informed them that, instead of DZ, they were MZ twins. Tom and Tim were delighted to find out they were identical. All through childhood they were not visually identical. Tom was born with a large birthmark on one side of his face. Looking at their faces, one could easily tell them apart. (Teplica would probably not be interested in this because it marks difference and not similarity.) Recently, however, when the twins were in their midforties, Tom was able to have the birthmark surgically removed. Not only had they recently found out they were

identical on the inside, but they are now identical on the outside—
and this is very important to both of them.

In the case of grown and mature men like Tim and Tom, who
proudly self-refer as "identical," their phrasing of the term is based in
complex histories, situations, and contexts that help to interactively
define their use of the term *identical*. Although dressed alike at our
interview, Tim and Tom, postsurgically, certainly do look alike but
are easily distinguishable to Dorothy and me. (This was not the case
for all the talking partners.) What the singleton researcher who kept
correcting me at the ICTS probably did not realize is that a story specific to and validating Tim and Tom's identity experiences underlay
their collaborative employment of the term *identical*.

Three related points brought up in Tim's short narrative introduce themes I employ to develop an alternative twin's-eye view of the
relationality of two bodies and embodiment of identity among identical twins. Among these are the notions that twins and twinship can
boggle the minds of "others." Growing up together and sharing space
and place shapes a kind of collaborative mutuality among twins. Environment becomes shared experience. Heredity, as looking alike,
becomes mutually interactive rather than dialectic. New, more nuanced and normative models for inhabiting each other's being are
called for. Moreover, Tim, although a numbers man himself, dis-
agrees with the notion that "everything can be quantified" and concludes that reducing all this to a single equation, although desirable,
does not work. Anecdote may not be science to the likes of Lykken,
but as Tim and Tom's lengthy, far-ranging, and experience-packed
conversation attests—not to mention the enthusiastic spirit in which
it took place—anecdote goes a long way to filling in the blind spots
of the hereditarian approaches (either old or new) that dominate the
beginnings of this chapter.

PRACTICE AND PRAGMATIC: HOW IT REALLY WORKS

Twins talk shows that, like the hereditarians, twins are interested in
how they are same and different. Yet molecular genetics or hidden
codes have limited relevance for the festival twins as they share space
and place with someone who looks very much like them. Moreover, twins talks shows relatedness not as shared or duplicate genes
but as actively and reactively co-constructed mutual and individual

identities while both challenging and confirming biologically oriented researchers' stereotypes about them. In the second part of this
chapter, I argue that there are alternatives to the hereditarians when it
comes to interpreting the biologies of twins' bodies as they relate to
the "Who am I?" and "Who are we questions?" of twinship. I develop
the notion of the body pragmatic, an alternative framework, which
puts some actual flesh on the bodies of identical twins and resonates
with what twins have to say.[10]

Prainsack et al. (2007) suggest that the greater acceptance of cloning among their large British sample of MZ twins, as opposed to DZ
twins, may lie in the MZ twins' firsthand familiarity and practical
experience with embodied sameness that has tangible implications
in the various spheres of their lives. Prainsack et al. (2007), however,
in their numerous publications, fail to follow through on what this
practical experience may be. I use the term *body pragmatics* to examine some key features of this practical experience of identity making among the Twinsburg twins. In doing so, I will return to notions
of self work and self styling introduced in chapters 1 and 2. As we
have seen, the cultural psychology approach features the idea of an
embodied self in which a perceiving acting body becomes both site
for apprehension of and setting in relation to the world (cf. Barth
1997; Battaglia 1995a; Burton 2001; Csordas 1994; Ewing 1990; Featherstone, Hepworth, and Turner 1991; Guarnaccia 2001; Kirmayer 1992;
Lock 1993; Merleau-Ponty 1962; Pálsson 2007; Reischer and Koo 2004;
Scheper-Hughes 1994; Scheper-Hughes and Lock 1986; Schildkrout
2004; Strathern 1992; Synnott 1993; Turner 1994; Weiss 1999). In what
follows I will draw on the ideas of personal enskilment and intercorporeality to explicate the body pragmatics of twins. Pálsson (1994,
903, 902) describes enskilment as "feeling at home in the body and in
the company of others," as a kind of "craftsmanship and agentively
acquired skills or bodily dispositions." It is how you use your body.
Enskilment implies active engagement with the natural and social
environment and immersion in everyday practice and has both individual and teamwork or collective dimensions. Weiss (1999) uses the
term *intercorporeality* to conceptualize the body as lacking definitive
boundaries. As such, intercorporeality derives from a gestalt of multiple and overlapping personal, interpersonal, and social identities and
images that are copresent in any given individual. Both ideas help to

demonstrate skills that pairs of look-alike twins interactively practice as they go about negotiating aspects of their embodied similarities and differences and as they negotiate their collective and individual identities in substance and action and language and reflection. But as Weiss (1999) and Pálsson (1994) also note, and as we have seen is the case for cultural psychology (Markus et al. 1997; Neisser 1997; Shweder 1991), twins construct (as do researchers) their identities within a wider sociocultural environment where biology and culture can be seen as mutually constructing each other. Here we must return to the notion of twins as a deviant persona or as on the fault lines.

Negotiating the Body Pragmatic

Twins must negotiate both individual (different or distinctive) and collective (mutual and paired) identities for multiple audiences in different situations and contexts. Yet this process takes place within a specific cultural context in which identical twins exist as a culturally deviant persona or fall on the faultiness of identity for "normative" bodies. Four key assumptions concerning the normative body are outlined below. Taken together, they lay out a kind of sociocultural terrain (or environment) or fault lines of self. If the self is realized through participation in cultural practices, what cultural practices may be relevant to the practical experience of twinship? What rules of the game or skills of self-presentation and negotiation must self working twins on the fault lines master? Although cultural themes are developed in more detail in chapter 6, here I focus on those related to the body or relationship of bodies. Twins and twins talk transgress, tweak, revise, or reject some commonplace assumptions about the body. These include assumptions about the nature of uniqueness, boundedness, self-consciousness, and relationality of body selves. Together, they provide an introduction to "environment" as the cultural construction of identity and a background for developing the notions of enskilment and intercorporeality, rather than shared genes, as central to the practical, everyday experience of living in twinned bodies.

Body Self as Unique. There is an unquestioned expectation that each member of humankind is associated with distinguishing bodily characteristics, a unique countenance or physique, or a relatively stable set of markers by which an individual can be recognized by others

(Burton 2001; Harris 1989; Sadri and Sadri 1994; Whittaker 1992). Visually, twins mark one of those moments during which the body and corporality are questioned or lose their self-evidence (Van Wolputte 2004). The analysis of the embodiment of self and identity as expressed among the Twinsburg twins represents an interesting twist in the body literature. For identical twins to assert their individuality, an important part of their body pragmatic is to mine their bodies for identifying differences and then educate their audience with clues of body distinctions as ways of telling them apart. This body pragmatic or example of enskiled identity management among twins, I will argue, means that identical twins actually craft a more finely tuned relational and refined sense of self than do singletons.

Body Self as Bounded. Assuming the outward manifestations of every person's body are unique, the skin is often portrayed as the boundary of the body or body self. In this sense, the skin thus summarizes or unifies the whole body and serves as an external sheath of self, a principal marker or boundary that differentiates self from other (Benthien 2002; Connor 2004; Reischer and Koo 2004; Scheper-Hughes 1994; Schildkrout 2004) and marks humans as discontinuous beings. That which is inside the body is me and that which is outside the body is not (de Munck 2000). Yet this visible surface or epidermalized sense of embodied self (Benthien 2002; Casey and Edgerton 2005; Fannon 1967) becomes problematic in twins. In the case of identical twins, the "duplicate" surfaces of their bodies can be seen as conjoining, confusing, or blurring the boundaries of their identities in the eyes of others (Konner 1991). Look-alike bodies can easily become "unit" bodies. Thus, physical similarities can conjoin bodies or render them interchangeable in the eyes of the observer. Twins talk shows how extra effort must be employed as twins agentively negotiate identities behind the face and from within the skin as they face an enhanced task of negotiating their respective identities from the inside out.

Body Self as Self-Conscious. In a consciousness model of individuality (Cohen 1994, 162), lived experience of the body self not only gives meaning to the personal, individual body, but each body has its own body-bound attributes. Each body also serves as a site of self-consciousness and personal awareness, reflection, imagination, creativity, and personal agency (Linger 2005). Not only are all children assumed to learn to distinguish where their bodies end and other beings and actions begin (Erchak 1992), but they are supposed to be able to describe their self in terms of personal attributes (Markus et al. 1997). Yet, in the case of twins, self-consciousness must be understood as coproduced. To the extent that self-consciousness involves a person's conscious and creative engagement with the sociocultural environment (Rapport 1997), then in the case of twins, one's twin becomes a key element in the sociocultural environment and thus a key element in the self-consciousness of the other twin. Common responses to our query "What does it mean to be a twin?" included "Only a twin can know" and "Never being alone." Twins talk shows how consciousness can also transcend bodies. Examples would include a twin's shared and mixed childhood memories (Davis and Davis 2010), and ESP stories.

Body Self as Relational. Bodies materialize in particular ways within specific kinds of relations (Taylor 2005, 769). The embodiment of self in other and other in self are important elements of the relational body self among twins. Twinsburg twins report that the twin relationship is like no other relationship, yet it also states that being too close, too interdependent, too alike (whether in looks or character) is held suspect in wider society. Twins are a paired couple who are assumed to share a unique relationship or bond. Twins may wear their twinship, but they also actively negotiate their individuality from within the embodied pair. Twins in childhood and adolescence coexist and coproduce body selves within a dyad so that another's body is not only always present but looks like theirs. Thus, twins see and experience self and "self in other" from a uniquely embodied and intercorporeal perspective that rests both on their embodied likeness and on the fact that they were born and raised together. When the Twinsburg twins sit side by side to co-construct their mutual and respective identities, there is a marked intercorporeal element of coexistence and coproductions of self that is expressed through discourse and can be directly observed.

When interacting with others as well as each other, twins must negotiate their identities in a way that both preserves the experience of being a special persona and normalizes twinship. Over-the-top characterizations of identical twins—such as being practically the same person (Bouchard and Popling 1993), being eerily similar creatures of fate (Teplica 2004), or even sharing DNA (new genetics)—do not mean that the likeness of twins is superficial or does not count. In contrast to singletons, who take their unique, bounded, self-conscious, and normalized bodies for granted, twins must explicate who they are to themselves and to others. They must connive with each other to affirm and validate their respective and mutual identities. Identical twins, on the fault lines, unlike singletons, face the task of *disembodying* their identities. A twin's self work involves differentiating his or her self or asserting her individuality in relation to the other twin who looks confusingly like her or him. At the same time, twins' selfways involve not only individuating in certain situations and contexts but surrendering themselves to the pair in others. This active agentive task of self working is the practical experience of twinship. This is a process that entails the constant education of the gaze or gazes of the observer, who is yet unschooled or in need of reeducation.

LIKE PEAS IN A POD:
ON THE BODY PRAGMATICS OF "BEING IDENTICAL"

Although we may disparage the phrase "as alike as two peas in a pod," meeting so many other pairs of twins at festivals gave Dorothy and me a new appreciation of the fact that it can be hard to tell twins apart. We certainly felt the frustration and sense of social awkwardness that comes from confusing or conflating identities of our adult talking partners. Our talking partners felt that other sets of twins looked more alike than they did. Similar or rhyming names (a common singleton complaint) make it even more difficult to distinguish each twin. But on closer view, as any pea sheller would know, peas in a pod do not look that much alike. We just assume they do. To abuse a metaphor, twins talk shows us further that not only is each pea same and different, but each pea's body is bounded, and each pea has its own place in the pod.[11] Moreover, although there are points of connection and separation, the peas are not interchangeable. They are self and other to each other. The "peas in a pod" analogy serves as an interesting departure point for further analysis of twins' own embodied, experiential worlds. What follows is a view from the pod.

Scientific politicizing over the terms MZ and *identical* does not negate the fact that Dorothy and I grew up and live in a real world where others, even today, cannot tell us apart. Being identical is not a superficial fact of twinship; it is central to the practical experience of twinship and demands some sophisticated self working on the part of twins. It is the visible surfaces or our bodies, not genotypes or hidden codes, that shape our senses of I and we.[12] When twins talk about their biology, they are hardly passive objects of the ruminations of others; they take control of the discourse. They assert likeness but will not be reduced to it. As they educate the observer's eye, their self work involves action, rather than abstraction, and stages an agentive, active, and creative co-negotiation of outer and inner logics of self and personhood. The analysis that follows shows the well-honed practical skills twins exercise as they go about dualing their selves as intercorporeal and distinctive in substance and action.

De-confusing and Confusing Identity

Although the remaining sections of this chapter focus on distinguishing and conflating identities, partners do report some identity confusion of their own in early childhood. The first two cases draw on family memory stories. For example, Dina and Jeana told us that when they were very young, they were each confused by mirrors, and each thought they were looking at their twin instead of their own reflection in the mirror. Dealing with identity confusion by others, however, is a far more prevalent theme in twins talk. Twins often talk about family members, particularly fathers, confusing them. For example, Dorothy and I are not even sure who is Dona and who is Dorothy. When we were infants, our mother could not tell us apart. When we came home from the hospital, she marked one of us by painting a little toe with red nail polish. One day she left us with our great-grandmother, and when Mother came back, we each had ten red toes. Mother always said she was never sure if the Dona and Dorothy who returned from the hospital are the same Dona and Dorothy of today. Being mistaken, when alone, for one's twin is also a common twin experience. One of the most lively confusion stories comes from Karen and Kristy, who recount an event experienced shortly before coming to the Twinsburg festival. This episode of identity confusion becomes an opportunity for public education or self working as a rather assertive expression of identity. Living in the same town at forty-six years of age, they are still mistaken for one another and must constantly assert their own identities. Kristy remarks on a recent trip to the gas station.

> Kristy: So, look, OK? She's [Karen] is little heavier than me. And he [gas station employee] says, "I thought you drove a blue Buick," and I looked at him and said, "I don't want to be rude. I really don't. Is fifty pounds totally invisible? Because I don't know why I work so hard to look like this if you can't even tell. I thought men looked at your bust. Do these look like double Ds? Am I wearing a double D? I don't think so." He was kind of like, "Arguhhh!" That was kind of funny. He was *so* mistaken.
>
> Karen: I'm going to kill her. I don't wear double Ds.
>
> Kristy: So, OK, but there was a point to be made.

But twins talk also shows that they revel in collaborating to actively confuse their identities. I use the term "trickster twins" to describe this kind of identity play. Such stories are common in twins talk. Trickster tales are the most common response to our requests to "tell us some of your favorite stories about being twins." They mark accounts in which twins play or satirize others' tendencies to confuse them. Twins are not passive objects of others' confusion; they actively set out to confuse. Dina and Jeana tell a graduation story that uses identity confusion to confound and then authenticate their own respective identities in the eyes of their classmates.

> Jeana: One of my favorite twin stories is that Dina was valedictorian at our school, and I was like third or fourth. We have always been competitive. We wanted to do something deceiving to the class. What we did was I dressed up in her valedictorian outfit and she wore the white honor's outfit. The valedictorian was supposed to give a fifteen-minute speech. I got up and, for the first five minutes, talked about the deceptions in life, how people will try to fool you, and you need to watch out. Just basically [I said] to

watch out when you go out into the real world and everything is not peaches and roses and all that. And then I said, "Now the real twin valedictorian will stand up and make a speech."

Dina: They still talk about that today.

Jeana: They bought it. It was a good one.

Taking each other's tests at school and confusing parents, teachers, and boyfriends were also popular themes of trickster tales. Many twins recounted stories in which one twin had done something bad, but the parent did not know which one it was. Twins reported that if neither claimed to be the culprit, both would escape punishment because the parent did not want to punish the "innocent" twin.

Trickster twins self-consciously play at identity confusion. Yet, most twins' tales of others confusing their identities are more commonly rooted in natural or everyday experiences. These are humorous stories in which twins do not set out to confuse, but confusion occurs anyway. As Kristy states at the beginning of the interview, "Being a twin means that in this life there is someone else running around with your face on," so that twins must operatively clarify their respective identities, together and alone, for the casual observer and even family members. Where the gaze of others tends to focus on their sameness, twins have to negotiate difference. This biosocial negotiation of identity features the surfaces of the body, but it also becomes a negotiation or coproduction of identities behind the face in terms, not only of asserting and positioning phenotypic differences but in self consciously linking those differences to identifying attributes or distinguishing characteristics of self. This practical aspect of twinship, body pragmatic, or dualing of identities as self work is depicted below. While Pálsson (1994, 902) refers to enskilment as "feeling at home in the body and in the company of others," enskilment for twins has the added dimension of self-consciously making a home in the body in the company of others.

DUALING IDENTITY: SAME AND DIFFERENT

Because they are so often and repeatedly confused in the eyes of others, twins report that they must mine their own bodies for identity markers that cue their individual identities for the gaze of others.

Bodily pragmatics here include enskilment in terms of embodied social strategies and practices associated with distinguishing each twin's respective identity, or training or educating the observer's abilities to discriminate identifying differences. The unobvious, in terms of small or obscure parts of the body or the body in motion (as in handedness or different smiles), comes to define personhood in twins. In the case of identical twins, one could well argue that twins' embodied individual identities are far more reflectively engaged and finely tuned than would be the case for singletons. Here we take a closer look at how the rhetoric of same and different is used to map identity on the surface of twins' bodies.

Talking about sameness comes naturally to our talking partners. When asked how they are same or different, Randi and Dante tell us that they are both traditional Italian males but that Randi wears Nikes and Dante wears Reeboks. This is not silly; it is an important aspect of the self work that Randi and Dante repeatedly do. It is, in a sense, an Intro 101 to their embodied selfhoods. A statement about shared ethnicity is important to Dante and Randi in their presentation of self. Also important is their self-coded distinctiveness in choice of athletic shoes as everyday wear. It is an idiosyncratic difference that makes a difference to them and materially defines and affirms their distinctive, individual identities. Randi will not wear Reeboks, even if they are a gift or on sale. Randi and Dante do not just talk about their shoes; they show them to us to validate this statement of difference between them. These idiosyncratic determinations are expressed in the twin vernacular as same and different. They are central to twins' presentation of self and identity negotiation. Unless they purposefully want to confuse the observer, Randi and Dante will diligently stick to wearing the identifying shoes because they have collaborated to train the gaze of the other.

In the open-ended free flow of the twins talk, three interesting things happened in response to questions about sameness. First, Jeana and Dina, Mary and Martha, and Chris and Carla were among those who corrected us at the onset of the interview. In effect, they questioned and changed the wording of the question. They said that they could only really respond to the word *similar*, since no one person could be the "same" as another.[13] Second, although I had initially planned to ask twins how they were the same and different in two separate questions, talk of *same* always entailed talk of *different* and vice versa. Third, although we did not raise the issue of individuality, it became an intrinsic part of the responses to the discussion we initiated on similarities and differences. Tina and Ginuh and Dina and Jeana illustrate how comments on same and similar move to comments on difference. For example, Tina describes how they are the same and Ginuh follows up with how they are different. Dina's account develops within a more elaborate explanatory framework, but as in the case of Tina and Ginuh, individuality is asserted.

Tina: Physically we're the same—same weight, same struggles with weight. We look similar.

Ginuh: And that sameness thing. I think it attributes to our differences too. I think that forcing us to be together, not being able to do things without the other there, and forced us to be different too.

Dina: I would say we are similar only because when we were growing up, when we were smaller, I would say we were the same, because my Mom dressed us alike, and we did everything alike. We can finish each other's sentences. Sometimes we will show up and be wearing the same clothes and stuff. I don't mind looking like her. I feel like I have identified who I am as a person. I would say we are just similar now, but we are very, very close.

The practical experience of living in the body makes twins even more aware (than singletons) of their collective and individual body traits. As we saw in the case of the twin game, mining the body for distinctive self-identifying traits not only clues the observers but helps to reinforce twins' own sense of embodied distinctiveness or the subtle natural and contingent differences between them. Body boundaries are at the same time permeable and fixed. Looking alike thus confirms twins' identities as twins, especially in a festival setting, but, simultaneously, contingent differences mark individual identities. The bodies described are relational; they have limited or no meaning if the twins are not together or being compared. Jean told us that she had "football eyes" (oval) and Carol had "basketball eyes" (round). Jean goes on to remark, "You have all these people looking at your eyeballs."

For us, as children, minor physical differences become self-defining. Dorothy has a dimple; I do not. Dorothy says, "We were always smiling like lunatics so that people could spot the dimple and tell us apart." I am left-handed; Dorothy is right-handed. I squint more than Dorothy. My fingernail beds are more oval than Dorothy's. My cowlicks twirl clockwise and Dorothy's twirl counterclockwise. One summer our camp counselors told us apart by our knees—apparently, one of us has larger kneecaps. This observation could only be made if we were standing side by side. How many singletons have a fine-tuned self-monitoring of the knee differences among their siblings? How many singletons have to stand side by side to have their embodied individuality determined and affirmed in the eyes of others?

The importance of the materiality of twin bodies is not limited to childhood. Nor are the physical markers of being same and different static over twins' lives.

> Arnette: Before we leave [the topic of] similar, there are
> certain physical [ways in which] we are similar—
> like we both developed this tremor at the same age.
> We both have high blood pressure. We both have
> a swelling disease that contributes to high blood
> pressure.

> Annette: That's congestive heart. And we both use bifocals
> and started dreading our hair at the same time.

Weight and weight differences were also issues that captured the attention of twins throughout their life cycles. Kristy's comment to the gas station attendant is an example of this. Yet from a life history or biographical perspective, physical differences such as health issues can become prime movers in a twin's life. Arnette and Annette talked about how Arnette's low birth weight and subsequent developmental problems and physical fragility in early childhood left her with a dependency on Arnette that she would need to overcome later in life (and did). Tom's facial birthmark made his life different from Tim's. A major turning point in Pete and Emil's life came during World War II when Pete failed his army physical because of a hearing loss.

The litanies of same and different as voiced by our talking partners also include character and behavioral traits or attributes. The idea is that once you can recognize the individual's body you can begin to affix same and different personal traits to it. Tom and Tim both like music; Mary and Martha have similar tastes and the same sense of twisted humor. Randy and Dante comment that they both have the same interests and enjoy watching the same TV shows. Chris and Carla say they share the same basic morals. Pete and Emil refer to being same and different across a series of behavioral traits that are important to their mutual and distinctive identities. These traits are important to twins because they give constancy (Sadri and Sadri 1994) to twin identities. Tina and Ginuh describe themselves as same in rather abstract terms. In contrast, Emil and Pete are highly specific.

> Tina: Generally, we are the same as far as spiritually, mentally, things like that. Everything is same as far as our social structure. We're both not millionaires.

> Ginuh: I would definitely think of us as same. We think the same. The same things irritate us. Our neuroses are the same usually.

> Emil: We have a lot of likes as far as food and everything.

> Pete: Except I don't like seafood.

> Emil: Right, he won't eat any kind of seafood. We clip coupons. We go shopping, shopping, shopping. We do the same things more or less although we live ninety miles away. We like going to ball games together, also going together on trips.

> Pete: We both volunteer in nursing homes and play bingo.

When it comes to personal attributes, discussions of sameness regarding physical features are often qualified by an assertion of individuality. When Dina states their similarities, Jeana interjects in a very authoritative tone, "Make no mistake, we are two distinct individuals." In twins talk, twins are not as close to being the same person as possible; instead, their personal attributes are identified, positioned, and contextualized. Behavioral traits or personal attributes not only differentiate but disembody identity and make the twin self, behind the face, more complex in the sense of "OK, we look the same or similar but we are two distinct people in terms of our character or personality." Yet these distinguishing characteristics are relational in that they are contingent on those of the other twin. They make meaning through a twin/twin comparison. This contingency develops from looking the same and being together. From this perspective, the resemblance of identical twins is not superficial.

Although twins take on self-identifying character traits, many of these come in the form of family labels that evolved over time to mark differences between twins. For example, Tina and Ginuh were referred to as "Tina weana" and "Ginuh meana." As children, I was called the "little football player" and Dorothy was the "little mother." Their grandfather called Annette "Miss Prissy" and her sister, Arnette, "Miss Sassy." Mabel says she is outgoing like their dad, while Bertha is shy like their mother. Later life experiences also shaped self attributes. Donna refers to herself as the "traditional grandma," whereas Dianne, who recently took up Harley riding, is the "motorcycle grandma." Lucy characterizes herself as liking cowboys and her sister, Linda, as liking auto mechanics and car racers. Ginuh characterizes herself as settled and domestic, while her sister, Tina, is the wild one. Lifetime attributes, such as being neat versus messy and being careful and fussy versus casual about physical appearance and clothing, were also differences noted by a number of twins. Arnette and Annette's litany of self attributes goes beyond character traits, as they move beyond being to becoming (cf. Ingold 2013), to include an accounting of their accomplishments.

> Arnette: We are both social workers. We both like to
> participate in community activities, especially in
> our churches. We have both worked in the youth
> department of our churches and in Sunday school.
> We both like to move around a lot. Travel and do
> different things. We both have a lot of grandchildren.
> Oh, man, we both love our grandchildren. We spend
> a lot of time with our grandchildren. We are both
> history buffs and are our family historians. We both

like current events. News shows and stuff like that. We are both artists and like to draw a lot. And like poetry a lot.

Annette: We both like to act.

Arnette: And we both like public speaking. We both are very good at public speaking. Does that cover everything?

Annette: Pretty much, that's all those things we like to do.

The disembodying of identity in twins talk is not always as harmonious as the examples above indicate. The contextualizing voice of complementarity can also take on a more oppositional tone. Remember Karen and Kristy's comments on bra size? In a sense, they were counterhegemonic in that they challenge others for confusing them. The following exchange between Karen and Kristy also illustrates a more assertive oppositional form of identity trait negotiation. Although they describe themselves as very close and always there for each other, Karen and Kristy state that they "look the same but that's it; otherwise, they are totally different people." The following exchange between Karen and Kristy draws on popular cultural stereotypes of twins. As they dual/duel their identities to become the "good" and the "evil" twin, they demonstrate relational identities in action. Being the good or bad twin was an important part of their identities, and they were very articulate about it. Both seemed quite proud as they bang out and proclaim their respective designations.

Kristy: We are similar in our looks. That's it. That's the only thing that is the same. We are totally different people. Don't you think? [It is worth noting that both women are dressed exactly alike.]

Karen: We argue a lot. A lot!

Kristy: That's because she's always cruel.

Karen: Someone else can be nice.

Kristy: We were never alike.

Karen: We don't like the same things.

Kristy: We don't like the same people.

Karen: I like good people; she likes bad people.

Kristy: Karen is the evil twin. She hangs out with bad people, jail time bad. What's wrong with you?

Karen: I'm evil.

Kristy: Mom always said that Karen could come out of a shit house smelling like a rose.

Karen and Kristy's self-portrayals were certainly the most oppositional of all the Twinsburg interviews in terms of being a consistent theme throughout the interview. Not only were they relating character differences, but they enacted the characters as they played out their respective good and evil roles. To refer to them as discordant for evil overlooks the playful, practiced, and highly enskiled quality of their exchange and would probably have bled all the life out of this data. Moreover, Karen's evilness only takes on meaning in contrast to Kristy's goodness.

Battaglia's (1995a, 674) rather rhetorical question, "Why should looking at yourself violate some profound sense of individuality?" is meant to be counterhegemonic. Yet it is the practical experience or body pragmatic of twins to enact, to manage identities, and to assert self in counterhegemonic ways as counterintuitive or against the grain of what is assumed to be normative. Normative, in this sense, posits likeness as a profound violation of identity. Twins talk as presented above shows how twins within and outside of the dyad actively assert unique, bounded, individual, embodied identities and distinctive self-conscious attributional selves. As mentioned previously, it could well be argued that identical twins have a more finely tuned sense of biological and attributional self than singletons. Although perhaps not as exciting as locating a new genetic loci or SNP that causes a terrible disease, an analysis of the kinds of embodied enskilment tools and practices that the Twinsburg twins bring to the table (literally, in the case of the Twins Talk Study table) provides a twin's-eye perspective on individual and shared identities and on twins as biosocial facts. When it comes to same and different, twins can be either one or the other or both at the same time. Twins are self-conscious of being on the fault lines. When it comes to self working their personal embodied identities, the Twinsburg twins explain, enact, and normalize themselves as unique, bounded, self-conscious, and separate. But if they distinguish and separate their identities, they also merge them.

Yet intercorporeality can also go beyond the notions of twins as a pair or twin-twin comparison from within the dyad. Some of the talking partners express and enact a form of intercorporeality that goes beyond look-alike selves referenced by some permutation or combination of self and other statement. The partners also show an ability to surrender one's self or reduce one's self to the pair. Rather than view twins as some sort of congenital duplicates, what follows describes intercorporeality among the Twinsburg twins in terms of a strongly felt sense of embodied mutuality, contingent identities, shared being, and a sense of open or porous body boundaries.

DUALING RELATIONSHIPS AND SURRENDERING TO THE PAIR

Certainly the very fact of dressed-alike talking partners, sitting side by side and enacting identities as a series of comparison and contrasts within the dyad, has an intercorporeal element to it in that one's twin's self is constantly referenced in terms of the companion twin's self. Paradoxically, however, embodied twinscapes also serve to join or conflate identities as well as separate them. Festival twins, by their very attendance of festivals, surrender self to the pair and express a kind of embodied, intercorporeal mutuality that transcends singularity. In what follows, I focus on (an embodied) intercorporeality as revealed in twins talk (the more psychological aspect of mutuality are the topics of chapter 5), not as mere duplication, but as a form of contingent mutuality that develops from time spent together or shared place and space. But I also focus on mutuality in terms of shared identities and practices, such as touching, gesture and movement, and extrasensory perception. All of these practices express intercorporeality as open, flexible, or fluid body boundaries and a readiness to surrender the self to the pair.

Conflating Selves: Names and Pronouns

An important way that twins confound the notion of a singular embodied identity is the extent to which they share space and place. Carol says that she and Jean are similar because they spend so much time together. A shared environmental copresence unites twins. Because they are constantly in the company of each other in the formative years of childhood and because they are look-alike identicals, twins often find themselves reduced to a paired identity in the eyes of others. From a singleton's perspective, attending to the self working of identical twins can be riddled with difficulties and confusion (or not worth the effort), and it becomes simply easier to reduce twins to a unit or paired kind of identity. For the Twinsburg twins, embodied similarities are often compounded by body identity labels or names, which often rhyme or otherwise sound similar. Given the opportunity to give themselves fictitious names, only three sets of twins came up with nonrhyming or alliterative names. Dorothy and I have often heard singletons complain that they can tell us apart but they get the names confused. Very often they do not even try. Expectations of pairness conflate identity. If names authenticate individuality, then being labeled collectively as "the twins," "the Davis twins," or individually as "Pete and Repeat," "Tweedledum and Tweedledee," "Twin and Twain," or simply as "hey, you" suggests confusion for an other who is unwilling to work out the separate identities. Twins are so used to dealing with confusion in the eyes of others that they report a lifelong automatic habit of responding to their twin's name.

Twins also conflate identities with the pronoun *we*. A "we-world" is a practical experience of twinship. Chris's statement that "we look alike" and Tina's that "we look similar" also demonstrate the tendency to "we" the body. Phyllis and Pat apologized for constantly saying "we" as they talked to us. We certainly understood them as they explained, "You know, it's a twin thing." One reason that twins get treated as a unit is their copresence. As a matter of fact, it is extremely difficult for me to write this book not using a constant "we." The we-ness habit, which can also characterize married couples, is impartible from the fact that twins' early lives are lived side by side. When Dina says "We are very, very close," she refers to both emotion and proximity. As Conley (2004) notes, identical twins, even within the family, occupy a unique social position in terms of their very togetherness. This togetherness can make twins more alike and can help twins distinguish themselves from each other (Conley 2004; Farmer 1996), but the distinctions are contingent. At the same time that Karen and Kristy sit dressed identically side by side and tell of their father insisting they always be together so he could tell them apart, they complain about a gas station attendant who cannot or does not care to tell them apart, all the while playfully arguing out their different respective identities. They rather aggressively assert their individuated identities as a counter to those who would confuse or conflate their identities by playing into and against stereotypes of good and evil twins. *Intercorporeality* in this sense refers to not only a "we" identity but the fact that, in the case of the garage attendant, one twin often stands for the other. This is all quite familiar to Dorothy and me; what follows is less so.

Gesture and Movement

It is important when focusing on twins talk not to see the body as static or frozen in form. The bodies of the talking partners move. They are in a constant process of action and interaction. I was thirty-three years old when I got married. My husband had never met my twin sister. He was rather anxious about doing so. When he finally did meet Dorothy, he felt relieved that he could easily tell us apart. However, this relief quickly gave way to being shocked by the extent to which our gestures and body language are the same. Although, through almost three decades, he has spent very little time in Dorothy's presence, I appear to have a facial expression that indicates when I am ticked off at him; he calls this my "Dorothy face." Yet gestures also differentiate. Growing up in a rural town, Dorothy and I shared the same classmates from kindergarten through high school. Although, in the lower grades, we were dressed alike, our classmates never had any trouble telling us apart (those who were not classmates were less able and far more likely to treat us as a unit). Because we walked differently (I with a slew foot), we could be readily identified from a block away, provided we were walking.

Touch and Touching

Touching as an expressive style of relatedness in twinship is interesting because it represents a way of transgressing body boundaries and is recognized as a form of intercorporeality. According to Weiss (1999, 121), touching bodies are nondiscrete; one is enveloped within the other. Touching selves are depicted as interpenetrating selves (Laderman and Roseman 1992), connected bodies (Benthien 2002; Bird-David 2004), and open, communicating bodies (Walby 2002). Dorothy and I, who do not have a "touchy-feely" relationship, were struck by the way that some of our talking partners were constantly in tactile contact with each other; we called them "tactile twins."

A touchingly "touching" story comes from Janet and Judy (age sixty-one). Janet and Judy would pause throughout the interview to hug each other. They would stop talking, look each other in the eyes, lean over, put their arms around each other's shoulders, bring their heads together (sometimes forehead to forehead and sometimes cheek to cheek), and embrace. When we finished the interview, Janet and Judy stood up and hugged and kissed each other. Judy and Janet realized that their physical intimacy was normatively transgressive. They remarked that at Twinsburg they were probably becoming known as the "gay twins." Yet they had not always been this tactile. This was something that had developed recently as Janet was undergoing chemotherapy for breast cancer. During Janet's treatment, Judy would come to her house to sleep with her, spooning together in the bed; Judy shared the strength of her healthy body with Janet's weakened body. Not only did Judy intercorporeally give the strength of her body to her sister, but she also gave to her hair. Still bald from chemo, Judy had given Janet snips of her hair to attach to her cap. Although they live a seven-hour drive apart, they claim to be "inseparable, as close as Siamese twins." They had come to Twinsburg to celebrate Janet's survival, to celebrate their joy, and to express their thanks to God for allowing them more time together on earth.

Karen and Kristy (age forty-six) were also in repeated physical contact with each other, but in their case the contact involved a constant barrage of mutual playful hits, punches, and pinches that punctuated their verbal performance of good and evil twins. Throughout their conversation, Karen and Kristy poked, hit, pinched, and thumped on one another, violating not only standards of appropriate adult behavior but also transgressing proximate norms of our culture by showing no respect for each other's personal space. Their behavior was so out of the ordinary that they caught the attention of those in research booths adjacent to us and across the aisle. In a different vein, Amy and Beth, throughout their conversation, would gently stroke each other's arms, touch hands, lean together shoulder to shoulder, and mutually perform a sort of one-armed hug. In a kind of mutual grooming, Amy picked a hanging eyelash off Beth's eye. When together, their body boundaries were open, not to make a point or to joke with each other as in the case of Karen and Kristy but as an unconscious form of mutual support and connectedness. Beth, the self-described take-charge twin, would answer a question or make a comment and simply sit quietly stroking Amy's arms until Amy, too, offered a verbal response.

> Beth: She's [Amy] dreading the seven-hour car drive home
> tonight. Her leg will be over me. And her arm will
> be around me. Then she'll start sleeping on my arm.
> Anyways, I don't know; we have a connection that
> [nontwin] brothers and sisters don't.

Among twins, touch in utero comes before seeing. Yet for the talking partners, touch is an active and interactive touching, whether in rough play, as in the case of Kristy and Karen; or intentionally comforting, as between Janet and Judy; or as habit, as with Amy and Beth. As they sit side by side, talking twins demonstrate the extent to which intercorporeality can be seen as overlapping body boundaries. They enact mutually defining body images as they position their respective identities as individual, contingent, and collective.

Extrasensory Perception

ESP, or extrasensory perception, is also a form of intercorporeality mentioned by some of the talking partners. It is not my intention to prove or disprove the existence of ESP. Touching can be observed, enacted, and felt. ESP is more ephemeral but emerges as a very real kind of intercorporeality to those who report experiencing it. Whereas touching is a habitual interactive process that physically joins or merges on the skin, ESP as a form of intercorporeality describes ways of joining or merging the minds, as in one twin's subjective experience of the other twin's mind and body. Dorothy and I did not ask about ESP. At the end of the talking sessions when we asked for comments about the interview or invited additional questions, we were both praised and criticized for not asking about ESP. Some of the talking partners were openly skeptical or found ESP as a topic for joking. Mary jokes: "I don't know about twin telepathy, but we were sharing spirits [alcohol] last night. Dorothy wisecracks, "No singleton in his or her right mind wants to play *Pictionary* with twins." At the end of their interview Tim and Tom actually thanked us for not asking them about ESP. They related a time when they sought to test the hypothesis. Tim was in Malaysia and Tom back home in the United States. Tim suggested that Tom pound his hand with a hammer and see if he (Tim) would feel it. Tom, in particular, showed little enthusiasm for the experiment.

Yet ESP is certainly real to the twins who describe it (Johnson 2005). Annette and Arnette, Lucy and Linda, and Phyllis and Pat describe ESP as a dramatic form of intersubjective connection or an open bond that exists between them. Annette and Arnette told us that both had troubled marriages at a time when neither could afford a telephone. When they needed each other, they would "phone," psychically sending dream distress calls to each other. Lucy and Linda matter-of-factly report that they can sit in a room, not say a word and carry on a conversation with each other. Lucy and Linda also report that because they feel each other's pains, they will, when necessary, call their twin sister to say, "You need to go to the doctor." After recounting a series of ESP-type experiences, Phyllis tells of the most dramatic one.

> Phyllis: The scariest thing that ever happened between the two of us was she was pregnant and she fell down a flight of stairs. She was in Auburn and I was in Jamesville. And I just flew across the room and landed and had bruises and stuff on me, but apparently the force of her body falling threw me right across the room.

> Pat: We had the exact same bruises.

Although hardly accepted by science, ESP as expressed in twins talk is interesting because it represents a form of intercorporeality that challenges the notion of a singular self, where self is bounded by our body so that which is outside the body is not me and that which is inside my body is me (de Munck 2000, 36). Although the Twinsburg twins report sensing or experiencing the other's pains or dilemmas, they seem to be able to discern that it is their twin's body and not their own where the "real" pain lies.

LIFE VERSUS LABORATORY

Twins are good to think with in a multitude of ways. In this chapter on the body, I have featured some major perspectives and assumptions of the hereditarians, as researchers who study twins or feature the twin method in their research, and then compared their perspectives to those of twins. Just as my introductory example illustrates, I have juxtaposed the perspectives, purposes, and assumptions of researchers, represented by those in attendance at the ICTS (where gene talk is privileged) to those expressed by ITA and Twinsburg twins (of which I am one). Whereas the former are rooted in academia and scientific research, the latter are rooted in the practical lived experiences of twins. Whereas the former focus on increasingly sophisticated research methods, the latter shift focus to the enskilment of identity practices among twins. While terms like *concordance* and *discordance*, as identified statistically or established in high-tech labs, characterize the discourse of researchers, twins negotiate same and different through interpersonal interactions. While researchers view twins as method or data, purge twins who do not fit the research criteria from their databases, and make claims of "same" if over 50 percent of the samples test the same on a trait, the anecdotal data suggests that twins recognize ambiguity and how a specific situation or context can influence and shape response.

I started this chapter with the example of my exchange with a twins researcher at an ITC meeting in which she sought to define my twin identity for me and I resisted her attempt. While she asserted that I needed to self-refer as an MZ twin, I insisted I was an identical twin. I was resisting not only her attempt to co-opt my identity but her denial of my being identical (and all the biosocial realties of my life that have sprung from it). Reading between the lines, and this is what we anthropologists do, I see her as disparaging or devaluing the term *identical*. She kept telling me that we must view twins as two separate individuals. I told her that she could not negate through word choice that, for twins, identical counts in the practical experiences of twinship. Both her position and my own invite cultural analysis, and I use the notions of embodiment of identity, intercorporeality, and enskilment to offer some additional perspectives on our positions in this debate.

What the researcher does not recognize is that her disparagement of the word *identical* is culturally rooted. Focusing on the body (there is much more of this in chapter 6) in a way that extends beyond the genetic debates concerning twins, I look at environment as affecting not only twins but those who research them. As a singleton and a product of the Western tradition, my researcher companion makes a number of assumptions about the embodiment of self and person-hood. Among these assumptions are the ideas that each person is or should be physically unique, each person's body is bounded by skin, and bodies are self-conscious with inner- as well as outer-defining attributes. Apparently, her assumptions about my twinned body being relational can be encapsulated with the acronym MZ. Her implied focus on my very first days of egged existence, rather on than what I have become—a twin expert talking to another twin researcher at an international research conference—irks me. I am no longer an egg, but I am still an identical twin.

What I am saying is yes, very well, I live in this society too and I should not be treated as or disparaged as identical to or the same as another person. I certainly know that I'm not Dorothy. Nobody who ever knew us, beyond the most casual of acquaintances, would make that claim either. Yet the fact is that Dorothy and I have had to deal with the practical experiences of looking alike and being on the fault lines or of having bodies where the uniqueness, boundedness, self-consciousness, and relationality of our embodied identities are confused, confounded, or transgressed in the eyes of others because, on the surfaces of our bodies, we look alike. As this chapter moves from the researchers' perspectives to those of twins, the embodied practical experiences of twinship, as they shape identity and identity practice, also occur within a specific historically derived environment or cultural milieu.

In part, this book is an artifact of the Research Pavilion's festival setting, where twins as twins are interviewing twins who are celebrating their very twinship. The talking partners sit side by side. Just as looking alike may be viewed as a kind of shared being, being together in shared place and space gives a contingency to twins' physical being that also becomes part of their twin persona. As the different sets of talking partners talk, they participate in a coproduction of self. They share experiences and memories, they touch each other, and they talk about ESP experiences they have shared. At the same time that they differentiate each other, they surrender to the pair.

Lock and Nguyen (2010, 334) comment that the wane of genetic determinism and rise of "the fuzzy gene" (epigenetics) has opened up new means for exploring interactions between nature and nurture. Others would argue that the very distinctions between nature and nurture should be collapsed (Pálsson 2013) or disappeared (Spector 2012). What my use of the concepts of enskilment and intercorporeality, combined with the more general perspectives of cultural psychology and theories of embodiment, bring to the analysis of twins' bodies is the idea that our bodies (as well as the biological assumptions of identity and personhood held by twins researchers) are shaped by culture. The idea that twins' bodies are contingent on and connected to the bodies of others applies to singletons as well as twins. Bodies and body images are also parts of wider systems of representation and meaning. Twins and twins researchers both exist in a social contest of multiple and sometimes discordant selfways. Not only are there multiple selfways open to members of a diverse society, but each member embodies his or her own multiple selfways and styles of relating. Twins are hardly creatures of genetic destiny or of their invisible and inborn natures. All the adult twins in this study have become who they are by making choices among different ways of presenting self and selves. These in turn are drawn upon, employed, negotiated, or enacted in different ways in different situations and contexts. This chapter has highlighted the embodied identity skills that twins bring to the process.

5

BOND

You are the company you keep.

—*Popular saying*

Being a twin means you're never alone or lonely.

—*Example of a pathological twin's statement in Schave and Ciriello 1983*

Phyllis has two grandchildren. I have thirty-five. I guess we can share. What difference does it make?

—*Pat*

AS AN ADULT TWIN WHO IS INVOLVED IN TWIN RESEARCH, I AM constantly asked by mothers of twins what I think are the best ways to raise twins so as to nurture both their special bonds and their individuality. At the ICTS, mothers or parents of twins groups like TAMBA and ICOMBO are particularly concerned with a host of child-raising decisions they must make.[1] Should they separate their children or let them be together? How special should the twin bond be? Are twins in danger of becoming too close? Similar concerns are expressed by educators and are widely discussed online and in how-to books on raising twins (Piontelli 2008; Stewart 2003). These concerns convey a core dilemma of popular and academic discussions of child and adolescent development among twins. It centers on how best to encourage what is good and enviable about twinship and how best to discourage the potentially negative and problematic aspects of twinship. Ironically, the good and the bad are the same thing: being together, an intimate bond, and a well-developed sense of mutuality. Although these are held to make the twin relationship special, they are also held to undermine or compromise the individuation of identities between twins. As we shall see, parents and educators have reasons to worry. Western social science, especially psychology, has not been particularly kind to twins (Harter 1999). Within the psychology literature, twinning becomes associated with multiple adversities that may affect the child's social world (Ainslie 1985; Parisi 2004; Tabor and Joseph 1961), lead to identity problems (Ainslie 1985; Joseph 2004), and continue to impair twin psyches long after childhood (Joseph 2002, 2004; Sandbank 2007; Schave and Ciriello 1989).[2]

This chapter moves from the last chapter's focus on embodied identities and the biological sciences of twinship to engage the twin bond and more psychological aspects of relationship and identity within the twin dyad. Of course, this is a rather artificial distinction when it comes to the lived experiences of twinship. As chapter 4 demonstrates and as Pálsson (2013, 24) notes, "The 'nature' with which we are born and which we develop is thoroughly biosocial, embodied through human activities." My artifice in distinguishing biological and psychological aspects of the practical experience of twinship nevertheless reflects two distinctive areas of scientific literature. Both bodies of thought, however, are similar in that they place identical twins on the fault lines of identity and medicalize twinship. While biology portrays twins as too alike or indistinct, psychology portrays twins as too close or too absorbed in one another or even as somehow cut off from the social world that surrounds them. Both approaches overlook or misconstrue the coexistence of twins as a social fact. Self working twins must negotiate their duality and unity in a culture that views autonomy and relationality as opposites and privileges the former (McCollum 2002). Moreover, the psychological imagination gives little sensitivity to or recognition of twins' own, largely counterhegemonic experiences and perspectives on their relationships. The twins talk partners certainly resonate with

Battaglia's (1995a, 674) question (although directed at clones) "Why shouldn't we ask what constrains mutuality rather than what constrains autonomy?"

Psychological research with nonclinical populations of twins actually shows that twins are at no greater risk for psychopathology than the general population (Levick 2004). Even clinical researchers note that most twins develop normally (Ainslie 1985; Zazzo 1978), that their codependence diminishes with increasing age (Penninkilampi-Kerola et al. 2004), and even that twinship confers advantages when it comes to handling interpersonal relationships (Besharat and Habibi 2004). Yet notions of twins as being too close or too self-contained within a single boundary dominate the twin psychology literature (particularly object relations psychology) in which the twin bond becomes a kind of psychopathological identity stunting, ego fusing, or unconstrained mutuality, which is purportedly rooted in overshared childhood environments (Joseph 2004; Klein 2003). What was problematic in chapter 4, a singular embodied identity, becomes a crippled or incomplete self in this chapter. Again as a kind of deviant persona, twins and their twinship, or relationship, reflect tensions between dependence and independence, between autonomy and mutuality, and between merging and individuating (Lindholm 2001). These tensions as styles of relating within the twin dyad become polarized or dichotomized in the psychopathology of twin literature, which in turn reflects unquestioned and hegemonic values of selving within the wider cultural milieu.

Although psychology is considered by biologists to be a softer science, the psychological literature also locates twins within a natural world that presumes a universal and universally developed human psyche.[3] Within this naturalistic framework, standards of normal and not normal styles of selving are developed and codified. As we have seen with the body, what is glossed as "natural" may in fact be cultural. Like the biolization by twos, the psycholization by twos overlooks four important social facts that shape and are shaped by the practical experiences of twinship as expressed in twins talk. First is the notion that there may be multiple and conflicting selfways, as well as multiple ways of constructing and enacting independence and interdependence, within any particular cultural context (Markus et al. 1997). Second, twins as a kind of deviant persona may take on positive as well as negative aspects (cf. Edgerton 1984). Third, twins actively organize knowledge about themselves and their twinship to educate the singleton in ways that both assert and legitimize their own alternative characteristic ways of being in the world. Fourth, one way to normalize twins' couplings of their relationships is to view mutuality both as a state of being and as a stratagem for relating.

TWIN DYNAMICS

Rather than see self as monolithic, a cultural psychology approach views self as composed of different parts, contexts, and interpretive stances that reflect the various places, social relationships, and social contexts in which the self lives (Markus et al. 1997). For example, "The self can be contingent and unique at the same time" (Cohen 1994, 21). Selves in action may oscillate between being ontologically secure, to being fulfilled with another, and to being overwhelmed or engulfed by another (Jackson 1998). In this chapter, I situate the idea and practice of what is commonly depicted as the twin bond in a variety of perspectives or interpretive stances. Twins talk demonstrates the practical experience of twinship from the ground up and shows how twins situate and negotiate autonomy and mutuality across a number of contexts in ways that reify, confound, and challenge their cultural persona and Western stereotypes (cf. Holland et al. 1998; Neisser and Jopling 1997). I use the term *twin dynamic* to capture this sense of the twin bond as a kind of intersubjective engagement, where within the dyad twins reciprocally negotiate and enact their individual and collective identities and interact to position and interplay their mutuality and autonomy. Rather than view mutuality and autonomy as abstract or rarified states of being, with one necessarily compromising the other, I view them as tools (cf. Harter 1999) strategically employed in the interactive processes of self working and self styling among the Twinsburg twins.

Starting with a section on the twin bond, I will briefly examine psychologically informed discussions of what I refer to as the *co-contemporarity of twins* and *troubled twins*. While the former views twins as a kind of closed society, the latter pathologizes the expression of interdependence or mutuality among twins. Using twins talk, I set forth an alternative perspective that views twinship, or the twin relationship, as a kind of enhanced rather than compromised self. I take a twin's-eye view of how twins respond to and adapt to being treated as twins by nontwin others. I then compare twins as a pair to other sorts of couples or pairs, and reconceptualize mutuality as a dynamic and situated tool for relating. This exploration of a twin's-eye view of his or her relationship will set the dyadic twin relationship within the complexities of a wider sociocultural milieu, setting the scene for the more culturally, anthropologically informed analysis of chapter 6.

THE BOND

Like the Twinsburg talking partners, Prainsack et al. (2007) report that what their British sample of twin informants see as distinctive about the twin condition or lived experience of twinship is not looking alike but the special bond or relationship that they share. This is not expressed as a genetic bond but as an interpersonal, experientially derived one. In *How Twins Grow Up*, one of the few book-length, cautiously positive portrayals of twinship in the psychological literature on twins, Rosambeau (1987, 83) refers to this special or mystical twin bond depicted by her informants as a kind of "double benefit" of twinship. Rosambeau's British twin pairs portray the bond as presenting a unified front to the world, having a confidante, someone who will always understand you, and someone who will defend or stick up for you. These phrases of British twins are echoed just about verbatim by the adult Twinsburg twins who also describe the bond in positive terms as strong and enduring links of affection rooted in the contemporarity and companionship that twins share during childhood.

What I refer to as shared place and space is expressed by the Twinsburg twins as a special form of coexistence. This coexistence operates through time and space and entails an active, interactive, and multifaceted copresentation and coproduction of selves. Interactive negotiations or enskiled (see chapter 4) practices of self and other, on the one hand, and pairness, on the other, exhibit their own relational intercorporeal elements and are rooted in the oft-repeated events of everyday experience. Crucial elements of this coexistence include having someone who is going through the same things at the same time as you, being regarded and treated as same or equal, and having someone who not only shares early experiences but also shares your memories of them. The popular saying "You are the company you keep" takes on special meaning when it comes to twins.

The positive twin's-eye view of their selves in relationship, however, finds little resonance with the negative views expressed in the psychological literature in which the twin bond is faulted and becomes a kind of relational glue that joins, fixes, fuses, locks, or traps twins together in their own society or dyadically defined world. In terms of relationships, the closeness of twins is referred to as interdependence, twin symbiosis, or the twin condition. Using a singleton model of the individual, parents are often advised by psychologists to nurture their twins' individuality through a process of "detwinning" that involves separate bedrooms, separate clothes, and separate classes at school (Piontelli 2008, 18).

Even those who caution that "physical identicalness does not imply psychic identicalness" (Gedda 1995, 7) or who describe the twin bond in terms of both exclusive and parallel identities (Rosambeau 1987) tend to objectify twins by regarding them as the preset or static objects of their relationships rather than as the enactors or shapers of it. When a set of twins talks together, Strathern's (1986) notion of interpersonal bonds as pivots of relationships certainly better characterizes twin relationships as they actively jockey with each other to position their identities within the dyad. Just as I described in the previous chapter on embodied identity, in this more psychologically focused chapter twins coterminously express their dual and collective identities as they speak of themselves as individuals while also representing themselves in their dyadic situation as a pair. When twins talk about their bond, they self-consciously express their mutuality as contained and situated rather than as constrained. Twinsburg twins realize that the dyadic bond between twins includes both a sense of collective mutuality that places them at odds with normative selfways and a sense of reciprocally negotiated self-awareness of self-otherness that, although uniquely positioned, conforms to conventional Western selfways.

CO-CONTEMPORARITY: PSYCHOLIZATION BY TWOS

In chapter 4, I discussed the biolization by twos that can characterize twins, whether the discussion is about phenotype, genotype, or behavioral traits. As I turn to a more psychological discussion of identity and relationship between twins, as in the "Who am I?" and "Who are we?" questions of twinship, I will again compare and contrast the twins researchers' psychologies of twinship to the practical experiences of twinship as revealed in twins talk. I start with psychological literature that features the contemporary or co-contemporary of twinship as bounded or shared lives. This is followed by a discussion of twins as impaired or enhanced selves. Finally, I bring twins talk and a more practical and normalized reassessment of dyadic or interactive expressions of autonomy and mutuality within the twin bond as I compare the twin pair to other kinds of socially recognized couples.

Closed Societies and Womb Worlds

We have already been introduced to the notion that twins are too close for comfort. The ambivalent dermatologist of destiny, Dr. Teplica, in his ICTS PowerPoint presentation (2004), started with a famous picture of twins kissing in utero (actually, one twin appears to be sucking the nose of the other). The photograph elicits both positive and negative responses to the twin bond. Like puppies, these snuggling twins elicit a warm, fuzzy feeling and were greeted with oohs and ahs by the plenary session's audience. Yet these "touching twins" also elicit a number of less positive notions about identity and relationship between twins. The first is an image of twinship as having rigid boundaries that are both literal and figurative. According to Kamin (1974), the twin relationship is a closed society of two with boundaries that separate twins from the world around them. Sandbank (1999b) describes twins as cutting themselves off from the outside. Zazzo (1976) refers to twins' twinship as a kind of secret garden, with its own private language and gestures, that none (except the twins) can enter. Second, twins who share common origins and an environment bounded by intimacy are characterized as close or too close. Identical twins originate from a single organism that duplicates itself in the first seven to fourteen days of fetal life (Piontelli 1992). Twins are depicted as having conflated or diffuse ego boundaries or as being incomplete selves (Ainslie 1985). Third, each twin is an essential element in the environment of the other. Each movement or action on the part of one affects the other. Conley (2004) benignly refers to the twin pair as like two pistons in a car engine: when one fires the other rests. Less benignly twins are depicted as two parts of a single whole. Sandbank (1999b, 177) characterizes twins as "like two pieces of a jigsaw puzzle, each needing the other to be complete." Gedda (1995,

24) refers to the twin bond, quite simply, as a twin society in which there is a leader twin and a follower twin. Piontelli (1992, 1999), however, who observed dominance differences within twin pairs through gestation into early childhood, focuses on unhappy twins who have failed the identity challenges of childhood individuation.

The picture of twins kissing in utero is a powerful representation of shared origins and prenatal companionships. It shows twins set apart together. Yet even after birth, if the Twins Days twins are any indication, they will remain physically together, interact primarily with each other, and share almost all their early life experiences and immediate environments. This constantly shared environment (usually during childhood) is termed, by twins researchers, *contemporarity* (Conley 2004). The meaning of contemporarity, or co-contemporarity, is fourfold. It refers to twins as given and occupying a unique space in society. It refers to twins spending so much time together. It refers to twins being treated the same. And, it implies a functional complementarity and unspoken coordination between the two twins (Conley 2004). Contemporarity is of interest because it shifts emphasis away from genetics to recognize that twins occupy a social place and interpersonal space that may provide for alternative configurations of relationship and identity. I have already introduced the "we-self" as a form of intercorporeality that refers to twins' physical similarities and constant copresence (especially among twins as children). While twins see "we-ing" in the sense of a plural of "I" to describe the practical experience of their shared and interpenetrating worlds, psychologists view the we-self as an indicator of an abnormal level of co-identification or interdependence between twins and refer to it as a "unit-self" or a "unit-identity" (Schave and Ciriello 1983, 45). The bond becomes a kind of relational glue that joins, fixes, fuses, locks, or traps twins together in their own society or dyadically defined world.

Unit Identities and Troubled Twins

There is a trend in the psychological literature to criticize twins as sharing an impaired or unit identity or we-self that sets them apart from the wider world around them. Ortmeyer (1970) refers to the we-self as a defining and pathological feature of twinship. A number of potential psychosocial hazards of a unit identity can lead to unhappy adulthoods among twins. Among these are the inhibition of efforts to act independently, the comparison of twins vis-à-vis each other when one is found wanting, and lack of a sense of where they stand in their family (Rosambeau 1987). In particular, object relations psychologists view the we-self as two individuals situated within a common boundary who function to a degree as one—as connected parts of a whole (Ainslie 1985; Burlingham 1952; Leonard 1961; Ortmeyer 1970; Segal et al. 2003; Schave and Ciriello 1983). The we-self (also termed *twin symbiosis, twin situation, twin reaction,* or *the twin condition*) connotes merged, fused, diffuse ego boundaries (Leonard 1961; Tabor and Joseph 1961; Segal et al. 2003). Undifferentiated, indivisible, or unit identities are held to pathologically produce split halves or mutual identification (Segal 2005; Segal et al. 2003). Schave and Ciriello (1983, 11, 19, 28) characterize twinship negatively as experiencing oneself as part of another person, self as shared or distributed between individuals of a pair, an unconscious process of partially merged identities, a special closeness, and a sense of belonging to another. Levick (2004), in a review of the clinical literature, describes how identical twins might be more prone to problems related to attachment, separation-individuation, and development of separate identities. Twins are noted to be at risk for delayed language development, slowed intellectual development, low achievement, and becoming a disruptive adolescent gang of two. Twinship itself is now considered to be a risk factor for abusive and neglectful treatment by overwhelmed parents (Piontelli 2008). Twins are also described as being at higher risk (than singletons) for mental health problems (Klein 2003), including a Borderline Personality Disorder (Schave and Ciriello 1983).

The bond or twin relationship also captures the imagination of psychologists who study twins. The clinical literature gives the impression that twins are not well bonded; instead, they are regarded as exemplars of a dangerous and potentially lifelong condition—that of overbonded, unconstrained mutuality. The twin bond becomes medicalized (Ainslie 1985). Not only can one twin harm the other (Zazzo 1978), but all emotional disturbances in all twins are held to originate in the twin relationship (Leonard 1961). The bond becomes associated with a pathological sense of empathy and dependency that, along with their merged identities, hinders development in twins and confuses or impedes relationships with nontwin others and their interaction with the outside world (Ainslie 1985; Burling-ham 1952; Tabor and Joseph 1961; Schave and Ciriello 1983). As soon as they enter school, twins exist in a kind of "double limelight" as teachers look to spot the potential for a host of problems. As part of the "detwinning" process mentioned earlier, psychologists often advise parents to nurture their twins' individuality by enrolling them in separate classes at school (Piontelli 2008, 18).

Please remember at this point that even the largely clinical liter-ature states that most twins develop normally (Ainslie 1985; Levick 2004; Zazzo 1978). Nonclinical samplings of twins studies show that, when it comes to indicators of social closeness, twins differ from the singleton population by being only one standard deviation closer (Johnson et al. 2002). I am not alone in my critique of the overween-ing negativity of psychological studies of twins. Piontelli (2008) de-scribes this pathologizing form of psychology with the terms "sloppy psychology" and "the twin gothic" (2008, 61, 5). Psychologists tend to look for, and isolate or feast upon, instances of twins and twin-ship gone wrong. No wonder the TAMBA and ICOMBO mothers (parents) of twins flock to the ICTS psychology sessions and are con-cerned about the personal and interpersonal development of their twins. Yet again, as we saw in chapter 4, scientific ideas of normalcy and deviance between twins are heavily influenced by Western cul-tural norms of self.

If twinship is suspect as a kind of trap that inhibits proper per-sonality development because it constrains individual autonomy, it is also suspect because it does not constrain connectedness and mu-tuality. Throughout these formulations of the we-self, the individual and pair, and autonomy and mutuality, exist in opposition to each other. The pair has the potential to impair the singular. Characteriz-ing twins as a closed society cuts them off from the rest of the world and overlooks the fact that twins must negotiate their duality and unity in a culture that views autonomy and relationality as opposites and privileges the former (McCollum 2002). Clearly one answer to Battaglia's question "What constrains mutuality?" would be Western notions of person and selfhood—our belief that the expression of au-tonomous individuality connotes self-mastery while mutuality does not. The psychology literature on twins cited above certainly seems to assume that interpersonal mutuality and independence are kinds of limited good, meaning that expressions of mutuality come at a cost to one's individuality and vice versa.

Psychological approaches to twinship have failed to recognize or investigate what are the positive aspects of twinship. Certainly the very features of identity and twinship that are viewed as disabling by the psychotherapists are seen by our twins talk partners as positive features of twinship. For example, Ainslie (1985, 95) uses the case of a young woman who describes her twinship as a feeling of close-ness—"I have an experience with her that no one else has—just between us. . . . It's like a fullness in my chest . . . just like I'm really happy"—to illustrate the pathological quality of twinship. Traits that twins relate as special, wonderful, and enduring aspects of their lives as twins—al-ways being best buddies or trusted friends, being able to call on the other, and sharing feelings—are portrayed as a pathological regressive pull toward each other (Schave and Ciriello 1983). In a "damned if you do, damned if you don't" fashion, according to Sandbank (1999a), the united front presented by twins is a way in which the uncomfortable or repressed feelings of rivalry and resentment are released. In con-trast, twins talk voices twinship as a kind of self plus, or enhanced self, rather than a self-minus or impaired self. Mutuality is expressed, not as a limited good, but as an unlimited, boundless good. Mutual bonds lubricate pivots of relationships rather than fix or glue them. In what follows, I use twins talk about the practical, grounded experi-ences of twinship as a kind of corporative endeavor that normalizes twinship, gives twins agency, and recognizes their self working skills in the microproduction of selves in the dyad, as twins act and interact to frame twinship within the predominant exigencies of the wider so-ciocultural milieu. As the analysis develops, mutuality will be seen less as a state of being (together or interdependent) and become more of a strategy employed in negotiating both autonomy and dependence.

Beyond Gothic Twins, Deficit Selves, and Shackled Bonds

When depicted as a closed society, unit, or incipiently pathological, twins—as a category of people—fit what Rogoff and Morelli (1994, 9) refer to as a "deficit model approach" to minorities or other catego-ries of people. Twins, it seems, just cannot win. Although romantic lovers are envied for their intimacy and the closeness of their bond or for being each other's soul mates, the similar mystical links that unite twins are seen as not so good a thing. A deficit model approach assumes that mainstream skills and upbringing are normal and the variations observed with minorities are aberrations that produce deficits. This can result in what Cohen (1994, 103) refers to as "anonymizing" or "homogenizing of characterization" in which "outsiders fail to take into account insiders' own views of themselves." What is needed is a way to theorize twin identities in relationship that offers more flexible and open-ended ways of construing self/other identities, as well as less rigid ways of addressing issues of affiliation and mutuality. Mutuality as shared space and place is a critically important aspect of the practical experience of twinship. Just as twins in an embodied sense accept being both same and different and have to negotiate markers for their individuality, twins accept their connectedness and their autonomy when it comes to the bond. They must actively do so, not as a society closed off from the singleton world but in response to a sociocultural milieu that puts them on the fault lines by conflating their identities or seeing them as somehow impaired.

Some Caveats

The Twinsburg twins are hardly a representative sampling of identical twins. Dorothy and I did not talk with children, but remembered childhood was a dominant theme among our adult talking partners, whether they were in their twenties or their seventies. Twins festivals, as we saw in chapter 3, serve as venues to relive or reinvent shared childhoods. The childhoods presented here are, however, childhoods remembered. Memories are not facts. Even the Twinsburg twins argue about what happened or even the respective roles they may have played in the remembered event. Twins talk does not limit their twinship to childhood; rather it features twinship as a kind of lifelong relationship in which memories move with them as they leave the family to venture out into the world. Yet memories of past experiences are informed by the meanings attached to those experiences. Not only do these memories reveal self-concepts or mental images of ourselves, but they also reveal what other people think of us (Middleton 2002). Clearly, the past informs the present, and the present informs the past. In this way, what follows differs from the clinical and observational childhood studies of the twin psychology researchers. Nevertheless, albeit from different standpoints, we engage the same themes.

None of our talking partners attribute personal pathologies or dysfunctions to their twinship, nor did we explicitly invite them to do so. They are, however, ready to critique parents and teachers for not understanding them or adding a degree of difficulty to their shared lives. Some of the talking partners do describe growing up in highly dysfunctional or abusive families (see chapter 7), being poor, or having experienced tough periods during their lives that called for personal strength and strong coping mechanisms. Twins who experienced the unhappiest or most traumatic childhoods, like Steph and Jenna, and Lucy and Linda, relate that the twin sister and twin relationship acted as a kind of buffer in an environment that may have crippled a single-ton for life. Being there for each other in times of crisis becomes a lifelong theme in twins talk.

Twins talk not only normalizes twinship, but by enacting their twinships, twins give twinship its own dynamic. Our Twins Days conversations involved at least four actors talking together. Side by side through collaboration, agreement, argument, and revisions, talking twins enacted their bond to coproduce selves. Twins talking to twins about their being twins and their twin relationship involves a great deal of what Goffman (1959) calls impression management. In this sense, identities are not only embodied imagined worlds (Holland et al. 1998) but are enacted through social practice and are continually produced and improvised in the flow of activity within specific social situations from cultural resources at hand. As in chapter 4, a large part of their discourse not only normalizes twinship, in the "only a twin can know" sense, but also includes that idea of the we-self—a counterhegemonic, enhanced, rather than compromised self—and the notion of the twin bond as a dynamic vehicle for balancing or coexpressing both mutuality and autonomy. Twins talk, as it accepts or questions wider sociocultural stereotypes and treatments of twins, shows an interactive engagement with the wider social worlds in which twins live.

CONTEMPORARITY, UNIT IDENTITIES, AND CLOSED SOCIETIES

When the talking partners reflect on their childhood together, contemporarity as shared origins, growing up together, and sharing space and place are common themes. Also common are the expressions of frustration and rebellion at being treated as a unit. Twins do characterize their lives during childhood and mature adulthood as an evolving bond that is like no other bond. Twins' accounts of their dyadic mutuality hardly cuts them off from the wider world. Instead, other nontwin relationships and their place within the wider socio-economic, historic, and regional contexts show them as integrated in memory and practice to the wider world around them.

Contemporarity

There is no denying the importance of contemporarity (Conley 2004) or the importance of shared environments as expressed in twins talk. For the Twinsburg twins, their twinship is the defining feature of their origins and of their childhood. But aside from jokes about once having been cell mates, womb mates, or, in one case, *blastosisters* (a reference to cloning), there is no philosophical reflection on common cellular origins or shared states of being in the womb. As we saw in chapter 4, twins tend to view their origins as natural facts or acts of god. Once twins are born, the processes of biopsychosocial becomings begin. The Twinsburg twins report distinctions in birth order and birth weight as well as in the early health states of each twin, which they and their families then use as self-descriptors. For example, in our family it was always noted that I was born first, but Dorothy was slightly heavier (we were each about seven and a half pounds) and therefore got the longer name. I must have made this statement thousands of times in my lifetime, and anyone who knows us both well today can state these facts about us. Twins also jokingly construct little womb-based scenarios of negotiating who will be born first. For example, as was the case for Pat and Phyllis, the firstborn twin will refer to being the brave and adventurous twin and the second born will self-reference as the wise, polite, and patient twin. The talking partners also report (Piontelli 1992) that parents and older siblings observe that their respective identities emerged at birth or soon thereafter. These themes were quite well developed in the talk of Annette and Arnette; Arnette was the low birth weight, incubator twin, who throughout childhood was smaller and developmentally slightly behind her sister. Jeana and Dina also tell a family story about their infancy that has become their own. It shows how their identities are expressed (as in the cases of Pat and Phyllis and Dona and Dorothy) in a positive fashion as unique and contingent at the same time.

Dina: We were born premature. I was like three pounds and something. No, I was like two pounds and something and she [Jeana] was like four pounds and something. And she got to go home sooner than I did because I had a heart murmur. I had an immature lung . . . and all this. So the way they told us apart when they took the armband off was they pierced her ears with stars because she was the star of the show. She got to go home first. Everyone got to see her. And I was in the neonatal intensive care, and so my mom, when I graduated from nursing college, she pierced my ears with hearts because I stole the heart of the family. And so I always thought that was interesting because she [mom] kind of symbolized me being the heart and her [Jeana] being the star, and how it's true. I'm the people pleaser and Jeana, even though she is not as outgoing as me, when she gets to a group of people she knows, she's the center of attention.

A shared childhood is certainly an important part of the practical experiences of twinship. It is a formative experience in twins' lives that has a lifelong effect. To the Twinsburg twins, the sharing of space and place is crucial to the idea of the bond. In our preparations for Twinsburg, Dorothy and I were worried that the Twinsburg twins, who went to so much effort to look alike, would not recognize us as identical twins. When we expressed our concern to our very first two talking partners, Chris and Carla, Carla, remarked, "Well, you're together here, aren't you?" Dina and Jeana offered that twins reared apart could not really be considered as twins nor as understanding the real meanings that get forged between them. Julie and Jenny, the only twins in our sample who were raised apart for the first five years of their life, are now living together at age sixty-nine to work at reinventing their twinship and experiencing the contemporarity that was denied them as children.

The Twinsburg twins had largely positive assessments of their lives together as children. According to Karan, "I have no idea what it is like not to have someone by my side all the time. To me and to us, we accepted it from childhood." During early childhood, the twins did not have much choice about sharing space and place. Like all Twinsburg twins, except Julie and Jenny, Dorothy and I shared a room as children (until we went to college). Most of us had twin beds. A few of the twins, like Tina and Ginuh, even shared the same bed during childhood. Like the other talking partners, Dorothy was my constant childhood and adolescent companion. As I joked with Tom, I said, "At least my invisible friend was real."

Units

Unit identities can be portrayed as coming from within the twin dyad (Leonard 1961) or being imposed from without (Conley 2004). Before I started my own research on twins, I had never heard of the term *unit identity*, although I was certainly familiar with the ideas it encodes. This was not the case among our talking partners. They were all familiar with the term and used it frequently throughout the conversations. As the partners spoke of unit identities, they did so with a counterhegemonic voice that expressed their resentment of being treated as a unit by nontwin others. Twins talk features growing up with unit identities as irritating rather than incipiently pathological. The following exchange demonstrates how in the practical experiences of self-working twins, unitizing is met with ambivalence and resistance. If the twins are to be treated as a unit, it better be on their own terms.

> Ginuh: I can't imagine not being a twin. I've always felt that. I couldn't imagine being like an individual, you know.
>
> Tina: Mother treated us like a unit, not like individuals.
>
> Ginuh: A unit, yes.
>
> Tina: I can't remember doing anything alone with my mother.
>
> Ginuh: I agree. She was, I could look back and say, the best mother.

Other twins, like Pat and Phyllis, refer to being born in the pronatalist postwar period of the 1940s. Pat and Phyllis also express the sense of a more forced convergence than Ginuh and Tina describe. They have this to say about their mother.

> Pat: Our mother wanted us to be together for her own ego instead of listening to what we wanted.

A page later in the transcript, Ginuh and Tina protest the consequences of being made to dress alike by their mother.

> Ginuh: We didn't dress alike; we *were* dressed alike.
> Everything was matching.

> Tina: It was a big fairness thing. I don't remember minding it so much. What I did mind was when other people, like our aunts, called us "twin." When someone would say "Hey, twin," we'd say "Hey, individual!"

Similarly, Tim and Tom said that they did not have individual names growing up; they were simply known as "the twins."

> Tim: I was five years old before I knew I had a name all to myself and it was Tim.

While Tom and Tim relate the conflation of their identities as a matter of fact, Karen and Kristy, the good and evil twins, have this to say, and the tone in which it is said expresses a marked protest.

> Karen: Dad never called us by name. He just called, "Hey, twin."

> Kristy: All our lives we never had a name. Twin, ha! I'd have to say, "Who you talking to—me or her?"

Although the we-self has been presented as a form of we-ing the body, it also was characterized as a kind of we-ing of the psyche, thus the we-self (Ortmeyer 1970; Stewart 2003) becomes a researcher's version of a flawed, unit self. As the talking partners express it, the shared experiences, copresence, and coexistence of twins, as well as the conflation of their identities by others, leaves twins with a lifelong habit of saying "we." We-ing as a problematic habit of speech that runs through all the interviews is voiced by Mabel and Ginuh. Mabel apologizes midinterview for their use of *we* in ways that are confusing. Well into middle age, they still use the referent even when apart and even when it doesn't really apply to both of them. Mabel uses *we* to refer to her twin, Bertha and herself, while Gina opens the *we* to other relationships.

> Mabel: What has really stuck with me, because we grew up together, is that people sometimes laugh at me

because I say "we." I'm sort of referring to me, and they kind of look at me and then I go, "Sorry, I'm a twin." Ha, ha. It's always been *we*.

Gina: We still refer to each other as *we* when we are talking to people. Even though we are by ourselves, it's *we*. A lot of people think I'm talking about me and my husband, not me and my sister. We still do the *we* when we talk, even though the other person is not there.

Pete and Emil, and Jeana and Dina, demonstrate an interesting case of a more ambiguous use of *we* that connotes togetherness and separateness at the same time.

Emil: We were always shy. Pete will tell you himself whether he was or not.

Jeana: Make no mistake—we are two separate individuals.

Dina: Right.

Despite their protests over being treated as units, Twinsburg twins (as we saw in chapter 3) parade around as a kind of in-your-face version of identical units at the festival. Certainly, despite issues with the ways that they are or have been treated, almost all the Twinsburg partners self-presented as being comfortable in their twinship. One would expect that twins who made the effort to come to Twinsburg would all be invested in their twinship and the performance of identicalness and identity that the festival expects. There was an exception. In one spirited interview, we talked to two sets of twins from the same family, born two years apart. The older twins, Karan and Kim, stated that they were happy to be twins, but their younger sisters, Cindy and Sandy, expressed having been "dragged" (by their well-meaning, older twin sisters), against their better judgment, to Twinsburg. Karan and Kim said that they were "into" being twins. They liked being dressed alike as children, are very close today, and had always gotten along with each other. They thrived on the special attention they got from others for just being twins. Their younger sisters, Cindy and Sandy, however, describe themselves as being *anti-* or *un-twin,* twins who could not care less about being twins. They resented being treated alike, never felt that they had gotten along all that well with each other, were always fighting, held grudges, and were highly competitive with each other. Cindy and Sandy most assertively claimed not to like being twins or being treated like twins at all. Although their contemporarity "we's" them, Cindy and Sandy have the most strongly expressed "I" in all the twins talk interviews.

> Karan: To me and to us [Karan and Kim], we accepted it from childhood on, but these two [Sandy and Cindy] have always rebelled against it.
>
> Cindy: We are very competitive, where my sisters aren't.
>
> Karan: They [Cindy and Sandy] are always fighting; we [Kim and Karan] work it out. We accept each other for who we are.
>
> Cindy: If she runs three miles, I've got to run five miles.
>
> Sandy: If she runs five miles, I have to run ten miles.
>
> Cindy: We are constantly in competition with each other.
>
> Sandy: Can we get a copy of this tape? I can't believe she admitted that.

A Closed Society of Two?

The contemporarity of twins' experiences of their childhood, where space and place were intimately shared and where one twin was a constant actor in the environment of the other twin, certainly comes through as a key theme in twins talk. Being together and being physically alike are both central to the practical experiences of twinship, as twins together remember the early years of their twinship. Rosambeau (1987), a mother of twins, remembers that when her twins were toddlers, her treatment of one twin always seemed to affect the other twin's feelings. The Twinsburg twins also express the dual challenges of presenting themselves as a united front vis-à-vis others and resenting being treated as a unit by others. As we saw in chapter 3, a key component of a twin's identity is that of being a twin. Certainly, as Sandbank (1999b) remarks, a twin's identity and sense of self are inextricably bound up in the partnership, both physically and mentally. The Twinsburg twins clearly agree that they have a special bond as twins and this bond is like no other type of bond they have ever experienced. However, this falls far short of twins being some kind of closed society, even when speaking metaphorically.

When the Twinsburg twins talk about their childhoods, they frequently mention other siblings as well as parents and friends. Tim and Tom report that an older brother became their major caretaker and they have always felt very close to him. Pat and Phyllis feature their very different relationship with each parent in their discussions of their own emergent childhood identities. Amy and Beth's as well as Chris and Carla's talk reveals a special and loving connection with their father. Steph and Jenna and also Lucy and Linda had much older siblings who became safety nets for one or both twins when things went horribly wrong at home. Both of these pairs of twins also spent time in orphanages. Arnette and Annette have nothing but heartfelt praise and appreciation for the grandparents who raised them when their mother could not. Arnette and Annette also place themselves in a gang of twins (other sets of twins in their school class).

Not only do the talking partners place themselves in an active field of relationships, but they talk about the wider worlds in which they lived during their early years. Several sets of twins were raised on a farm where, even as children, they had daily chores to perform that not only made the animals they cared for important to them but also provided them with important roles, skills, work values, and identities when it came to the family business. Many twins talk about the socioeconomic status of their families as children; themes of being poor repeatedly emerge in the narratives. Gina and Ginger talk about being raised by a single mother who struggled to keep her family together. Dante and Randi, Judy and Janet, and Peter and Emil cite their ethnic identity as an important feature of their childhood.

As twins' reactions to the term *unit identities* show, the experience of twinship grows from twins' shared worlds but is also shaped by the societal stereotypes of expectations of what twins are like. As Rogoff and Morelli (1994) note, others' socially shaped opinions of twins can become an important element in their own sense of self. For example, during the ICTS conference in Belgium, I was very excited when attendees, especially those connected with mothers of twins organizations, were invited to tour a nearby fishing village whose local historical society had recently completed a book on twins in local families (Baete 2007). About twelve of us signed up for the afternoon excursion. After a lunch and before a local tour of a fishery, we were shown a PowerPoint presentation of pictures of twins from local families. Some pictures dated back almost a hundred years. While many of the photos showed twins at ritual occasions such as marriages and confirmations, a good number of photos were of twins posed with the rest of the family. Family pictures were intergenerational and many of the photographs captured large families. In the photos, either all children were dressed alike or all were dressed differently. There was no tradition of dressing twins alike or of posing them side by side for the camera. What I found very interesting was that, as an audience consisting of a twin and mothers of twins, our major challenge was not to tell the twins apart but to determine which two individuals in any one picture were actually the twin family members.

This search for the twins among large families became a topic of the liveliest discussion of the day's outing (no one but me expressed interest in the fishery). On the one hand, the photos were an interesting reminder that twins are embedded in other relationships, not to mention wider historical and social contexts from their very beginnings. On the other hand, it is also interesting that when I asked some mothers of twins to show me pictures of their own twins, their photos featured only the twins—and not other family members—standing side by side and looking into the camera. After viewing the photos from the mothers, I saw these wallet-size photos of twins posed together, dominating the subject field of the photograph and bounded by a white border, as encoding the very essence of a "unit identity." This was nowhere near as obvious in the pictures from Belgium.

Beyond a Deficit Model of Twinship

In chapter 3 on performance and festivals, we saw how twins talk can be used to challenge stereotypes of them in the wider cultural contexts in which they live. Twins must contend with being seen as another configuration of identity (Murray 1993), another type of social arrangement (Besnier 1994), or kind of deviant persona (Holland and Leander 2004). One of the problems with the psychopathological perspective is the assumption that "unit-ness" stems not just from shared space and place but from the twin bond itself (Ainslie 1985; Burlingham 1952; Schave and Ciriello 1983). Yet twins talk also shows that from the practical, everyday, commonplace aspects of the twins' experience as "unitizing" are situated in wider cultural contexts that conflate their identities and treat twins as a unit. That the Twinsburg twins expressed resentment about being treated as a unit demonstrates an awareness of themselves as existing within what wider society sees as a deviant or deficit model of self.

At the same time that society expects every twin to do his or her duty as a symbol of closeness, loyalty, mutual concern, and social harmony, twins are marginalized as compromised or somehow partial selves. As a deviant persona on the fault lines or as another configuration in their own familiar worlds, twins have a lot of self work to do in a wider society that holds both their mutuality and autonomy as suspect. The following quotation from Dina, expressing her relationship with her sister, Jeana, is an example of this kind of self work. Dina delivers her statement in a very assertive tone.

> Dina: People think we're crazy because we flew all the way to Twinfest, and I said, "You don't understand what twinship is. It's not just my sister. It's not just my best friend. It's something you're born into. You can't pay to be in it. You can't be invited to be in it. It's a bond that will never break." We've had our differences. When she got married we had our rocky times, but we made it through. We still call each other every day. Her and her husband were talking about moving out of state, and I was like, "Well you got to let me know because where you're moving, I'll be following behind." And it's so amazing how you can lean on someone and you can truly bare your soul to that person, whereas people have sisters, they have best friends, but I don't care what people say. I can't bare myself to my older sister. I can't bare my soul to my best friend, but yet to Jeana I literally have no secrets and I'm pretty sure she feels the same way.

Discussion of a twin's-eye view of their twinship necessitates a more open-ended and functional modeling of self than we see in the psychological literature. Cannot contemporarity function positively to adaptively fine-tune interpersonal skills or broaden styles of relating to others? Must a coproduction of twin selves connote a closed society? The Twinsburg twins talk shows them as very much embedded within conventional Western selfways. In twins talk the partners not only challenge the hegemonic individualism of Western society but also offer an alternative version of self and relationship or bond. This takes the form of an enhanced self that reprioritizes autonomy and affiliation. Twins use the idea of a kind of lifelong enhanced self to normalize their selves by asserting that within our society there are multiple ways of selving, or constructing interdependence and independence. This enhanced self flows through twins talk as same and different, contingent and unique, and fluid and fixed. It becomes a relational stratagem enacted over a lifetime, both within and outside of the twin dyad.

Enhanced Self

Instead of expressing their twin bond as a kind of bondage or "glue" for mutual attached identities, twins talk enacts a more positive and complicated and practical (as opposed to abstract) version of twinship. The partners' perspectives do resonate with the few positive portrayals of twinship to be found in the twin research literature. The sociologist Rosambeau (1987) notes problems of unit identities but also describes the twin bond in terms of having both exclusive and parallel or unit identities. Similarly, Gedda (1995, 7), a biologist, states that "physical identicalness does not imply psychic identicalness" and rephrases the twin bond in nonstigmatizing ways as a kind of "behavioral solidarity." Even the French psychologist Zazzo (1978) argues that within the twin pair, one does not lose an aspect of self but enhances it, and pairness acts to differentiate each twin's identity. These more positive aspects of twinship, however, remain underdeveloped and underanalyzed in the twin literature. In contrast, the idea of a special bond and enhanced, or augmented, self flows through and is very positively expressed in twins talk. In what follows, I focus on ways in which the Twinsburg twins express twinship as a kind of value-added "self plus other and other plus self" relationship.

We have already seen in chapter 3 that Twinsburg twins have a positive view of their twinship as something special. They challenge stereotypes of themselves as impaired by asserting that they are a kind of enhanced self. When Dorothy and I asked our talking partners what it meant to be twins, they offered heartfelt but rather clichéd statements like these: "being best friends for life," "having an alter ego," "a special form of connectedness," "being really, really close," "having someone who knows your mind and understands you like no one else ever will," "a very special sense of sharing," and "someone who will always be there for you." As we have seen, these are the same statements that indicate pathology in the view of some researchers. The Twinsburg twins are all adults. Twinship for them is a tenacious and desired state. The talking partners do view their twinship as forged in their childhood years, spent in a day-by-day interactive, intimate kind of togetherness; but they also note how their twinship develops or changes during their lives. According to Mabel and Bertha, twinship evolves. Jeana and Dina describe their twinship as maturing. As we will see in chapter 7 (on kinship), a number of the younger Twinsburg twins are negotiating a time of their lives called "the split," and older twins are working to spend more time together.

As they get older, proximity becomes more a matter of choice (see chapter 7) among the talking partners. For example, Cindy and Sandy, at age thirty-six, revel in going their separate ways in life, whereas Julie and Jenny, at age sixty-nine, chose to retire together. Yet, perhaps with the exception of Cindy and Sandy, the twin bond is expressed by the talking partners as a lifelong sense of affinity that they characterize "as always being together"—whether they are in each other's physical presence or not. This sense of togetherness transcends place and time; it connotes a lifelong continuance of communication, intimacy, and sharing that results not in an impaired self but in an enhanced one. A sustained sense of connection and mutuality makes twinship special. For example, adult twins report feeling they are still together even when living separate lives and located long distances apart. Twinsburg itself is an opportunity to renew this sense of togetherness. As Martha says, each twin went her separate way when Martha got married. Yet she and Mary continued to "remain in touch with each other every day, even though [their] phone bills are huge." Although Mary jokes, "We have AT&T unlimited," they make a point to equally share their phone expenses, no matter who calls whom. All the twins who lived close to each other say that their twin had a key to their house with no knock required and unrestricted access. Pat and Phyllis have adjacent summer cottages where their families spend the summer months together. Their grandchildren may choose to sleep and eat at either sister's house.

> Pat: We have keys to each other's camps. All the grandkids share. She has a paddleboat and I have all the tubes and stuff. We have freezers. We just go and use each other's freezers. Phyllis has two grandchildren. I have thirty-five. I guess we can share. What difference does it make?

Pete and Emil tell us about their strategies for sharing expenses for the trip to Twinsburg.

> Pete: Now we're making up for lost time.

> Emil: We go on these trips now.

> Pete: We go on trips. I'll just say to him, "You take care of everything." And when we are all done, [I say], "Let me know what I owe you." Whether it's for gas—

> Emil: And he does this—

> Pete: —or meals.

Janet and Judy describe how the twin bond can be revitalized in times of crisis. Janet's battle with breast cancer has brought them both together in their sixties. Their current relationship is more intimate now than ever.

> Janet: When I found out I had cancer, she went to the doctor's with me, and she stayed with me all through my chemotherapy, and all through my radiation—

> Judy: [She had a] mastectomy.

> Janet: My mastectomy, my surgeries, everything. Or I would have never made it as well as I did without her.

> Judy: And every day—

Janet: And she was always there when I needed her. It's
         just hard to explain with twins. It's just a bond that is
         there. We have an older sister, three years older. Sisters
         aren't the same as identical twins.

Judy: The bond isn't the same.

Janet: I'd look forward to my chemo treatments just to have
         her around.

As we saw in chapter 4, Janet and Judy go on to describe how they
would sleep together in the same bed during the chemotherapy treatments. Judy would spoon her body next to Janet's, hoping to impart
her strength and also absorb some of Judy's pain. Their talk is punctuated by holding hands, mutual embraces, and kisses. Both twins shed
tears as they remember these hard times. When asked how their respective husbands, who were also featured in their narrative, reacted
to their renewed closeness, Janet remarked that "it didn't matter;
it wasn't even relevant; it was all about us." Judy adds, "After thirty
years, what's he going to say?"

While Janet and Judy have faced death head-on and won, Mary
and Martha joke about facing death alone, and Tina and Ginuh talk
about surviving their twin. In a heartfelt exchange, Martha and Mary
refer not to life before reason (Piontelli 1999) but to life after reason.
Mary and Martha jokingly refer to the contentment of continued
contemporarity when one of them dies.

Mary: I say, if I ever go old and senile and they have to put
         me in a nursing home—

Martha: They'd have to put us in the same one.

Mary: Ha ha. And we'd sit there and just giggle at each other.
         And then if one of us was ever gone, we wouldn't
         have to tell the other. We'd just put a mirror there.

This touching scenario captures the sense of shared mutuality and
corporeal interidentity that our talking partners see as a positive
feature of their lives. Certainly twins talk shows that twins are close
and others expect them to be close or we would not get Mary and
Martha's joke. Yet losing a twin takes a less humorous turn when we
asked Tina and Ginuh what it means to be a twin. Tina responded,

"I'm with her [Ginuh]" and went on to reflect on a conversation they had with a twinless twin the night before.

> Tina: I feel so bad for them [twins whose partner twin is dead]. I felt it deep within me. I just thought, you know I could lose my husband and recover. I would be heartbroken. But if it were her [Ginuh], you'd have to string me up. I don't know if I could ever recover from that. It would leave a permanent hole there [points to heart]. What does it mean to be a twin? I repeat. I'm with her.

Tina's statement evokes themes already covered but also introduces new ones. Although the thoughts expressed are hypothetical, it reflects the contemporarity of twins and the emotional closeness of their bond. It may also be viewed as carrying undertones of being too close or emotionally crippled by interdependence. As Tina alludes, she could not be or feel to be herself without her twin. Ginuh's death would be a death beyond getting beyond. Tina is more than just Tina; she is Tina and Ginuh together—self plus other and other plus self. Moreover, Tina says, "I'm with her," not "I am her." Their selves also have boundaries. Tina and Ginuh are thirty-six years old. They have very different marital histories. Each has her own household, career, and children. At various times in their adult lives, they have lived in the same community and in faraway states. Tina does not deny her individuality but she does privilege togetherness and forms of interconnectedness that come from being together in both a real and a figurative sense. Ironically, if Tina spoke of losing her husband in the same way she felt about losing her twin, the statement would not be exceptional.

Tina's reflections about deaths in the family bring up three points that have not yet received a great deal of attention. First, Tina presents her sense of self and twinned other ("I'm with her") as a kind of "interexistence" or "inter-action," or "inter-est" or what Jackson (1998, 3, 28) collectively terms "intersubjective engagement," not simply as linked or somehow static (glued) or connected identities or even some highly abstracted common soul. Tina and Ginuh's identities are positioned, in this case a hypothetical deceased and survivor twin in the twin relationship. Second, Tina refers to her twinship, not in comparison to being a singleton but in comparison to another close, intimate, long-term, contemporaneous, and important relationship—the bond that she shares with her husband. Third, Tina's heartfelt statement addresses themes of separation and connection as well as divergent forms of mutuality. Although Tina's statements are hypothetical, they also emerge in the more practical interactive narratives of the Twinsburg twins as they address negotiating mutuality and identity both inside of and outside of the twin dyad.

Twin Conundrums and the Practice of Twinship

Because they are located on the fault lines, when twins talk, they make explicit the largely tacit, taken for granted, implicit, and invisible assumptions that people share with others of their group or carry around inside them. Appellations like "indivisible by two," "the pressures of pairness," "unit identities," and "a closed society" not only conflate, objectify, and stagnate twin identities in the dyad but regard mutuality as a kind of zero-sum phenomenon that only occurs at a cost to autonomy. Yet in the television movie *Rudolph, the Red-Nosed Reindeer*, Hermey, the elf who wanted to be a dentist, proposes to Rudolph that they "be independent together," suggesting that self can be contingent and unique at the same time (cf. Cohen 1994). The twins' statements below illustrate the simultaneous expression of twins' selves as contingent and unique.

> Tom: Parents want to do the best they can. They read these books that say, "You should treat them as individuals." Well, they are individuals but they still are identical twins. So don't try to fix something that happened.

> Dona: For our fifty-third birthday our mother sent us both copies of the same card that said, "There's nobody like you in the whole wide world." The irony here is that she really meant it.

> Janet: What one didn't think of, the other one did.

＊＊＊

Emil: We were always shy. Pete will tell you himself whether
         he was or not.

In what remains of this chapter, I aim to develop a more positive, agentive, and interactive approach to the twin bond that sets self
work among twins into a more dynamic and interactionist framework. This entails a less oppositional approach to the negotiation of
self and other within the twin dyad. My aim is to address interactive
processes of selving and othering as expressed in twins talk. In what
follows, I consider how Jackson's (1998) idea of the oscillating self and
Harter's (1999) notion of mutuality as a tool for negotiating connectedness and autonomy lead to new insights into the twin dynamic as
the enactment of identity and bond within the twin dyad.

THE TWIN DYNAMIC

I find *twin dynamic* to be a useful term. Tim coined this phrase to depict the dynamics of the twin relationship as a "competition between
twins or the ways in which parents can set siblings against each other
or not." In Tim's phrasing, the twin dynamic involves twin-twin interactions that promote individualism and competition as well as
mutuality and cooperation. Tim's term implies interaction between
two seemingly contradictory forces that become intensified within
the twin dyad. Posing the dynamic of the dyadic relations as one of
competition or the absence of competition, Tim sets individuality
and mutuality as not necessarily mutually exclusive dualisms but at
least as the opposite ends of a lineal continuum. What is missing from
Tim's explication of the twin dynamic, but not from his wide-ranging
conversation with his brother, Tom, is what happens at midline or at
interstices of this continuum. Does the middle become a point of
oscillation (Jackson 1998) between the two opposing extremes? Or
does the middle consist of interwoven strands that somehow act to
negate or compromise the very notions of opposition, as in Harter's
(1999) notion of the conditional negotiation of mutuality in a paired
relationship? Let us start with Jackson (1998), who poses a tension between relatedness and self as a difference shared by all human beings
but differently emphasized in diverse sociocultural contexts.

Jackson (1998) notes it is characteristic of all persons that a sense of self oscillates between an ontologically secure sense of self, to being fulfilled by being with another, to being at times overwhelmed or engulfed by another. Jackson (1998, 8, 4) refers to this "intersubjective nexus of self/other" as a kind of "interexistence" characterized by a give and take, or "push and pull," between fellow feeling and antagonism. In twins talk, the gives and takes of inter-est among twins, or Tim's dynamic, are evidenced in terms of variable interactions between the talking partners. The examples presented cover different points of the continuum from being engulfed by other to a secure sense of self. These include twin positioning of self and other in memory, twins' practical experiences of sharing names, issues of dominance within the pair, and twin-other relationships.

Oscillations of selves (Jackson 1998) are enacted and emerge in twins talk when they co-remember and attempt to position their shared pasts. Memories can reveal how twins position themselves as they interactively recall incidences in their lives along a continuum where at one end twin identities are confused (if not conflated) and at the other end, ontologically distinct. Twins who shared the same environment and were always together also share their memories. For the most part, as in their trickster tales, the Twinsburg twins agreed upon and shared the telling of events or experiences of their shared lives together. But, memories also get confused, not in terms of what was real and what was imagined, but in terms of what happened to whom, as Janet states below (note the use of pronouns).

> Janet:　Sometimes we would be reminiscing and something would remind us of something we did that was silly. Judy would say, "Oh, do you remember that?" But the funny thing is we always thought it happened to us. Like I'll say, "Oh that happened to me," and Judy will say "Oh no, it happened to me." We can't remember which one it actually happened to.

Other memory accounts are more self-affirming and are clearly agreed upon. These accountings of past memories position the twins vis-à-vis each other and helping each other out for major events in their lives. For example, Donna and Dianne share their adult memories of Dianne running off to get married. Left behind, Donna not only financed the elopement but had to reveal it to their surprised and anxious parents. In this shared enterprise, it was Donna who remembers having to suffer all the parental disapproval from her parents, although it was Dianne who had asserted her independence and run away. Yet the partners also report memories that are distinct to one twin only. Pat and Phyllis surprised each other as they were reminiscing about a shared childhood experience, and Phyllis revealed her feelings about a particular event in their past. Pat's surprised response was "I never knew that." This was not uncommon; at numerous junctures of our conversations, the talking partners would remark to each other in similar fashion, "You never told me" or "Why did you never tell me?" When discussing disparities in memory stories, short term as well as long term, Dorothy and I will comment to each other, "What planet were you raised on?"

Naming

Issues of naming, or more explicitly name response, also illustrate oscillating selves of twinship—as Meyerhoff (1978, 64) asks, "If I should be someone else, then who would be me?" Like our other talking partners, I have always responded to my twin's first name (Dorothy) as well as my own. Although, separated for over forty years and living in different parts of the country, we still respond when hearing each other's names. Even today in our sixties, Dorothy's body label is me and is not me. There was a time in our earlier years together when it could have meant me anyway or may have required a clarification of "I'm not Dorothy—I'm Dona." If our names position or clarify our identities, then I appear to be forever a Dona-Dorothy and she is forever a Dorothy-Dona. If I hear her name, it means I have been both identified and misidentified.

When it comes to naming, Amy and Beth raise another issue. They relate that they referred to each other as "Hey, you." Karen and Kristy report that they never call each other by name, and it seems strange when they do. Likewise, I use Dorothy's name to refer to her when talking to other people, but I never address her directly as *Dorothy*. To look at her and call her *Dorothy* somehow seems strange to my tongue. If I use any term of address at all, I call her by her relationship to me, *Sis*. She calls me the same name. The word is the same, but the *Sis* is intersubjectively situated as either sis-*you* or sis-*me*. Thus, the named self oscillates from secure, fulfilled, and en-gulfed by the twin other. The problem in terms of Jackson's model is that this amounts more to a practical learned mode of code switching rather than to a tension or antagonism between self and other. The closest twins talk gets to this kind of Jacksonian tension or opposition is with positioned identities and relationships that enjoin themes of dominance. Yet even here, dominance is tempered by well-honed equanimity within twin relationships.

Questions of Dominance

Dominance has been regarded by twins researchers as an important dimension of the twin relationship. Issues of dominance among the Twinsburg twins come up in response to queries of "How are you same or different?" Dominance is a central theme in the twin research literature (Piontelli 1992). Gedda (1995) refers to leader and follower twins. Yet from the perspective of adulthood, twins talk reveals dominance and dominance remembered to be a complex and shifting phenomenon. Most twins recognized dominance and submissiveness in the twin dyad as complementary rather than oppositional. Any totalizing remarks Dorothy and I made about her being the dominant twin were met with resistance or correction by our talking partners. For example, when we stated that Dorothy always answered the phone and made travel arrangements, our talking partners would reverse our presentations of self and ask who was the real master and servant, noting that I never had to do any of this work for myself.

The Twinsburg twins tended to respond to the questions of dominance by situating dominance in particular situations and circumstances. A common theme was that dominance flip-flopped between them. For example, Annette and Arnette talk about the flip-flop of dominance during the life of their twinship.

> Arnette: Basically, we had different personalities that we
> flipped. OK, so sometimes I would say I'm Annette
> and that is why I thought I was Annette for a while.
> Because I could act like Annette and Annette could
> act like me. So we didn't know we had different
> personalities until we got bigger and figured out
> there was a difference in personalities. I was a lot
> quieter than Annette and she was more outgoing and

talkative. She makes friends easily. I was not that way
at all. Didn't want to do it, didn't want to try.

Dorothy: Would you agree with that, Annette?

Annette: Yeah, I think we flip-flopped. Yeah, I think we kind of
flip-flopped around like that.

Arnette and Annette's comments show how dominance is not a simple case of leader twin and follower twin, bossy and bossed or manipu-
lator and manipulated twins. Nor does dominance describe a more
aggressive and less aggressive twin. What is expressed, when the topic
of dominance emerges, becomes who is the more outgoing or assertive twin. For example, a few minutes later in their conversation,
Annette discusses how Arnette has blossomed and developed over
the years as an active person and community leader in her own right.

Other Relationships

Twins are not hermits in the dyad. As twins reflect on their relationships together, other relationships or actors enter the picture.
For twins (and singletons), discrete, individual identities coexist in a
nexus of nontwin self/other relationships. More is said about this in
chapter 7 on kinship, but for now, I note how Twinsburg twins talk
places them as, in Cohen's (1994, 2) words, an "active manager and
creative agent in view of a plethora of obligations that trigger them
in different directions." These include nontwin siblings, and themselves as parents, neighbors, friends, employers or employees, and so
on. Dorothy makes this point below, as do Tim and Tom.

Dorothy: Although Dona and I stay in constant contact
with each other and are in the same discipline,
we have had very different lives. Many of my
friends and colleagues have never met her. Some
of my acquaintances don't even know that I'm a
twin. Even though I enjoy myself as a twin, I also
celebrate my individuality. I prefer to think of
myself as dually acculturated.

Comments by Tim and Tom also illustrate the flow between autonomy
and relatedness that exists between twins and coexists in other types
of relationships. Note Tom's use of present tense and Tim's use of

past tense and the way Tim balances his success in business relationships to his brother's married state.

> Tom: But in another fashion we are very different because of our personal relationships with other people. I'm married. He's not.

> Tim: I didn't have a wife. I didn't have a girlfriend. So I just focused my relationships into the business. I was pretty successful in doing that.

This exchange between Ginger and Gina (age twenty-five) captures both the tension and the flow twins experience between autonomy and relatedness in a fashion that takes into account other nontwin relationships. It is an interesting example of Jackson's oscillating self and the interexperience or the active and evolving and negotiated state of twinship.

> Ginger: I think it's neat [being twins] because a lot of people, they think it's—they like it. We work in the same town but at different stores. People will come into my store and ask, "Did we just see you down at Yonkers?" They think it's neat, and I don't know. I like when we talk in the whole "we" thing. It's always "we" not "I."

> Gina: Yeah . . . and it's you and not you too.

> Ginger: Not you too, Boo-Boo.

> Gina: People sometimes get comfortable.

> Ginger: UNcomfortable!

> Gina: Because they can't tell us apart, because we look so alike. But I don't think they really understand. I mean, I can't imagine not being a twin. I've always felt that. I couldn't imagine being, like, an individual, you know. I've always felt like I couldn't imagine, like, going places by myself where, you know, I wasn't with her. Although I am a little more independent than she is. She's always the one—am I right, Ginger, that you depended on me? She's always had someone around her—me or her husband. You know, she's never really been by herself. I have. I'm not married. I'm alone.

Ginger: Sometimes my husband gets jealous and he'd blow up. Usually, when I want to go out, it's always with my sister. It's not always with him. I think he gets kind of jealous about the relationship we have together. And he didn't really know when he married me that he kind of married Gina.

Gina: Yeah, he does get very jealous. I mean, when we go on—we plan a road trip. Like this is our road trip for this year. We always try to plan a road trip every year. So I think he thinks this is kind of crazy.

Ginger: He makes too big a deal of it.

Gina: He thinks we're children.

Ginger: Yeah, but *who*, exactly, is being the child here?

Gina: Not who, whom.

It may be tempting to psychologists to intimate that there is some sort of problem evidenced by Gina and Ginger's exchange. These twins are twenty-five years old. One could suggest that there is some sort of inadequate identity differentiation between them and that Gina is somehow compromising the success of Ginger's marriage, let alone her grammar. Another way to see it is that they are working out new challenges in their own relationships, as well as making new spaces for new significant others. Self in Jackson's (1998) parlance is not engulfed by the other, but self in this case is fulfilled by the other. I would also assume that Ginger's relationship with her husband is one of being fulfilled by the other.

Gina and Ginger's exchange also reminds us that twins are one kind of couple among other kinds of couples. As Rosambeau (1987) states in her book *How Twins Grow Up*, our human psyche seems programmed for pairing. Twinship certainly does not exhaust all forms of accepted mutuality, and at least in the case of female twins society provides some space for connectedness and mutuality. Why then are twins as overbonded most often compared to singletons? When Gina and Ginger reflect on their relationship, their twinship, or twin bond, they do so by comparing themselves not only to singletons but to other kinds of co-contemporary paired relationships, including best friends, other siblings, and, most often, married couples.

The French psychologist René Zazzo (1978, 24) coins the terms "couple effect" to describe twinship as one of multiple coexisting styles and modes of relationality and selving within a society. Zazzo's couple effect approach both normalizes and values mutuality but also explains psychological differences between a pair of twins. Two twin partners, even when raised together, live in two different environments, where one twin is the environment of the other. Twins' personalities are, according to Zazzo, the consequence of relations between self and other. While the term *pair* connotes sameness, twins as a couple connote difference as well. Despite his recognition that twins cannot be compared to singletons apart from understanding the couple effect, and despite his assertions that each twin is a part of a pair, Zazzo's discourse on the couple effect (and as used by others like Sandbank [1999b]) remains embedded in the meta narratives of clinical psychology that place twins on the fault lines of identity and selfhood by pitting mutuality as a concept against individualism as a concept. In this model, expressions of mutuality come at a cost to one's individuality and vice versa.

When twins are compared to other kinds of couples, they can appear as far less exotic. Marriage connotes a kind of emotionally exclusive bonded pairing. Spouses, like twins, are actors in intimate, cocontemporaneous, and (ideally) long-term relationships. Thirty-three of the Twinsburg twins are or have been married. Harris (1995) argues that an ideal of inhabiting each other's being and a desire to merge with (rather than be passively engulfed by) the other is a universal characteristic of romantic love or passion. This certainly finds resonance with the experience of twinship as revealed in twins talk. When speaking of the processes of identity and selving in married couples, anthropologist Anthony Cohen (1994, 24) also offers some analytical insights with which to explore the practical operational dynamics of the twin bond. He states that on a micro social level, when the "I" requires transformation to the "we," as in, say, a marriage, the married "we" does not entail a contradiction of self but places limits on it. According to Cohen, "I take a particular version of myself to the we and hold back others. I have not lost an aspect of myself, but have augmented it." How then does all this relate to the expression, negotiation, and enactment of mutuality and autonomy in the twin relationship?

Susan Harter (1999) stands out among psychologists for her innovative modeling of autonomy and mutuality. Whereas Jackson's universal self oscillates between a dialectically posed self and other, and Cohen's married self gives and holds back, Harter's self flows and bridges. Although she is not interested in twins per se, her work certainly finds resonance in the twin experience as voiced by the talking partners. In her book on childhood social relationships, Harter notes that within Western society, socialization toward an autonomous independent self has represented the predominant theme in developmental accounts of child rearing. Harter, however, argues that autonomy and connectedness are not dichotomous (should not be polarized) but are actively integrated through mutuality. Mutuality in a paired relationship, according to Harter, is conditional and utilized to negotiate both individual competition and collective cooperation. Using the example of spouse- or partner-paired relationships, Harter refers to a trichotomy of styles that defines self in a relationship. These include (1) a self-focused autonomy, (2) another focused connectedness, and (3) a mutuality that reflects a healthy balance of autonomy and connectedness. The task, according to Harter, is to understand the dynamics among all three of these. These dynamics, Harter suggests, would include connectedness expressed as loyalty, trust, emotional support, mutual understanding, conflict resolution skills, and clarification of thoughts and feelings.

Harter (1999) views mutuality as a negotiated intermediary between an autonomous and connected self. According to Harter, mutuality connotes a mutual style and empathy and validation of one's self from one's partner. As a style of relating, mutuality involves compromising or balancing needs, and clarifying feelings with those of the partner. Further mutuality is wanting both closeness and separateness and balancing them with other concerns. Mutuality, in this sense of a skill or process, as opposed to a static state of being, implies skillful self work and negotiation. This more processual and strategic approach to understanding mutuality as part of a trichotomy of associations can be found in the following exchange between Pat and Phyllis. In our conversations Pat and Phyllis talk about how similar they are. Phyllis relates that both like to swim, and they share tastes in clothes and music and have husbands who are alike. Yet, as in all the interviews, talk of similarity merges into talk about difference. What follows is a positive portrayal of how their personalities interactively function to complement each other.

> Pat: Yeah, it's how it [growing up twins] affects you is how you remember it. It doesn't affect you both the same. You really are different. I do tell people that I think brothers and sisters are more alike than twins are. I think twins are opposites. We really and truly know each other well enough and are intimate enough to really know each other, but basically I think we are opposites. I'm my mother and she's my father. That's why we get along. If she was like my mother, I wouldn't like her.

> Phyllis: This is the first time she's ever admitted that I'm like my father!

The practice of mutual selving, of being alike and of being opposite to each other, illustrates, in Harter's words, a balance between self-focused autonomy and other-focused connectedness that flows in and out of Pat and Phyllis's conversation. It also illustrates Cohen's (1994) point about taking a particular version of oneself to the "we" and holding back others.

Tom's recalling of a childhood memory of an insect bite illustrates the flow between a mutual and individual sense of self in his relationship with his brother, Tim, and calls forth themes of independence and mutuality as caring and sharing. But in the end, Tom has also learned to weigh or balance his concerns about his brother with those of his own self, discovering a new meaning of mutuality as a healthy balance of self-focused autonomy and other-focused connectedness.

> Tom: We all knew Tim was allergic to insect bites because when we were like six or seven years old, he got bit and swelled up big-time. Because we were identical (we didn't know then but assumed we were), we just assumed that some day I would have a reaction too. Tim was supposed to always have his medicine with him and we worried about him. Then guess what? In my early twenties, I was out mowing my grandfather's lawn and ran over a bee's nest with the mower. I got

stung but so did he [Tim]. And this is the interesting thing. I still didn't know if I was allergic to it. So when he got stung and I got stung, I was more worried about him than me. But guess who had the worse reaction? I did. Our brother-in-law drove us to the hospital where they saved our lives. It's kind of interesting that I was more worried about him because I knew he was allergic too, and I guess the fear of me being allergic too had not kicked in until after the problem.

The Twinsburg twins realize that the dyadic bond between twins enacts both a sense of collective mutuality that places them at odds with normative Western selfways and a sense of reciprocally negotiated self-awareness of self-otherness that, although uniquely positioned, conforms to conventional Western selfways. While this chapter started with a critique of the psychological literature that sees twins as at risk for being too close, we have also raised Battaglia's (1995) question of what constrains mutuality in Western culture. The exchange below enacts the interflow of connectedness, mutuality and autonomous, bounded, controlling selfhood as exemplified in the twin dynamic—the interactive practice of twinship. Yet Arnette and Annette's discussion of how their twinship plays over into their counseling skills as social workers also shows how Annette and Arnette strategically act to both express and constrain mutuality that characterizes their experience of twinship. Here are two mature, award-winning social workers as they interactively identify and evaluate what their respective abilities in the counseling field involve. Not only do they position self and selves in different kinds of dyadic relationships, but they put forth an interactive strategy for playing mutuality against autonomy in the context of their careers. In their narrative, mutuality becomes a kind of interactive tool or strategy for communicating both empathetic connection and authoritative distance. These are self-working and self-framing or positioning skills that both twins have honed in their twinship and that can be adapted into nontwin relational arenas.

> Dona: As social workers, as specialists in human relations, in your work is there something from your twinness that

you can bring to other people? Or is there something that just can't be done unless it is your twin?

Arnette: I think that when you're a twin and your clients know you are a twin [because Arnette has a picture of herself and Annette displayed on her desk], somehow or other they think you're going to be more sympathetic. I've used it. They feel like, "Well, if she's a twin, she's been close to somebody. So she's going to be more sympathetic."

Annette: With me, I think it's more of a style I developed on how to relate to people, how to get close to them. I was so close to my sister. It seemed like I could always just kind of sit there, figure out how you move your head and automatically kind of mark it, but not in an intrusive way, but in a way that says, "I'm like you." After a while people will say to me, "It's easy to talk to you." You understand just what I'm meaning to say. "Even abusive men will say this to me. They feel I understand them, but I don't really understand them. Working with clients like abusive men, however, you must also set limits, you have to set limits. I'll say, "This is your limit, understand?".

Arnette: I said the exact same thing last week.

Annette: I deal with some real violent people. They felt I was being real close to them, but I've learned to set my limits too. They can't use me because I set my boundaries. You learn being a twin how to set your boundaries.

As the exchange between Annette and Arnette illustrates, practice of autonomy and mutuality of twins is situated and positioned. Twin identities are produced and improvised across multiple vectors and in multiple contexts and situations at different points in one's life. Arnette and Annette view these skills as adaptive—an ability to relate to others, to come close, as well as to set limits on or draw back from that relationship. Their twin-shaped use of mutuality as a relational tool is not viewed by Annette and Arnette as pathological. In fact and practice, their twinship has provided them with interpersonal styles of interacting that translate adaptively to the extremely difficult therapeutic encounters they face daily as social workers. They oscillate between empathy and antagonism with their wife-beating clients. They take certain versions of their selves to the therapeutic encounter but hold back others. But most importantly, their exchange certainly enacts what Harter (1999, 8) terms as a healthy expression of mutuality that balances a "self-focused autonomy with an other-focused connectedness," and this Arnette and Annette attribute to their twinship.

AN ENHANCED SELF AND A WELL-PRACTICED BOND

According to Ingold (2013, 15, 17), our identities are continually produced by our own actions, relationships, and pronouncements. Just as physical resemblance both separates and merges twins' identities and experiential worlds, the same is true for the bonds between them. In this chapter, I have focused on the "Who am I?" question in terms of the twin bond and how contemporarity and proximity of twins shape their individual and respective selfways. As in the chapter 4, I have juxtaposed the concerns of parents of twins and twins researchers regarding the twin relationship or bond with what the talking partners have to say about the same topic. There is overlap and there is difference. While both researchers and twins view the bond in terms of intimacy, mutuality, and shared space and place, they each bring a differing perspective to these features of the bond. In this chapter, I have documented and addressed two major differences between the two perspectives. The researchers, particularly those interested in the psyche and child development, tend to medicalize or pathologize the pressures of pairing or twin bond. They tend to view the bond as being too close and too much together. Psychologists also portray the twin relationships or bonds, forged in shared childhoods, as a risk factor for potential pathologies, rooted in a regressive pull to each other that may lurk over a twin's entire life span. The talking partners, on the other hand, both normalize and celebrate their twin bond. They refer to the bond as something only a twin can know and portray it in highly positive terms as having a friend for life or someone who will always understand and is always there for the other. The partners also reflexively view their twinship as developing or maturing over their life cycles. In a sense, the psychological researchers seem to imply that it is better to be lonely than to be two who are too close. But as the case of Kristi, our student research assistant, who, on returning home from Twinsburg, reported feeling a profound sense of loneliness or that something special was missing in her own singleton life, tells us, there can be a very positive aspect to twinship as a lifetime sense of never being alone.

As we have seen, psychology, like biology, often presupposes a natural world, wherein what is healthy and normal for the Western self and psyche is a panhuman phenomenon. Yet, as we have seen in chapters 3 and 4, as well as this chapter, notions of identity and normality in relationships are culturally constructed and subject to variation both within and among particular sociocultural contexts. Identical twins do exist on the fault lines of these largely hegemonic, singleton, dominant Western notions of relationship and identity. Twins' identities and relationships emerge in this chapter as a kind of deviant persona with positive, as well as negative, attributes. Ironically, when psychologists take into account the social or cultural worlds of twins, they offer metaphors of twins as *a closed society* or *culture of two*. Twin pairs in this vein of thinking are portrayed as being so close that they actually cut themselves off from the surrounding relational world. Yet a twin's relation or bond reflects a tension between dependence and independence, autonomy and mutuality, and merging and individuating (Lindholm 2001) and is actually well embedded within wider society and history. Self-working twins must negotiate their duality and unity in a culture that privileges autonomy over relationality (McCollum 2002).

Twins who celebrate their bond and mutual identities and find themselves located on the fault lines of Western sociocultural constructions of identity and relationship (far more so than would be the case for those who study twins), exemplify Markus's (et al. 1997) notion that there may be multiple and conflicting selfways, not to mentions multiple ways of constructing and enacting independence and interdependence within any particular cultural context. The talking partners do not self-refer as truncated or compromised selves. Instead they portray their relationship as a self-enhancing, unique and contingent, value-added self-plus-other or other-plus-self. Normalcy emerges from the bottom up as they face the challenges of self work to interactively and self-consciously orchestrate their relationship rather than become passive objects of it. In so doing, the partners act not so much against each other but against stereotypes about them and their bond. Twinship becomes expressed as something that hones, refines, and defines their respective identities within and beyond the dyad. From a cross-cultural perspective, however, twins hardly exhaust cultural models of unconstrained mutuality. Yet limiting analysis to intracultural variation falls short of giving serious play to the concepts of culture and even more wide-ranging intercultural variations in styles of selving. In chapter 6, a more cross-culturally informed investigation of alternative, certainly less constrained, modeling of mutuality, interpersonal connectedness, and shared identities is introduced and compared and contrasted to the culturally based "Who am I?" assumptions made by, and core cultural values held by, both twins and the scientists who study them.

6

CULTURE

Twins are a biological and a social fact.

—*Stewart 2003*

One must avoid the error of locking twins in their twinhood.

—*Zazzo 1978*

What is physically double is structurally single and what is
mystically one is empirically two.

—*Turner 1969*

We are simpatico for all our lives.

—*Caroline Satchell and Janice Morris, NPR StoryCorps twins, 2007*

At the 2007 ICTS research conference, in his presidential address to
members, Jaakko Kaprio (2007), also representing the Finland Twin
Registry, presented a lecture on the current status of twin research.
He summarily concluded that the future of twin studies lay in longitudinal studies based on collaboration of those who had large,
national databases on twins. In his PowerPoint presentation, Kaprio
projected a scattergram that featured a clustering of twin research
specialties. The largest centered cluster consisted of related medical
fields interested in twin research with genetics being the central core.

Psychology and education were small clusters that were set apart from the centralizing cluster of genetics. What was most interesting to me, however, was that ethnology was also a category on the chart. Yet ethnology was located on the margins, relegated to the farthest point in the lower right corner of the chart. Ethnology was the most isolated and distanced "special field" on the chart. There were no other clusters associated with it or even located in the vicinity.

On the chart two references exemplified the field of ethnology. These were the names Quetzalcoatl and Clytemnestra. Both are twins. Quetzalcoatl is an Aztec god of the sun, and Clytemnestra, a woman of Greek mythology.[1] Now, even taking into account that Finnish ethnology is more similar to folklore than American usage of the word, why does Kaprio refer to ethnology in terms of named entities—one, a figure of religion, and the other, a figure of myth? Both of these mythical historical personages come from centuries past. They are far removed from the "real" and the here and the now. Yet, as a seasoned ethnologist, I found every presentation I attended at the ICTS in 2007 to be a proper topic for ethnological analysis. They all evidenced expressions of core values embedded in Western historical and cultural constructions of individualism, competition, and control, as well as the triumph of scientific rationalism over common sense or mythical beliefs. In my view, the entire underlying background of all the clusters on Kaprio's chart should have been ethnology.

This chapter utilizes the cross-cultural comparative method of anthropology (as ethnology) and cultural psychology to illuminate some cultural blind spots of twins researchers. Already we have seen cultural factors being denied by geneticists and ignored by psychologists. Kaprio (2007) deserves credit at least for keeping culture—that is, ethnology—in the picture. There is a bit of irony here because the ICTS social programs planned for participants actually celebrate the cultures and heritages of the places where they hold their meetings. Local food and wines are served during evening events. In Denmark we were treated to Hans Christian Andersen plays, and in Ghent an evening in the local castle was hosted by actors in the garb of medieval lords, ladies, and fools. My purpose throughout this chapter on culture is to embrace the task of anthropology not only in terms of its mission to make the strange familiar and the familiar strange (Lindholm 2001, 369) but also to shake complacencies of those who think only their world exists.

We have already seen that culture shapes beliefs about the body, and psyche as well as science. Yet at the ICTS conferences, culture—however it is defined—receives limited attention. Even foreign twins researchers buy into Western models that separate the domains of biology and culture. Despite the fact that the ICTS includes twins researchers from Sri Lanka, Japan, and Iran, for example, if their studies are to be considered good ones, researchers must design them to include methods and research instruments that have been developed within increasingly sophisticated Western traditions of scientific research. Recently both geneticists and social scientists have begun to critique twin studies for rather naive approaches to the concept of culture (Walters 2006). In this chapter, I hope to build on what I have presented in previous chapters to expand on what twins talk reveals about who we, as a Western society, are, individually and collectively, and how this, in turn, encodes key values forged in our own social, economic, political, and historical traditions.

Two interesting "cultural" exchanges that took place at the 2007 ICTS also exhibit a lack of cultural sensitivity or a naivety on the behalf of twins researchers. One exchange I witnessed was at the end of a presentation by a researcher who sought to document a "father effect" in twinning rates. His research was among an African population with high twinning rates. Although the audience politely listened to his presentation, it was clear, although the study was of interest, that his methodology was not up to snuff. An audience member, referring to great apes studies, suggested that the researcher collect data on testicle size. The presenter claimed, forcefully, that collecting such data would not be strategic, would be unethical, and was an unwarranted intrusion into the privacy of his sample of African men. I was sitting close enough to the questioner to hear him whisper to the person next to him that "you have to do it anyway or it's not science." My second example comes from an exchange with a mother of twins attendee at the Ghent conference. We sat together listening to a Swiss woman, with a heavy French accent, give a presentation on Swiss maternal leave policies. When the presenter finished, my companion asked me, "What was that all about?" I briefly explained that she was arguing that parents of twins should have double benefits and double leave time from work. Using my knowledge of the welfare state and maternal leave policies in Norway, I elaborated on these policies.[2] My companion responded with disbelief, "You've got to be kidding. They can't get all that." She was shocked, both by her own sense of relative deprivation and by the Swiss woman's sense of entitlement.

As Markus et al. (1997, 15) claim that all experience is individual and cultural, how do we go about a cultural analysis of twins in Western society? How can we go about convincing twins researchers that they have a culture too? How do we approach "culture" (and the nature of human relationships that activate it), not as an unexamined "given" but as a baseline for analysis? We have already introduced and dealt with the notions of culture as talk, cultural psychology, and culture in practice and selfways. Rapport and Overing's (2000, 93) definition of culture as a specific, historically contingent way of life will serve well for the analysis that follows. Culture, in this sense, pertains to that huge proportion of human knowledge and ways of doing things that are acquired, learned, and constructed—that is, not innate to humankind. This chapter brings a kind of informed cross-cultural analysis to the "Who am I?" question. Key components of the cultural psychology approach that guide the analysis are worth restating at this juncture. First, it recognizes multiple constructions of self or selfways within particular situated, social, sometimes divergent or competing contexts and multiple layers of self within a single individual (de Munck 1993; Jopling 1997; Lutz 1990; Markus et al. 1997; Mageo 2002; Murray 1993). Second, it recognizes individual agency and employs a culture in practice approach (Ortner 2006) in which twins become constructors and actors in their own dramas. Twins practice in the world and produce the world through practice (Casey and Edgerton 2005; Csordas 1994; Ortner 2006; Markus et al. 1997; Neisser 1997; Shweder 1991). Third, it views the self as situated and contextualized within the wider society and culture. Selfways may be defined as characteristic patterns of sociocultural participation or as characteristic ways of being a person in the world. As such, selfways include key cultural ideas and values, including what makes a good, appropriate, or moral person (Markus et al. 1997). Yet selfways are also situated within hierarchies of power and structural constraints. As Rosch (1997, 195) states, "The so-called self is not independent of anything."

Although twins are recognized as a biological and a social fact (Stewart 2003, 3), they have received short shrift in analyses of how culture mediates the experience of twinship or vice versa. Even studies of behavioral genetics that dichotomize and contrast heredity and environment fail to consider the cultural aspects of environment or even confuse genes and culture (Marks 2002, 2004). Most European and American twins researchers assume that science exists above and beyond culture and that while "others" have a culture, they as researchers do not. When Wright (1997) raises the questions of what twins tell us about who we are, the "who we are" or "wider society" remains unexamined.

Previous chapters have discussed the extent to which festival twins push the boundaries of normalcy in a positive as well as negative sense. By pushing the boundaries, they raise a host of complex cultural questions about self and identity in terms of biology, psychology, and issues of relatedness. Because they are exceptional, identical twins' self stylings challenge or conflate a number of dualisms that characterize Western traditions of thought. Among these dialectical distinctions or tensions are those between self/other, unit/individual, pair/single, same/different, connected/separate, and independent/dependent. I will argue in this chapter that although the twin bond and a twin's sense of person and selfhood fit within the range of alternative constructions of self that exist in our society, any difference is a difference in degree, not a difference in kind.

This chapter continues with an examination of the concept of culture as it is employed, either unconsciously or naively by nonanthropological twins researchers. I then turn to consider a sample of more anthropologically informed, biosocial depictions of twins from a comparative cross-cultural perspective. Next the focus shifts from cultural analysis of twins, per se, to a descriptive consideration of differing sociocultural constructions of self in a variety of societies, but most importantly the Wari of the Amazon and the Nyaka of India. Both of these tribal societies illustrate the practice of selfways in which mutuality lacks the kinds of constraint that typify the cultures of twins researchers. All of this sets an informative background for presentation of the argument that we (Westerners) have a culture too. My analysis of twins' narrative self stylings then proceeds to draw on a comparative discussion of the sociocultural construction of egocentric and sociocentric selfways. The last section of the chapter addresses twins talk in terms of core Western values. These include individualism, the right to privacy, equality as fairness and balance, choice making, and self-development.

CULTURES OF TWIN RESEARCH

As Kaprio's (2007) chart illustrates, anthropological studies of twins are highly stereotyped when it comes to twins researchers. Cultural studies or ethnology is so far off the beaten track as to be inconsequential. There are no feedback arrows or loops linking ethnology to other specialties of twin research. With its referencing of characters from Aztec mythology and classical Greek legend, culture is relegated to nineteenth-century armchair anthropology or presented as a topic perhaps of interest to some throwback scholarly dilettante in jodhpurs and a pith helmet. Yet some kind of cultural reference to twins is standard on the first page of any book-length or comprehensive review on the topic of twins. These references include culture in its most generalist or generic sense and overlook any potential for culture as an analytic tool or concept. For example, Klein's (2003, 1) introduction states that "probably since the beginning of human history, twins have been a source of wonder and fascination or repulsion and fear." The Italian geneticist Luigi Gedda (1961, 3), in his classic, much-quoted book on twins in history and science, states that "so impressive is a twin birth that it has not failed to leave its mark in the imagination of men in every ethnic group and every epoch of history." Even Sadri and Sadri (1994, 204), in one of the best sociological analyses of twin identity issues I have read, start their article with this formulaic tip of the hat to culture: "Numerous myths, fairy tales, urban legends and novels explore the horrifying or hilarious possibilities of physical, psychological or supernatural duplicates of unique individuals in forms of imposters, doppelgangers, robotic replicas or evil twins."[3] These works illustrate a lack of imagination when it comes to a contemporary take on cross-cultural aspects of twinship among contemporary twins researchers.

Twins researchers' notions of culture have remained static over the last fifty years. In his recent review article on the scope and history of twin research, Parisi (2004) continues the tradition of glossing culture as exotic customs and traditions. Anthropology continues to be conflated with mythology, religious studies, history, legend, and literature. The same outdated sources, like Harris's (1913) hundred-year-old depiction of twins in Greco-Roman traditions and Gedda's (1951, 1961) short fifty-year-old chapters on twins in myth and folklore and twins in literature, repeatedly provide enough cultural background to sufficiently cover the anthropology angle for contemporary twins researchers. When any kind of cultural analysis takes place, it tends to be formulaic and predictable. Culture tends to be limited to a fairly standard two-point universalizing analysis. The first, a psychological shock argument, posits a psychic unity model of humankind and focuses on primitive peoples. Supposedly the shock of the twin phenomenon, described as the birth of two babies instead of the expected one, arouses particular feelings and customs among primitives that become explained in terms of the intrusion of supernatural forces (Gedda 1961). A second approach usually entails some note of the symbolic duality of twins, as depicted in myth (mainly origin myths) and folklore, as representations of good and evil, cursed or blessed, harmony and disorder (Parisi 2004). Cultural practices also become reduced to attitudes and practices toward twins, usually reflecting an armchair approach to the subject matter (with a reliance on texts, not fieldwork). There is no voice of twins themselves, and the "cultures" of those who study twins go unremarked. In the popular and scientific literature, however, books by two prominent twins researchers, Elizabeth Stewart (2003) and Alessanda Piontelli (2008), stand out as exceptions to this rule. They are of interest not only for their attention to cultural factors but as prolegomena for future twin research endeavors.

Stewart, in her book *Exploring Twins: Towards a Social Analysis of Twinship* (2003), brings what she calls a constitution (not constructionist) approach to her ethnographic or cultural/anthropological analysis of twins. Like Gedda (1961), she sees twin birth as a surprise and shock to family and community that must be addressed. Yet Stewart brings ethnographic specificity and depth to her analysis. For example, she focuses on the issues twins raise in the context of specific aspects of traditional social systems, such as kinship systems, characterized by the practice of lineal descent and primogeniture. In these descent patterns, the birth of twins may shock and surprise, but twin births also present classificatory problems. These problems may center on issues concerning paternity and identification of the firstborn twin. Stewart also looks at cultural practices such as taboos, infanticide, and ritual enacted to normalize the effects of twin birth. In Stewart's analysis, while twins may disrupt, cultural systems restore, or rectify. Not only does she address how cultural stereotypes of twins in British culture (that they are identical) raise issues of identity in modern society and shape people's perceptions of twins. She also notes that different cultures deal with the duality of twins in different ways. Stewart engages the anthropology of twins on somewhat of its own terms by citing works of famous, midcentury anthropologists like Victor Turner (1967, 1969) and Claude Lévi-Strauss (1978). Her examination of twins in the contemporary Western media features scenarios of self as deeply enculturated, socially premised, and nonstatic or emergent. Through media analysis she briefly explores issues of personality, social identity, mistaken identity, bond (we two as one), duality of competing selves, the fragmented nature of self, and alternative selves.

In her fascinating and disturbing book *Twins in the World: The Legends They Inspire and the Lives They Lead*, Piontelli (2008) draws on her firsthand personal accounts of twins and parents of twins she has encountered as a physician working in many places for brief periods. She also draws on her work with various immigrant groups at a twin unit of an Italian hospital. With a unifying focus on customs, treatments, and beliefs, Piontelli describes twins, or more often, parents of twins (particularly mothers) in different areas of Africa, the Brazilian Amazon, Papua New Guinea, and Thailand, as well as twins among subpopulations of gypsies and Nigerian prostitutes living in Italy. Although Piontelli (2008, 6, 9) makes "no claim to the depth of an anthropological or ethnological inquiry," she does state that her descriptions of twins in different societies reveal a great deal about "broader beliefs about children, reproduction, pregnancy, motherhood and gender." Like others, Piontelli couches her cultural analysis in the big shock value or highly traumatic event of an unexpected twin birth in societies without access to modern medicine. She also develops analysis along the lines of the dangers of twin pregnancy and birth for both mother and twins and high infant death rates, as well as the potential for abnormalities in twins, such as one born healthy and one not and the physical appearance of a premature child (as in large head, bloated body, or body hair). This very haunting book associates twins with death, good and evil, and danger. Piontelli (2008, 9) notes the positive aspects of twins as representing closeness, companionship, and union. She also emphasizes the "dark side" of twinship, including contemporary cultural practices and beliefs associated with infanticide of one or both twins, twins as sorcerers or practitioners of voodoo, twins in the sex trade, twin-twin marriage, good and evil twins, and the selling of children, as in use of orphaned twins as organ banks. Throughout her book, Piontelli poses rational science as the antithesis of myth and superstition, stating, for instance, "From the heights of our scientific knowledge we can now have rational explanations" (2008, 160). Her focus, however, centers on issues of maternity and motherhood. She actually talks to very few twins. She does, however, situate her discussions of twins within the contexts of global capitalism, human rights, culture change, and the inter- and intranational divides or inequities that exist between rich and poor.

TWINS AND TWIN CULTURES: ANTHROPOLOGICAL PERSPECTIVES

Interest in twins dates back to the beginnings of anthropology. For example, Frazer's early work, *The Golden Bough* (1900), sets varieties of cultural and magical reactions to twins within the framework of anthropological analysis. Twin infanticide was one of the earliest aspects of childrearing to receive cross-cultural analysis (Granzberg 1973). Researchers interested in human fertility have had a long-standing interest in how the biological, demographic, environmental, and cultural factors may influence variations in twinning rates between different "natural" populations (Dona Davis 1971; Dorothy Davis 1971; Chakravarty 1994; Grantzberg 1973; Madrigal 1994). Most of these rely on secondary databases like the Human Relations Area Files (HRAF).[4] Anthrosource, a search engine for anthropological sources, reveals only a handful of hits for a twin/twins search; most are mid-century and all focus on symbol and myth. Even the best-known anthropological studies of twins focus on meaning and ignore what I have posed as the more grounded, practical experiential aspects of twinship. Twins as actors are pretty much limited to discussions of the divinity (twins as gods) or analytically engaged as imaginary characters in myth and folklore.

Three of the most famous early to mid-twentieth-century anthropologists—Victor Turner, E. E. Evans-Pritchard, and Claude Lévi-Strauss—have discussed the paradoxical qualities of twins. All three share an interest in twins as a unifying pair of opposites in relationship to some sort of universal classification system. Lévi-Strauss (1978) discusses of the dualities (good and evil) of divine twins or twin myth in native North and South American cultures. Turner (1985, 1969, and 1967) describes identical twins among the Ndembu of Africa as existing betwixt and between. The paradox of twinship, according to Turner, is that twins are conceptualized as a single entity in the sacred order, while they are recognized as two or a dual entity in the secular order. Thus, "what is physically double is structurally single and what is mystically one is empirically two" (Turner 1969, 45). Twins, in particular opposite sex twins, according to Turner (1969), exist in a kind of liminal state. They are not only same and different; they are dual-singular-monadic and paired-united-dyadic. Evans-Pritchard (1967) makes a similar point for the African Nuer, who classify twins and birds as beings of God. Twins, like birds, although being many or multiple, also have a supernatural quality of being a single social person. Thus, twins as a symbolic social entity are set against their physical duality.

Diduk's (1993) more recent ethnography of Kedjom twins in Cameroon goes beyond myth and ritual to set traditional beliefs about twins within wider frameworks of culture change and the structuring of relations in the wider political and economic contexts. Diduk notes that, although twins are regarded as special in Cameroon, they are hardly an uncommon occurrence. Not only are twinning rates high but all anomalous births are regarded as "twins." Distinctions are made between "double twins" (two babies) and "single twins" (a single baby born with a caul, birth defect, etc.) (1993, 552). According to Diduk, contemporary Cameroon is characterized by great disparities of wealth, power, and privilege that divide a small elite from the masses of the impoverished poor. Since the exploited poor are afraid to accuse the elite of sorcery (because the poor fear the elite's powers), they take redress in the powers of twins. Twins have taken on a kind of middle ground role as supernatural actors. Kedjom twins (double and single) occupy a status somewhere between regular people and sorcerers. Although mischievous, they are considered to be more benign and controllable than sorcerers and therefore less dangerous as supernatural actors. Although Diduk places Kedjom twins within the wider frameworks of social relations in Cameroon, she tells us little about the twins themselves.

Like Piontelli (2008), Diduk (1993) places twins within wider frameworks of cultural analysis that include globalization and culture change. They both point a way for future efforts in culturally informed twin studies that go beyond the customs, beliefs, and practices era of ethnology. My interests, however, are not twins in exotic places, but twins at home. In many ways, it is far easier to explicate cultural factors in unfamiliar settings than it is in taken-for-granted and familiar settings like the ICTS. Clearly cross-cultural analysis shows us the importance of culture in shaping beliefs and practices surrounding twins and twinship. What is largely missing from these types of analysis is how these beliefs and practices are grounded in the everyday experiences of twins and affect their relationships and senses of self. Twins, even in the ethnographic literature, remain literally voiceless.

BEYOND QUETZALCOATL: THE WARI AND THE NYAKA

One day as I was driving to work, I listened to a conversation between two middle-aged twin women on National Public Radio's StoryCorps series.[5] In searching together for a term to describe their twinship, the women, in their self-self interview, agreed that being twins meant that they were *simpatico* for life. I found it interesting that during this interchange of two twin voices trying to come up with a word to describe their twinship, these StoryCorps twins resorted to a foreign term that has been adopted into English. In Spanish, *simpático* refers to likeability, congeniality, and sympathy. In what follows, I do not use ethnography to describe twins in differing cultural settings. Instead, I look at how people in other cultures model and express identity and relationship in ways that, by comparison, will make Western twins seem less exotic. Piontelli (2008, 15) states, "Twins break down some of the rules dominating our daily social contacts, such as keeping a safe distance and respecting each other's space." Yet Harter (1995) asserts that within any couple relationship, a self-focused autonomy coexists with another-focused connectedness. Do the kinds and expressions of mutuality, as a state of shared being or as a relational tool, as so far related by the Twinsburg twins, find any kind of resonance that transcends a couple effect, when viewed across a wider cultural spectrum? With the dictum that by learning about others, we learn more about ourselves, I now begin a process of making more explicit some of the tacit cultural assumptions held by twins researchers. I do so by comparing our selves and other selves and by searching across the ethnographic spectrum for examples of ways of being that normalize alternative constructions of a sense of connectedness and affiliation with others.

The anthropological literature is replete with discussions of sociocultural and historical variations in constructions of embodied and relational self styles. Notions like the open, permeable self (Battaglia 2000; Stewart 2003); the divided, fragmented, or multiple self (de Munck 2000); the dividual self (Strathern 1988); the contingent self (Murray 1993); the fluid self (Marriot and Inden 1977); the fractual, particle, or composite self (Fowler 2004); the transcendent self (Kapferer 1984); the saturated self (Gergen 1991); the body as shared substance self (Conklin and Morgan 1996); the situated, active, intentional, talking self (Holland et al. 1998); as well as a host of other "others" (Hardman 2000; McCallum 2001, Overing and Passes 2000; Landrine 1995) represent potential points of entry into a more culturally informed analysis of twinship. Two recent studies help demonstrate alternative constructions of mutualities in the selfways of the Wari of Amazonia (Conklin and Morgan 1996) and the Nyaka of India (Bird-David 2004). The processual shared substance body of the Wari, as described by Conklin and Morgan, and the bodies of the Nyaka that both join and come apart, as described by Bird-David, demonstrate that bodies and persons are products of cultural practices and that relations between bodies may be constituted in multiple ways. As ethnographic examples, these two studies serve to make twins' bodies, bonds, and social contacts, whether seen from the perspectives of researchers or twins themselves, seem like less of an exception in the human condition.

Beth Conklin and Lynn Morgan (1996, referencing Csordas 1994b, 3) ask, How is personhood worked through the body, and how can we use the body to think with? In their fascinating discussion of personhood and identity on the fault lines, Conklin and Morgan (1996) take a look at gestation, birth, and infancy in two cultures, Western and Wari, to show how concepts of personhood are contingent on the social meaning given to bodies. The Amazonian Wari view the body as interconnected, or interrelated, to other bodies through interpersonal exchanges of food and the body fluids of breast milk, semen, and blood. The Wari conceive of interpersonal attachments as shared physical substances that link body selves in an organic unity that transcends the boundaries of discrete physical forms. Person-hood among the Wari develops over time to become a shared product of these fluid exchanges. The Wari thus have an image of processual, relational, interconnected bodies. Conklin and Morgan characterize Western bodies, rather than merging into one another, as separate from other bodies, as bounded by the skin and as a kind of private property. They argue that it is the gene, as substance, that provides the blueprint for biological identity and individual uniqueness and that is increasingly considered to be the body substance most funda-mental to Western personhood. They employ the term *bumper car bodies* to describe Western personhood. Bumper car bodies merci-lessly attempt to protect their space while at the same time bumping into and rebounding off one another.

Like Conklin and Morgan (1996), Nurit Bird-David (2004) explores the ideas of relationality and intercorporeality from a cross-cultural perspective. Bird-David models intercorporeal mutuality among the Nyaka, not so much in terms of shared substances, but in terms of a kind of joined being or pluralized individual rooted in a Nyaka sense of togetherness/distance from others. As for the Wari, however, among the Nyaka, personhood predicates engagement with others. A forest-dwelling tribal group in India, the Nyaka see themselves as plu-ralized individuals or as an inseparable many (Bird-David 2004). They talk about themselves in first-person plural pronouns, as in *we* and *us*. This joinedness, according to Bird-David, is based in physical proxim-ity or close communal living and is expressed in a number of ways in spiritual and material/environmental, as well as in interpersonal realms. There is a strong sense of egalitarianism in the community, and stress is placed on living amicably with others. All community members are seen as relatives and refer to each other with kinship terms, as relational rather than distinct individual identities. Bird-David describes relationality among the Nyaka as webs of connections and mutualities to other fellow beings that must be cultivated to avoid misfortune and sickness. Among the Nyaka, the surfaces of the body, the skin, connect bodies rather than divide them. Personhood, is this sense (Bird-David 2004), focuses on persons in touch rather than on a singularized skin-bound body.

Conklin and Morgan's (1996) and Bird-David's (2004) discussions of less constrained forms of mutuality and selfhood in unsteady states are in accord with a much wider literature of the natures of self and selfways in anthropology. I have chosen to present them because of their focus on shared substance, sense of connectedness, and close living. I have already argued that in their own self-perceptions and certainly in the gaze of others, twins embody intercorporeality in the sense that they are joined in the skin; they share genes and look alike. The Wari and Nyaka, both exotic, ethnographic others (and there are other others [cf. Celtel 2005]), show that notions of porous, processual, transcendent, or joined bodies as forms of embodied connectedness or mutuality are the norm rather than the exception in some societies. Conklin and Morgan's (1996) analysis highlights social contexts in which personhood is called into question by focusing on gestations and infancy. They focus on prenatal and early infancy as life stages, to compare and contrast Wari and Western conceptions of personhood. Bird-David (2004) uses the Nyaka to critique Weiss's (1999) idea of intercorporeality as rooted in Western assumptions that the individual's body is autonomous and skin-bound. A less constrained mutuality (as contrasted with the West) also shapes Bird-David's depiction of the Nyaka.

Examples from ethnographic studies of the Wari and Nyaka demonstrate that what we (Westerners) see as abnormal about twins is actually, in some cultural contexts, normative for all societal members. Yet even among the Wari and the Nyaka, individualism is stated as (although not developed or given any dynamic in these two articles) coexisting with the kinds of mutuality the authors describe. Conklin and Morgan (1996) posit that the relative values ascribed to social ties and autonomous agency among Westerners and the Wari do not suggest a radical difference in the subjective experience of self. They note that in the praxis of everyday life that Wari are individuals. Rather, these two anthropologists see selfways as departure points for exploring differences and parallels in societies. Similarly, Bird-David (2004) sees autonomy and mutuality as a matter of nuance, closeness, and distance. Yet lacking in the accounts of the Nyaka and Wari is an elaboration of how, from the ground up, these people negotiate independence and interdependence within specific contexts of their individual and collective personae. Both sources deal with collective, rather than dyadic, identities and relationships. They focus on states of being and worlds of meaning in the abstract, as sociocultural constructions rather than the practical realities of identity making and interpersonal relationships. Nonetheless, they echo themes expressed in twins talk and put forth as normative for some cultural contexts what the twins voice as special to themselves.

Western twins, although they share some of their characteristics, are neither Wari nor Nyaka. Like the Wari and Nyaka, Western twins live in a society where multidimensional models or multiple renderings of self are recognized, as are needs to merge and separate (Barth 1997; de Munck 2000; Fowler 2004; Lutz 1990; Mageo 2002; Markus et al. 1997). One can be independent and connected at the same time. To Lindholm's (2001) statement that independence or connection is a matter of emphasis, I would add that it is also, for twins, who stand betwixt and between, a matter for negotiation. Twins and twinship exist in, shape, and are shaped by a sociocultural milieu that goes beyond the twin dyad. A twin's body, mind, and bond exist on the fault lines of two seemingly discordant selfways within Western traditions. As Stewart (2003) notes, twins are placed at the center of a modern dilemma—being an individual while society perceives them as being a supra-individual. These comments attest to what Fowler (2004) describes as a lack of middle ground or limited elasticity of our own concept of personhood. As I have argued in chapters 3, 4, and 5 on festival, body, and bond, twins and their identical bodies represent challenges to the ethos of autonomy and individualism that predominates in Western culture, and this has profound implications for the self work that takes place between and among them. So far in this chapter, I have critiqued nonanthropological twins researchers for their naive or uninformed use of the culture concept, including the idea that the science they practice is not culture-bound. I have critiqued the ethnographic literature on twins for its focus on customs and beliefs rather than on the practical, grounded experiences of twins. I have used cross-cultural case studies to validate the mutuality already expressed by the talking partners in chapters 2–5. In the sections that follow, I bring a culturally informed analysis of twins and twinship in terms of the configuration and expression of seemingly contradictory selfways commonly framed as the *egocentric* and the *sociocentric* self. I then look at how twinship highlights core Western values such as equal opportunity, fairness, and rights to dignity, personal privacy, self-development, and choice.

WESTERN SELFWAYS:
SOCIOCENTRIC AND EGOCENTRIC SELVES

The paradox of twinship is that twins exist as both a single and dual entity. As Victor Turner (1985, 1969) states, twins are in a liminal state of betwixt and between. Similarly, Piontelli (2008) notes that twins break rules when it comes to notions of keeping a safe distance and respecting each other's space. In Harter's (1995) formulation, twins would diffuse boundaries between self-focused autonomy and other-focused connectedness. If twins constitute selfhood in an unsteady state or an unsettling presence, what tacitly held cultural assumptions are they transgressing or challenging? If twins are impaired individuals, what exactly constitutes an unimpaired individual? If twins exist on the fault lines of multiple selfways, what exactly are these selfways? The Twinsburg twins and researchers at the ICTS share and express commonly held cultural assumptions and values concerning what can be called a normative Western or egocentric self (Gaines 1992; Landrine 1995; Mageo 2001).[6] Whether they challenge these norms (as in the case of the Twinsburg twins) or worry that twinship can compromise these norms (as in the case of twins researchers), the Western self is implicitly understood as indicating a predominant selfway in Western culture. These implicit understandings, however, are seldom articulated either by the talking partners or researchers, yet they are embedded within the academic and conversational discourse of twins and twinship. There is a large body of literature on Western constructions of self that includes cultural psychology and bridges multiple disciplines. The cultural analysis of twinship that follows begins with a brief description of this Western self and then compares and contrasts it to its opposite, the so-called sociocentric self.

The anthropologist Clifford Geertz (1975, 48) offers one of the more classic descriptions of the Western self.

> The Western conception of the person is as a bounded,
> unique, more or less integrated motivational and cognitive
> universe, a dynamic center of awareness, emotion, judgment,
> and action organized into a distinctive whole and set
> contrastively both against other such wholes and against its
> social and natural background.

This value of personal distinctiveness has been a constant theme of the previous chapters. A Western sense of being special and unique in the world, and elaborated as having one body and mind per person, as having private thoughts and desires, and as having experiences that no one knows or can share, is also commonly referred to as the *egocentric* self. The egocentric person is independent, autonomous, self-assertive, contentious, highly competitive, and in control of her or his destiny. In contrast, a *sociocentric* self is interdependent, has permeable or open mind/body boundaries, is group oriented, has a strong sense of place vis-à-vis others, is publicly shaped by others, and is fatalistic (Landrine 1995). Although the terms have been used to describe intracultural variation in typologies of self or selfways, more often they are used to compare different cultures. For example, although egocentric has been used to distinguish middle- and upper-class Protestant men from sociocentric underclasses, including ethnic minorities and women (Gaines 1992; Landrine 1995; Lutz 1990), the two terms are most often employed to describe intercultural variation.

During the 1980s and '90s, a substantial body of literature emerged to contrast the so-called North American or Euro-American, egocentric/independent self with the so-called Japanese sociocentric/interdependent self or selfways (Kitayama and Markus 1995). The independent American self is individualistic; he tries to be separate, autonomous, and bounded off from other individuals. He has attribute-based traits that are stable and consistent. His self is privately turned inward yet is also self-assertive and contentious. While he may experience intense emotions, he tries to be in control of them. He has preferences and goals and maintains self-esteem through a sense of self that is positive and unique. In contrast to the egocentric self, the Japanese interdependent, sociocentric self is posed as more permeable and processual. He is group oriented and feels a sense of connection to and harmony with others. He tries to fit in and fears exclusion. He has a strong sense of place vis-à-vis others and is sensitive to the expectations, preferences, and feelings of others. Although he tries to improve his self, the Japanese is obedient rather than self-critical. His demeanor is calm and his behaviors in public are flexible, context-dependent, and shaped by others. Additionally, emotions among the Japanese are subdued and accompanied by anxiety over expressing them. The Japanese fear being egotistical.

More recent accountings of these two constructions of self have focused on breaking them down (Gjerde and Onishi 2000; Lebra 1992), recognizing that these distinctions can be overdrawn, that contradictions coexist in any one culture and that selves are situated and multiple. Not only can the Euro-American be conforming—wanting to fit in, be other directed, and participate as coequals working for the common good—but the Japanese can be, in certain contexts, remarkably individualistic. Thus, many critics of these selfways as somehow opposing or mutually exclusive note that in practice people invoke different interpretations to suit different purposes (Battaglia 1995b; Conklin and Morgan 1996; de Munck 1993; Neisser 1997). As Lindholm (2001) notes, a Westerner can be an independent, bounded self in one situation and a conforming and other-directed self in another. These constructions, therefore, represent a degree of emphasis rather than a difference in kind (Conklin and Morgan 1996). As Lindholm (2001) describes, it is a matter of text and subtext. The subtext of sociocentric interdependence is the reinstating of an independent bounded self; the subtext of independence is interdependence.

These two constructions of self, however configured, encode key cultural ideas and values of what makes a good, appropriate or moral person (Markus et al. 1997). Those twins researchers and popular science writers who pose science as a rational unbiased phenomenon fail to query the ideas that the so-called Western individual self is not a fact of nature (or even genetics) and that somehow by looking too much alike or being too close, twins transgress their natural environment. The Western self is not a de facto self; it is a product of a culturally and historically shaped environment. As we saw in the case of the Wari and Nyaka, it is one way among many of being in the world. Moreover, however co-occurring the egocentric and sociocentric selfways may be, a hierarchy does exist between them. The egocentric construction of personhood is hegemonic. Exemplifying this hierarchy would be the following statement from the twins IQ researchers Plomin et al. (1997, 279): "The basic message of behavioral genetics is that each of us is an individual. Recognition of, and respect for individual differences is essential to the ethic of individual worth."

Conceptions of personhood described above dominate moral peoplescapes of Western culture. This includes our assumptions about what constitutes a healthy, normally functioning self. In a sense, identical twins embody an exaggeration of the positive and negative attributes of both constructions of self. Although twins researchers and twins themselves coalesce and focus attention on these competing tendencies between autonomy and togetherness, the cultural challenges they face are hardly unique to twins. All children must learn to negotiate autonomy and togetherness (McCollum 2002), but constructions of appropriate selfways are not politically neutral and neither is the science that fails to interrogate them. The egocentric self is prototypically Western, masculine, and capitalist (Landrine 1995; Gaines 1992). It is considered as normal, desired, healthy, and mandatory in democratic societies. The answer to Battaglia's (1995a) rhetorical question "What constrains mutuality?" is the superior value that is given to the egocentric self. It is one thing to describe how twins negotiate autonomy and interdependence within the twin dyad, but they must also do so within a wider cultural framework where these are seen as in opposition to each other.

Socio-Egocentric Twins

So far throughout this book, my focus on multiple twinscapes—including twins festivals, twins' narratives, twins researchers and research conferences, and my own self-reflections—show that confounding the binaries of sociocentric and egocentric selfways is a signal experience of identical twins. Twins are identical as a pair in ways that encroach on our Western sense of being special and unique in the world (Wright 1997); yet each twin has a far more finely informed sense of his or her individual, distinctive phenotype than does a singleton. Although others around them tend to merge their identities or treat them as a unit, twins take great care to differentiate between their respective personal attributes and personalities. Our Twinsburg talking partners collaborate to negotiate and express their individuality. Festival twins turn the tables on cultural values by celebrating the very closeness that outsiders condemn as compromising their individuality. Whether en masse, by pairs, or individually, identical twins attest to the existence of a milieu of competing or overlapping models and practices of self. From a twin's perspective, sociocentric and egocentric constructions of self are not merely multiple constructions or renderings of selves, or text and subtext. Given the facility with which twins jump from one conversation topic to another as they both merge and individuate their identities, both self-constructions are important; one does not take a back seat to the other. In what follows, I use the notion of American core values to illustrate how twins actively situate their constructions of self.

AMERICAN CORE VALUES

The value of personal distinctiveness has been a constant theme of the previous chapters. This ideal of the Western self in the United States, according to Lindholm (2001), has deep cultural roots. Among these are the moral premises of Puritanism, personal mobility, and an entrepreneurial spirit. This prototype of individualism also has deep roots in Western philosophical traditions. Lukes (1968) describes this Western self as rooted in a combination of New Testament Christianity, European Enlightenment, political liberalism, and German Romanticism. The idea of Western individuality (Lukes 1973) derives from four core values: the dignity of man, autonomy, privacy, and self-development. The dignity of man refers to the supreme or intrinsic value of individual human beings. In New Testament Christianity, it is a moral imperative that each individual has his own relationship with God and that all Christian men are equal in the eyes of God. In the United States Declaration of Independence, the dignity of man is also associated with equality and becomes a moral axiom that overrides all others. From the European Enlightenment comes the moral valuation of autonomy and independent rational reflection. Autonomy includes the idea that an individual's thoughts, intentions, and actions are self-directed. They are his own and are not determined by agencies or causes that are outside his control. Each person must make his own choices. The core value of privacy is central to liberalism and a political philosophy. Privacy entails the idea of boundaries in a private sphere, in the sense that an individual is or should be left alone by others to think and act as he pleases. Within the private sphere, within himself, each individual has sovereign rights over his body and may do and think whatever he chooses. The tradition of German Romanticism implies not only qualities of individual uniqueness but self-development as the ability to shape one's life course and be the best person possible (Celtel 2005; Lukes 1973). Each man represents humanity in himself and in his own special way. In short, this historically derived, culture-based, modern Western self requires respect for each person's autonomy, privacy, and freedom for self-development (Celtel 2005). These core values are all evidenced in Twinsburg twins talk. In the narratives that follow, the twins reason and reflect together over issues of privacy, equality (as in autonomy and fairness), and choice (as in personal freedom and self-development).

Privacy

In Western culture a right to privacy is considered essential to the development of a proper egocentric self. Erchak (1992) states the solitude of an American middle-class baby, who sleeps in his or her own room, is a key indicator of Western individualism. Here, the individual exists as a sovereign, personal sphere of thought and action wherein intrusion or interference is ideologically prohibited. Lindholm (2001) also notes the Western assumption that privacy in childhood is essential to the development of autonomy, self-esteem, and self-expression. Western children need privacy. Educators worry about whether school policy should separate twins or allow them to be together. Piontelli (2008) makes much of the idea that though twins may be envied for their closeness and ability to understand each other, they also break down two cardinal rules regulating daily social contacts: keeping a safe distance and respecting each other's space. Much has been made of the contemporarity or co-contemporarity of twins, their sharing of space and place, treatment as a unit, and even the idea that their own thought processes (as in secrets, lies, or ESP) can be open to each other. If the opposite of privacy is groupism (Celtel 2005), then twins together comprise a kind of dyadism. Clearly festival twins do not conform to society's expectations, as two look-alike selves challenge the idea of bounded private spheres of identity and co-create their own private dyadic sphere of twinship. For example, Judy and Janet consciously transgress norms of social distance and respect for each other's space as they hug and kiss each other.

As we have seen in former chapters, self work among twins includes the dual processes of authenticating twinship as a special kind of close relationship and the process of drawing boundaries between self and other, both within the dyad and within the wider milieus of social relationships. On one hand, an individual twin's personal space or privacy may be compromised by the other twin. Yet, on the other hand, twinship is a private relationship, if not a closed society. Twins-burg twins remember their childhoods with shared rooms and the proverbial twin beds as "periods of never being alone" or as "having a constant companion." Dorothy and I experienced our own version of culture shock when our college roommates reacted with horror when we admitted to sharing underwear. Rosambeau (1987), a mother of twins, states that she cannot remember a time in her twins' child-hoods when what she did to one twin did not affect the other twin. This exchange between Linda and Lucy demonstrates how same and different are co-negotiated within the dyad to create a sense of mutu-ally agreed upon privacy, both as shared space and place, and a space and place of one's own.

> Linda: When we were little, another thing that really
> bothers us was like at Christmas times and birthdays.
> Everyone wanted to give us something alike so we
> got two. And we would sit there until we could find
> something different about them. My grandmother
> gave us outfits one year and said, "You're not going to
> find anything different," but we did.
>
> Lucy: Buttons, hems, or something—we always did find a
> difference.
>
> Linda: So we had our own outfits.

Whether natural, allowed, or forced, the contemporarity of twins leads to a kind of hypercognition of same and different among the twin pair. To Lucy and Linda, a sense of privacy is expressed by a sense of entitlement to each twin's personal possessions or private property. They express resentment at their grandmother who en-gaged their twinship by treating them exactly the same. By giving them outfits that matched exactly, their grandmother equated same with equal. Would it be fair if the outfits had been different, and both twins preferred the same outfit and one twin ended up getting her second choice? This dilemma is avoided by giving each twin the same gift. Not only does twins talk about being same and different transgress and confirm Western notions of privacy and distanced or bounded identities, but it is interwoven with talk about equality—another core Western value.

Equality

Western children, even as babies, according to Lindholm (2001) in his discussion of the American self, are trained to have authentic identities. Authentic here implies a profound journey of self-discovery leading to a sense of autonomy and of being not the same as everyone else. We have seen how the twin game or twins' self work includes fine-tuning one's own self/other identity by mining their bodies for distinctive, identifiable traits and by attributing to each other different character traits. Jean tells us that one way to tell her apart from Carol was that Jean "had football eyes" and her twin sister had "basketball eyes." When it comes to personal character or behavioral attributes, Karen is the evil twin, and Kristy is the good one; Dianne is the logical critical thinker, and Donna is more laid back; and Helen is more family-oriented than June. Yet Western culture also includes core ideals that we are all born as equals on a level playing field. Unlike other kinds of relationships, the identical twin relationship is seen as a relation of co-equals. As intensely intimate relationships go, twinship is the most equal. The bond between mother and child is a hierarchical or vertical relationship (Farmer 1996, 45), and even most marriages are compounded by issues of gender.

Egalitarian individualism may also be conceived as sameness (Gullestad 1997). Twinsburg twins show a comfort, acceptance, and even pride in being same. Tina and Ginuh tell us, "Physically we're the same, same weight, same struggles with weight; we look similar." They add, "Generally, we are the same as far as spiritually, mentally, things like that. We think the same. The same things irritate us." Same and different, however, are two sides of the same coin. Not only do festival twins differentiate themselves from singletons by performing same, but they conterminously assert the uniqueness of the twin state as well as their personal and interpersonal individualities. Kristy states, "Although we are similar in looks, we are totally different people." Westerners, like twins, are same and different, but for Westerners same and different must somehow be balanced so that some state of equilibrium ensues.

Same and different are hardly abstract or static concepts. They are lived experiences and must be dynamically negotiated. The dilemma faced by Lucy and Linda's grandmother, who made their outfits exactly alike and challenged the twins to spot any difference, is hardly unique. According to the twins researcher Joseph (2002, 9), society expects that identical twins should be treated more similarly than fraternal twins; as Pat remarks, their mother was obsessed with treating her and Phyllis the same. I had thought that my own understandings of treating twins the same were carryovers from my own 1950s experiences as a twinned child. Yet my contemporary students are also very sensitive to the idea of twins as co-equals. When I ask my psychological anthropology students to tell me about their own personally, experientially familiar stereotypes of twins in Western society, I usually get the standard positive and negative characterizations of twins and twinship, but they also repeatedly say that twins are equal, must be equal, or must be treated as equal.

This notion of being equals is not limited to identical twins; it also reflects what Lindholm (2001, 393) refers to as one of the challenges of Western culture to validate the reality of difference with everyone according to the cultural ideal of equality. This sample of American twins reflects the wider egalitarian values of their society as they voice their concerns and strategies for balancing their experiences of being same and different with an overriding ideal of fairness. This is true whether the talking partners are speaking of times past, present, or future. As twins talk, notions of equality as sameness and of authenticity as difference must be balanced through standards of fairness. Flowing through Twinsburg twins talk are ideas that twins should be treated as equals with equal opportunities. A sense of equilibrium between twins must either exist or be achieved. For example, Tina and Ginuh complain about being treated the same, but they explicitly mention how this sameness is intertwined with ideas of fairness and balance. Tina and Ginuh express equality as "forced sameness." Pat and Phyllis express equality in terms of complementary personal attributes.

> Tina: Mother tried to treat us as equal but ended up treating us the same.
>
> Ginuh: We didn't dress alike. We were dressed alike.
>
> Tina: Our mother made matching clothes, matching dolls, and matching toys.
>
> Ginuh: Everything was matching.
>
> Tina: It was a fairness thing.

Pat and Phyllis claim that despite their mother's agenda to treat them the same, by modeling themselves on their parents, they were able to develop a complementary distinctiveness. Pat grew up to be like her mother and Phyllis grew up like her father.

Phyllis: Our parents got along OK.

Pat: And that's why we get along so well today.

Not only are twins treated equally or the same, they expect it from their parents. My mother says that one of the hardest parts of rearing us was how to be fair. As with the same yearly birthday cards we received, our mother's idea of fairness is to treat us, even in middle age, as the same. We certainly internalized this and came to realize same through sharing. In the United States Declaration of Independence, the dignity of man becomes invariably associated with core values of freedom, liberty, and equality. Yet equality not only connotes fairness and equal opportunity but also a kind of unselfish mutuality or sharing and caring that ties individuals as co-equals together (Lindholm 2001, 383–85). Even now, when one of us has, for example, a pack of M&Ms, the other will shout "fairzies" in a plea for sharing, which is always reciprocated. In every paper or article we have written concerning the Twins Talk Study, issues of fairness, in terms of our respective contributions to the efforts, have been a point of contention between us.

Twins, as they express co-equal mutuality, exaggerate a positive aspect of selfways in the sense of the mythical ideal of everyone being equal or starting out with equal opportunities. A key concept here is what the linguist Anna Wierzbicka (2005) describes as the modern Anglo ethic of fairness as equal shares. Wierzbicka, a Polish native speaker, recounts how her bilingual, Polish American children demand fairness from her, when Polish child-rearing lexicons have no linguistic equivalent. *Fairness,* according to Wierzbicka, is not a language universal. *Fairness* is an English word that emerged under specific historical circumstances during the Enlightenment to become a key concept in modern Anglo ethno-ethics. Fairness, as equal shares, also implies tensions between reciprocity, mutuality, and cooperation and between what a person wants to do and what can be bad for others. Rules and procedures to regulate fair conduct are recognized as good, but they must also be the same for everyone. Not being fair implies doing something that is bad for another. Yet Lindholm (2001) also notes the cultural nexus of individuality and equality as complex since Western power or authority relations can be hidden behind trappings of equality. Equality, as sharing, coexists with more rivalrous forms of co-equality. Among these are competition to gain resources and a market economy that fosters rivalry rather than cooperation. One's freedom becomes limited by the interests of others (Wierzbicka 2005).

Western core values, in terms of mutuality such as sharing, flow through twins talk, but so do expressions of rivalry among equals. Although they state that their father's child-rearing agenda set a priority on guiding the development of each twin's individuality, Amy and Beth told us that they willingly shared as children. In their view, it is better to go without than to not be equal. They recount an episode of an uncle who took away Amy's birthday party plate, hoping to raise discord between the pair. The twin who still had her plate simply shoved hers between them so they could share. Interestingly, in contrast, Lucy and Linda, who grew up with fewer material resources, highlight having to share a birthday cake as one of the unfair things of their lives as children.

> Lucy: When I was little, every time we got a birthday cake it'd always say happy birthday Twins or Happy birthday, Linda and Lucy. I was sixteen years old before I got my own birthday cake.

> Linda: It doesn't bother me, but you got to recognize a lot of kids, especially right before being a teenager, they want their own things. They don't want to share.

Dorothy and I could certainly sympathize. As children, we always each had our own cake. Our grandmother made the cakes. They were exactly alike, except that we each chose our own color of frosting. Although we had two cakes, we were also told that, because we were twins, we could only have a party with friends (as opposed to only family) every other year. Our singleton siblings, however, were allowed to have a party with friends every year.

Yet negotiating fairness also engages tensions that constrain or limit mutuality in the twin relationship. Ginuh provides a rather benign account of these tensions. Arnette and Annette and Emil and Pete recognize the tensions inherent in the twin relationship but assert that fairness and equality must prevail. The following quotations feature balance as achieved through rather harmonious forms of cooperation:

> Ginuh: I think these differences came from childhood. That's a natural thing that God put within us to balance and offset each other.

Arnette and Annette state that even opposites must ultimately be equal.

> Arnette: Sometimes it's [being a twin] an oppositional type of thing, a negative and positive pole type of thing.
>
> Annette: Yeah, a yin and yang.
>
> Annette: What twins need to understand is that it's not so much that you're different but that your differences fit together like a puzzle.
>
> Arnette: Why waste energy arguing or fighting? It all balances out equal in the end.

Similarly, Pete and Emil say they do not fight; they "cooperate."

> Pete: We don't fight over it. We don't try to outdo each other, outwit each other, or cheat each other.
>
> Emil: That's right. Everything's equal and that's right.

Remember Karen and Kristy, the self-described good and evil twins? Despite their posturing as opposites, a sense of fairness also flows through their conversation. Even Karen, the "evil twin," gets equalized.

> Kristy: Mom always said Karen could come out of the shit house smelling like a rose.

Similarly, Lucy and Linda comment on the way that dominance gets equalized within the dyad. As adults, they remark that sharing has evolved its own rules.

> Lucy: As for dominance, if it has to do with what we are buying or what we're cooking or what we're having for dinner or something around the house, she's dominant. But the other stuff, I'm more dominant. I

> do the yard work. I bring money in. The bills are all set. We know which to which this goes to that [who pays how much for what].

> Linda: Anything that's left over goes to Twinfest.

Similarly, Arnette and Annette even portray the history of their relationship as dominant and submissive twins as having an inner dynamic of fairness and balance. In discussing how their personalities have changed over their lives, Arnette admits that as children she was the more outgoing and positive twin but also states that who would be considered the dominant twin has flip-flopped over the years. Annette agrees.

It is one thing to present a united front to the world as a form of empowerment. Yet sharing or cooperating to ensure fairness or maintain equality can also take a more dissonant, overtly rivalrous, or negative, turn. Although Amy and Beth state that if they could not share, they would each go without, many sets of twins mention less harmonious scenarios similar to that of Jean and Carol as they describe fairness as equality. Jean and Carol compete to be equal, making sure that through the process of sharing one twin does not receive more than the other.

> Carol: If you poured Pepsi in a glass—

> Jean: You'd better get out your micrometer because nobody got an extra drop.

> Dona: Were you competitive?

> Jean: No, we just had to be even—

> Carol: Just fair.

On fighting, they have this to say.

> Carol: We would fight and pull hair and bite each other.

> Jean: Whoever started it did the biting. When all was done, you just had to put your arm out to get a bite mark just like you gave your sister; the same amount of damage was done and we were even. We always had to be even.

The Twinsburg twins also express Wierzbicka's (2008) construction of fairness as an Anglo ethno-ethic in that fairness entails the idea
that what is good for one is good for the other. This mutual sense of
shared good is expressed by Mary and Martha as they discuss their ar-
tistic talents. When it comes to juried art competitions, they admit to
being very competitive with each other. Yet Martha goes on to say, "I
never lose to her. It's better for her to win than someone else." Mary
responds, "As long it is one of us, we don't care who wins." Yet what
was good for Karen, the "evil twin," was not so good for Kristy. Kristy
says, "Life isn't fair; Karen never got caught." As examples of unfairness,
the Twinsburg twins also relate tales of the wrong twin being punished
for a misdeed. Yet, more often, both twins would mutually choose to
either deny or confess the misdeed. This was a strategy to avoid punishment that usually worked because parents were reluctant to punish
the wrong twin. Here the notion of fairness trumps equality. This raises
additional themes or expressions of core Western values noted by Lindholm (2001): the right to choose and the duty to accept the consequences
of your choices. As twins mature, themes of same and different and
self-development as a matter of choice find expression in their talk.

Self-Development: Choice and Choice Making

Given what they remember as the equal playing fields of childhood,
the adult talking partners also describe same and different in terms
of individual agency and the life choices that each twin has made as
he or she has moved away from the natal family and into the wider
world. Likewise, successes and failures are believed to result, not from
destiny, but from one's own agentive actions and choices. Adult twins
also act to validate the reality of difference in terms of narratives
of choice or the decision-making strategies they have made largely
during their adult years. As Lukes (1973) states, principles of self-
development—freedom of choice, the right to choose or fix one's
destiny, and the very idea of liberty—are core Western values. When
expressed as an egocentric self, this means being in control and being
responsible for one's actions. These core values of choice and agency
are embedded in the competition, rivalry, distinctions of rank, and
corporate authority that characterize the Western capitalist market
system (Markus et al. 1997). North Americans like choices, and American capitalism is good at providing them. Choice in the Twinsburg

narratives illustrates a number of themes. Twins do not view their twinship as a matter of destiny. Twin life stories always include reflections of the time of their split or declarations of independence from each other. Choice, however, like fairness, encodes concepts of both balance and rivalry.

In contrast to the genetic determinism expressed by Teplica (2004) as he asked, "Do we have no control over our destiny?" twins talk shows that in terms of the wider society, mature twins see their life trajectories as the products of the choices they have made. Our talking partners want and choose to achieve success and live well. Their narratives reveal the importance of choice and agency in their lives—not in terms of abstract philosophies but in terms of everyday experiences and on-the-ground challenges of navigating a complex selfways within. Some portray choice as something that comes later in life, as Tina and Ginuh demonstrate in their conversation about how best to follow up on the Twins Talk Study.

> Tina: A study of life choices between twins would be fascinating.
>
> Ginuh: You hit the nail on the head. There are many things in our childhood that we did not have control over, and when you get older you can make choices.
>
> Tina: To be similar and do similar things, go to college together, work together or move away from each other.
>
> Ginuh: One choice sets a pattern of choices.

Jean and Carol also forcefully make statements about choice.

> Jean: Being identical doesn't mean you will make the same choices in life.
>
> Carol: Once you're married and you each have your own families and careers, it just leads to different people and situations that you deal with day in and day out. It leads you to a different place.

The following conversation of Tim and Tom starts with choices they both made to play the trombone and ends with a discussion of class and social mobility in America.

Tim: This doesn't have anything to do with being twins.
        Tromboning was a family habit. We chose to play the
        trombone because we liked trombones.

Tom: All our brothers and sisters have musical talent.

Dona: Do you ever think it's genetics over environment?

Tim [who has previously talked about being poor as children]:
        I think we all live in different environments and people
        will blame environment for a person not being the right
        type of person. I don't think environment has anything
        to do with it. It has to do with a person's ability to
        make whatever environment they are in to succeed
        or not succeed. We're all dealt the same hand, OK? If
        you're born into a poor family, that doesn't mean you're
        going to be a poor person when you grow up. Basically
        you have to have the attitude of changing your own
        environment, take advantage of the environment you
        live in, you know. It's your choice.

In short, the Twinsburg twins' answer to Teplica's destiny question would be a resounding no. Yet self-development as choice, as with finding one's own way in the wider worlds, takes a slightly different twist among the Twinsburg twins when it comes to stories about leaving home. Although these stories will receive more detailed attention in chapter 7, all the older talking partners recall key choice-making episodes in their lives, and a number of the younger twins are currently negotiating this stage as twins. These are accounts of what twins refer to as "the split"—a specific event or time in their lives when they ceased living together and went their separate ways. The split becomes a kind of declaration of independence from each other. The split for Donna and Dianne and Jenna and Steph came in their teens when one sister ran off and got married, leaving the other at home. Donna and Dianne lived in a happy home; Jenna and Steph did not. Placed in various foster homes, with family, and at orphanages, Jenna ran away from home at sixteen to get married, and two years later her sister, Steph, left home to join the navy. Also placed in an orphanage, at age thirteen, were Lucy and Linda. They have this to say.

Linda: I only stayed there six months and then I left.

Dona: Did you run away?

Linda: No, I just chose to leave.

Amy and Beth, ambitious and career oriented, are twins in their early twenties who now have to make choices concerning their split. These include career and partner choices. Beth, who has started teaching, and Amy, who is in public relations, are adjusting to living apart in order to pursue their respective careers. Below Beth compares her career to her sister's career.

Beth: I'm a teacher, my dad was a teacher and everyone says I'm following in my dad's footsteps. I chose to do what I wanted to do. But you also change to remain constant. As I make choices about career and new relationships, I will still remain close to Amy.

The examples above show an agentive choice to move toward greater independence in line with society's expectations of their selves as individuals and as twins. To realize their human potential, to take control, and to make their way in life, it is expected that each twin will eventually go her or his separate way. Yet when twins reflect on their life choices, the sense of balance and competition that runs through talk of same and different and fairness also characterizes talk about choice. Complementarity coexists with competition and rivalry. Tina and Ginuh talk about life choices they have made. Ginuh, who recently received her PhD in business, sees herself as the role model twin and her sister as playing catch-up.

Ginuh: I'm a corporate woman all the way; I've gotten just a little ahead of Tina. I've been married to the same husband for sixteen years and have lived in the same house for eleven years. Tina chose another route in life.

Tina: I've been married three times and I've lived in several different houses.

Ginuh: I got my master's degree one week before her first baby was born. I couldn't imagine why anyone would stay at home with children and she did that. I just

couldn't deal with it. But I'll admit that I had it easy.
Tina didn't have it easy when she chose to pursue a
master's degree as a single parent.

Tina and Ginuh both view life, however, as having equalized them as
they both have two children, are now both happily married, and have
successful careers. In more general statements about choice, Jeana
and Dina recall how they developed their respective personalities. Referring to her sister's lack of assertiveness, Dina has this to say.

> Dina: It's funny how you can pick and choose different
> characteristics from your parents that come out in us.

Bertha and Mabel describe competing to be equal when it comes to
self-management in terms of weight.

> Bertha: We got to talking about competition last night with
> the other twins.
>
> Mabel: We all talked about weight.
>
> Bertha: There's a certain amount of competition when it
> comes to our weight.
>
> Mabel: When Bertha says she is going to lose weight, I'd say,
> "I'm going to do it too."
>
> Bertha: When we start to get heavier, then we say, OK, one of
> us has to make a choice to stop eating.

Choice, as in a competition to be equal, is well developed in the
narratives of Mary and Martha. Mary and Martha both describe
themselves as graphic designers and their talk encompasses their lives
together and apart. They see many of their similarities as rooted in
shared closeness and shared child rearing, yet they see differences in
choices they have made in later life. For example, Mary married a military man, traveled widely, and had children, while Martha remained
single and stayed in the United States.

> Mary: I've picked up habits like being on time from my
> husband. I'm the one who got married. I would say
> the fact that I got married so young and moved away
> and developed new circles, new independence, and

> had to change in a lot of ways. Not just being married, but being a military wife, you're sort of a single married person a lot of the times and you have to take care of everything yourself and have to take care of a small child and having all those ties and binds. It changes me a lot. At the same time, she [Martha] had to take care of herself financially and all that. Our priorities shifted. Mine were holding my family together and hers were, do I have enough money to keep the car running?

Despite each twin feeling she had grown through different responses to different life challenges, Mary and Martha hold each other to account when it comes to moral personhood.

> Martha: It's a self-reflection kind of thing. At certain times in our lives, we look to each other, see where our strengths lie, and judge whether one of us shows that the other twin should be working to become a better person.

Other Cultural Considerations

Within the United States, constructions of self, personhood, and core values can vary in terms of region, ethnicity, social class, age, and gender. Although, according to Lindholm (2001), Americans do not see class, styles of individualism are mediated by class structure. As we have already seen, twin studies have been criticized for their middle-class bias (Charlemaine 2002; Joseph 2000). For example, recent studies in behavioral genetics (Harden, Turkheimer, and Loehlin 2007; Turkheimer et al. 2003) demonstrate that when social class becomes a variable, twins of lower socioeconomic standing show more difference on traits once supposed to be genetic than do middle-class twins. In middle-class North America, a primary goal in life is to establish an independent and unique self and at the same time bond with others (McCollum 2002). Yet, according to Kusserow (1999, 210), the middle classes are characterized by a "soft individualism" in which children are seen as blossoming to reach their full potential, while children from working-class families—which are characterized by a "hard individualism"—are expected to stick up for themselves, follow the rules, and not be too sensitive. The psychoanalyst

Dorothy Burlingham (1952) also recognized differences in the ways midcentury middle- and working-class parents treated their twins. Burlingham medicalizes the working classes. Working-class families, according to Burlingham, unlike middle-class families, stress similarity and dependence in their twins, thereby putting twins at risk for pathological ego development.

When it comes to gender, girls and women are critiqued as prima donna twins. Parents create a prima donna problem by dressing their twin girls alike and showing them off. This, according to Koch (1966), puts female twins in the role of being cute and entertaining. This, in turn, creates a dysfunctional lifelong hunger for attention. Not letting male twins off the hook, Koch (1966) faults them for veering toward the feminine. Male twins, when compared to singleton males, are more passive, less rivalrous, and less aggressive. Koch (1966, 163) labels male twins as "milder males"—like prima donnas, a potentially pathological, inappropriate gendering of twins.

Actually, the Twinsburg twins have quite a bit to say about gender and class. Some of this comes through in chapter 7.[7] As Murray (1993, 16) notes, when Western diversity is considered, the tendency is to look for alternate or "other configurations" of self in terms of class, gender, or race. Other configurations or forms of diversity that lack clear structural markers are often overlooked. It has been my intent in this chapter to present identical twins as one of these other configurations that embody and enact multiple stories of self in Western culture.

THINKING BEYOND AZTEC GODS

It is a standing convention in any book-length oeuvre or comprehensive review of twin research to make some sort of introductory tip-of-the-hat reference to twins from a historical or cross-cultural perspective. As Kaprio's (2007) chart, mentioned at the beginning of this chapter, illustrates, all knowledge is positioned. In his case, ethnology or cultural analysis of twins exists on the margins, or periphery, of twin research. Somehow, we find the notion that culture must be mentioned, whether to provide a little nonlocal color or to set the scene for twins as an exotic entity. Afterward, however, culture can be summarily ignored as having no relevance or analytic utility. I would place ethnology on the margins too if it could be summarized by Aztec gods and characters in Greek epic poems. But as an anthropologist who has conducted anthropological fieldwork in a variety of Western settings and who has critiqued the unexamined assumptions of cultures of science in fields of women's health, sexology and psychiatry,[8] I find twins and those who study them ripe topics, begging for more sophisticated forms of ethnographic or cultural analysis. As I have already argued, identical twins as a biosociocultural phenomenon challenge distinctions between nature and culture.

This chapter starts with a critique of twins researchers' understandings that although others have culture, they as scientific researchers do not. At the least, they merely accept the idea that their culture is a given. Not only do their samples represent a Western middle-class bias but so do their methods and goals of study. At the ICTS, even non-Western twins researchers work within assumed Western models concerning the nature of the body, bond, and kin.[9] Culture is seen as relevant to exotic practices, beliefs, and rituals of faraway peoples or exotic others, such as voodoo twins. As Marilyn Strathern (1992, 189) notes, "Although we strive to recognize the complexities of engineering relationships among the tribes of Papua New Guinea, we fail to recognize them at home." I find it of interest that despite the overweening interest in environment espoused by twins researchers, any attempts to deal with the cultural aspects of environment remain exceedingly naive. This is particularly true when it comes to any kind of argument that twins researchers, in terms of themselves and their research, are shaped by and reflect historically derived cultural values. Some of these culture-based assumptions and values are made explicit while others are more tacitly held. For example, twins challenge researchers to rethink what the term *individual* means, but as I have argued in this chapter, the idea that scientific rationalism is culture-free is itself a historically derived, culture-bound concept, as are assumptions about the nature of the individual.

How can we convince twins researchers that they too have a culture and that culture is central to twin studies? I have tried to do this in this chapter through a number of strategies familiar to anthropology. Using the supposition that cross-cultural comparisons can be a tool that makes us more familiar with our own taken-for-granted culture, I draw on exotic other cultures that exemplify alternative cultural constructions of self and personhood among the Wari and Nyaka, where notions of porous or joined body boundaries or the ideas of inhabiting one another's being are commonplace and normative for all members in the culture. I then turn my focus to cultural variation in terms of widely recognized and controversial cultural typologies of self. Conceptualizations of egocentric and sociocentric selves are used to describe variations of selfhood among and within particular cultural contexts. Twins talk demonstrates how self stylings characterize the practical experience of twins, and the Twinsburg twins distinguish between and blend both sociocentric and egocentric versions of their selves. As twins talk about being twins, they do frame their twinship within the wider Western sociocultural contexts. American core values, such as need for privacy, equality, self-development, and choice, all find expression in Twinsburg twins talk. Like other middle-class Americans, the Twinsburg twins express an intense desire for union and togetherness and a pressure from society for individuation and self-definition. Unlike other middle-class Americans, the partners are far less likely to view these different forms of self styling as unequal or as in opposition to each other.

Although Westerners do not necessarily consider themselves to be bounded and autonomous all the time (Murray 1993), and although psychic tensions to merge and to separate are recognized as panhuman (Lindholm 2000), twins are faulted, not just for being too sociocentric but also for failing to validate sociocentrism and egocentrism as opposites. Twins confound the supposed opposition of egocentric cultural ideals that glorify individual difference and autonomy and sociocentric ideals that value affiliation and mutuality. Twins and twinship thus subvert or jumble up a number of dualisms key to Western cultural traditions. The opposition of egocentric and sociocentric constructions of self is one of any number of key dualisms in Western culture relevant to the experience of twinship. Among these are nature/nurture, public/private, self/other, mind/body, unit/individual, pair/single, same/different, connected/separate, autonomous/mutual, independent/dependent, rational/irrational, and normal/abnormal. What twins researchers fail to recognize is the extent to which these constructions of self as culture-based have come to influence, unlike the mythological Quetzalcoatl, the so-called value-free, objective sciences of twins researchers.

7

KIN

We find that we have got closer as we got older. We are more close today than ever. There's no separation and there will never be a separation.

—*Janet, Twinsburg 2003*

I think that it's almost like you mature; just like you mature in a relationship, you mature in your twinship.

—*Dina, Twinsburg 2003*

We're going to the same retirement home.

—*Martha, Twinsburg 2003*

TWINSHIP IS A BIOSOCIAL FORM OF KINSHIP. CERTAINLY THE genetics of relationship dominate at the ICTS, but given the salient presence of mothers of twins groups, twins in terms of parent/child relationships also receive a great deal of attention. As twins move into adulthood, it seems to be only pathological forms of relationship between twins that captures the attention of twins researchers. Once again any kind of cultural analysis or voices of twins themselves are absent. This is interesting, considering that anthropology has experienced not only a renewed but a reformulated interest in kinship topics (di Leonardo 2008; Gullestad and Segelan 1997; Franklin and

McKinnon 2001; Franklin and Ragone 1998) that relates to how the talking partners express their twinship as the experience of a lifelong form of kinship. Much has been made of the new genetics as paving innovative ways to trace novel kinds of relationships (Pálsson 2007; Strathern 1995) in terms of shared substances, hidden codes or markers, and / or bundles of genes or even entire imagined communities. Yet, as we have seen in previous chapters, these invisible biological links are of limited interest to the talking partners. There are, however, four innovative trends in the anthropology and kinship literature that do capture the gist of twins talk about twinship as a special form of kinship. These include, first, a marked shift from concerns with lineal descent to an interest in collateral, consanguine, or intragenerational kin relationships (Hirsch 2003; Stone 2010). Thornton (2001, 157) refers to this type of collateral family analysis as "doing history sideways." Twinship, as an age-graded pair, has got to be the *sine qua non* of collateral kinship. Second, another area of interest in reformulating kinship highlights nongenetic ways of sharing or the interpersonal-social relational aspects of kinship. For example, kinship is discussed in terms of other forms of sharing (as in Miller's [2005] discussion of the Wari) that are characterized by a sense of human relatedness that is close and intense. Third, Micaela di Leonardo (2008) reassesses kinship as a matter of work or effort (see also Pálsson 2007) to maintain links across households that result in frequent contact, feelings of intimacy, emotional vitality, and emotional fulfillment. A final new direction in anthropological kinship studies focuses on the notion of kinship as choice (Stone 2010). For example, Weston (1991) looks at how gays and lesbians construct their own families based on choice. In this chapter we will see many of these new themes of kinship reflected in the narratives of the adult talking partners. *Twins Talk,* not only goes beyond a centralizing perspective on lineal parent-child relationships but shifts attention from childhood to adulthood.

What these new approaches to kin and kin relationships share is an approach to family histories of competing assumptions about identities and relatedness, which in kinship become a complex and processual phenomenon (Pálsson 2008, 61). In this sense, Pálsson argues kinship is no longer fixed or abstract but is continually under construction. Similarly, Franklin and McKinnon (2001) imply that kin maintenance from the ground up draws on a process of creative negotiation in which points of connections and relationships are brought into being through personal agency and practice. This kind of social practice approach to kinship entails a dynamic aspect of being related to another person. Kin becomes a study of the contexts of relationships—how and why who interacts with whom and how it changes through different circumstances and over time (Miller 2005). In previous chapters we have explored issues of self work among identical twins as it relates to the experience of identity, relatedness, and sharing, from a combination of biological, psychological, and cultural perspectives, as expressed and reflected in the narratives of the Twinsburg twins. Although twins can hardly be biologically untwinned, the narrative-based, life-cycle perspective that follows shows how twins work to make choices about the different directions their twinship will take throughout their lives as they negotiate both closeness and distance in their twin-twin relationship.

A TIME TO TELL

Every other year when I teach my psychological anthropology class, I hand out three pictures of twins of different ages and ask the students to write short stories about them. Students' stories are varied and often quite humorous or fantastical.[1] Writing about Diane Arbus's (Arbus 1972, 54) famous and haunting picture of identical twin girls, one student ended his story with the question, "What will become of them?" Another student remarks,

> One wonders how life will affect these girls. Will they strive to
> be different, fight for their sense of individuality, or will they
> remain two halves of the whole, one person with two bodies?
> How much will their culture affect these choices, and will
> they blend different and same into a medium that makes them
> happy? Maybe one will be different while the other will try to
> emulate her sister. Only time will tell. (Dodd 2005)

In this chapter, I give the talking partners their time to tell. A fascination with adult twins as persons is relatively absent from the literature.[2] This is especially true for twins who grow up to become self-involved in relationships and modes of caring and sharing that transcend the dyad through marriage, careers, separate residences, happenstance, etc. Yet, as we will see, twinship as expressed in the

Twinsburg twins narratives and festival attendance evolves and matures over the life cycle. In my opinion, it is with the narratives of this chapter that the talking partners come through as persons in their own right. This chapter, more than any of the others, belongs to the Twinsburg twins. It is shaped by their own narratives and revelations about their experiences of twinship.

Besnier (1994, 203) describes narrative as a constant foregrounding and backgrounding of different aspects of individuals' identities as they move across and negotiate time, space, and social contexts. While Besnier depicts narrators as protagonists of their own stories, our Twinsburg talking partners, positioned side by side, became "cotagonists" as they simultaneously and interactively told their individual and collective stories. The narratives that follow show how, as already argued, self emerges out of social practice (Holland and Leander 2004) and persons exist in continuous states of construction and reconstruction (Gergen 1991). As cotagonists of their own stories, the Twinsburg twins show that whether together or apart, they continue to enact dynamically positioned identities that are lifelong.

ACROSS THE AGES

One advantage of the "tellings" is that as twins copresent their twin-scapes from a life-cycle perspective, they put some ethnographic meat on the bones of what *kin work* means. Our talking partners represent different age groups and social classes. They have differing life experiences and different stories to tell, as twins and as individuals. As they relate their life tales, there may be sections that seem abnormal to a singleton, but twins see them as normal. As attendees of a festival, they have a vested interest in maintaining their twinship. That is not necessarily the case for all twins. In the case of the Twinsburg sampling, they provide both a cross-sectional and longitudinal perspective on the practical experiences of twinship and self work as a lifelong process of identity management. Twins manage and sustain twinship as a special type of kinship, even though their life choices and selfways may take them far from each other.

TWINSHIP AND TWINSCAPES: LIFE-CYCLE PERSPECTIVES

What can a life-cycle perspective reveal about self stylings and feelings of affiliation and sharing between and among twins? The talking partners included six men and thirty-eight women who (in 2003) ranged in age from twenty-two to seventy-seven. The Twinsburg twins reported that their twinship was important to them but had its own twin cycle that "matured" (Dina) or "evolved" (Mabel) over their adult lives. The Twinsburg and ITA twins depicted twinship as a matter of work and negotiation that faced different challenges at different points in their lives. While the twin research literature tends to focus on childhood and separation at adolescence or early adulthood, the twinscapes revealed in twins talk employed a more long-range perspective. Four postchildhood life-cycle stages emerged from twins talk narratives (see table 2). They are as follows:

1. Negotiating "the split" (twins ages 22 to 26)

2. Negotiating other relationships and careers (twins ages 36 to 46)

3. Twin kin work, renegotiations, and reprioritizations of twinship (twins ages 54 to 58)

4. Retirement and renewal, investing in the idea of twinship, plans for reunion, or actuating coming together again (twins ages 61 to 77)

TABLE 2. Talking partners by age stage			
Stage 1	*Stage 2*	*Stage 3*	*Stage 4*
22 Chris & Carla	36 Tina & Ginuh	54 Carol & June	61 Janet & Judy
23 Amy & Beth	36 Sandy & Cindy	54 Lucy & Linda	62 Pat & Phyllis
24 Jeana & Dina	39 Karan & Kim	55 Dona & Dorothy	64 Dianne & Donna
25 Gina & Ginger	41 Jenna & Steph	56 Annette & Arnnete	69 Jenny & Julie
26 Randi & Dante	45 Tim & Tom	58 Mabel & Bertha	74 Helen & June
	45 Mary & Martha		77 Pete & Emil
	46 Karen & Kristy		

Some cautions, however, should be noted for reading what follows. The "staged" narratives are drawn from twins at a contemporary stage and from the memories of similar stages among older twins. It is perhaps the fact that these "stages" stand out in the memories of twins that gives them their definitive features. But understandably the sociocultural and historical context (as well as class, region, ethnicity, urban/rural residence, and gender context) is different for those born toward the beginning and those born toward the end of the twentieth century. Coming of age in the 1940s is certainly different than coming of age at the birth of the new century. In addition, a myriad of other contexts and situations shapes differences in the experiences of twins. For example, Emil and Pete were first-generation Italian Americans, born ninth and tenth of eleven children into a poor immigrant family. Steph and Jenna and Lucy and Linda came from dysfunctional (their term) families and were put into orphanages in their early teens. Janet married a rich man and Judy a poor one. Kim and Karan and Cindy and Sandy are two sets of twins in the same family; Kim and Karan like being twins, and Cindy and Sandy say it means nothing to them but they attend the festival because of their love for their older twin sisters. Furthermore, there is a good deal of serendipity in the life stories as one twin "gets lucky" and "shit happens" to the other. Moreover, twins from very large families, like Pete and Emil, and Tim and Tom, remember their childhoods in terms of a collective shared intimacy with all their siblings or a special caretaker sibling, remarking that their twinship begins to emerge in significance as they leave the intimate, crowded spaces of their childhood behind.

STAGE 1: NEGOTIATING THE "SPLIT"

While collecting background data for our talking sessions, Dorothy and I asked all our talking partners to describe their histories of co-residence as twins. We expected to simply write the number of years lived together in a box. The question, however, raised a host of issues for our talking partners, which begged for (and got) further verbal elaboration. As in the case of other terms we were not initially familiar with (e.g., *singleton, twindom,* and *twin dynamic*), the term *split* emerged as a key component of their stories. The split entails each twin going his or her separate way and maintaining or renegotiating the twin relationship. Previously Dorothy and I would have referred to this as *separating* or *going separate ways in life*. The split entails the end of shared place and space, a physical movement away from the immediate domains of each other, and entry into nonshared activities and other relations. The split is a popular topic of conversation among twins as they casually talk to each other inside and outside of the pavilion.

When twins were asked to comment on their lives as twins, split or break stories mark an important transition point in our talking partners' lives as twins. Leaving home is one thing; leaving your twin is another. Chris and Carla, Randi and Dante, Amy and Beth, Gina and Ginger, and Jeana and Dina, all in their twenties, are dealing with the split as being currently negotiated or as having recently taken place. Chris and Carla continue to live together but are pursuing their respective careers and different interests. Randi and Dante and Amy and Beth are in the process of establishing separate residences, establishing careers, and adjusting to significant others in their twin's relational world. Gina and Ginger and Jeana and Dina are dealing with the marriage of one twin.

Chris and Carla

Chris is a part-time student and works in a day care center. Her sister, Carla, graduated from college and works as a commercial credit analyst. They live together and have spent a total of only three summers apart. They state that it is cheaper to have a roommate, and Carla makes more money, which helps subsidize Chris's education and part-time employment. They are both at a stage where they are financially independent and feel that since they would need a roommate anyway to share expenses, they might as well have a roommate with whom they can get along—someone with the same basic morals. Despite living together, Carla and Chris say that they have their own identities and very different personalities that lead them to interests and non-overlapping sets of friends. For example, while both are athletic and participate in community sports leagues, Carla plays basketball and Chris baseball. At age twenty-two, they figure that living together and looking alike does not compromise their individual identities. Carla states, "When we were younger, up to age ten, we were a lot more similar than we are now. We liked everything the same. We wanted to be exactly the same. We referred to each other as twin or 'my twin'; now we just say 'sister.' We live together because we get along so well, but we are separate now and go our own ways." Carla and Chris state that they realize eventually career or love interests will lead them further into their separate ways, but for now living together is a matter of convenience. They do not anticipate any problems with the split and expect that they will always maintain a close relationship.

Randi and Dante

Randi and Dante, age twenty-six, are both recent college graduates who are beginning careers in accounting. Despite advice from their mother "to mix it up a little bit," Randi and Dante went to the same college, took the same courses, had a common set of friends, and had girlfriends who always got along with each other. At present they live together. For a while, they even worked at the same place, although they eventually found this to be a disadvantage since the bosses, for reasons of fairness, were unwilling to promote one twin over the other. Randi and Dante felt that working at the same job was holding them both down. Randi and Dante are currently facing a lot of pressure to split up. Dante says, "Everyone always says to split up. I don't know. They [friends] ask, 'Why are you always hanging out with your brother? Why don't you establish your own identity?'" Randi adds, "A lot of people just don't get it. You can't explain it. I have a brother that is two years younger and I'm not like that with him. If you're not a twin, you just don't understand." When they get back from Twinsburg, however, Randi will be moving out of the apartment that he and his girlfriend share with Dante. Randi's girlfriend seems to be instrumental in this split. Randi will not be moving far away and will stay in close contact with Dante. It will be the first time in their twenty-six years that they have not lived together.

The big issue when they return from Twinsburg is splitting up all of their (copurchased) extensive and valued CD and DVD collections in a manner that is fair and does not lead to fighting. Like Chris and Carla, who liked living together because they shared the same moral values, Randi and Dante feel that a key strength in their relationships is the values they place on being traditional Italian males, and family is of central importance in their lives. This means the continued cultivation of their twinship in terms of established, emergent, and anticipated relationships, including the spouses and children each might have.

Amy and Beth

Amy and Beth, age twenty-three, have always been close. Beth says, "We grew up so close together. We went to a very, I guess you could call it preppy, snobby, rich kid school. And we are by no means preppy, rich, or snobby. We learned to lean on each other a lot in high school because everybody else was like a flirt. We had friends, but we didn't have that many friends. We learned to really depend on each other in high school." They are currently, however, negotiating separate residences, separate careers, and new relationships, while each is pursuing her individual lifelong dream. Beth is working on a graduate school degree and is an eighth grade teacher. Amy, a college graduate, works in public relations and aspires to be a writer. They went to the same college and roomed together but chose different majors. Beth majored in elementary and special education, and Amy majored in English with a minor in public relations. They currently live together but had lived apart for the last year while Amy did a professional internship. They had separated for the first time, in college, when Beth did her student teaching. Beth describes their recent separation as awful, while Amy states that the excitement of the internship made it less awful for her. Nevertheless, she missed her twin and her family, but she missed her twin more. When separated, they call each other three or four times a day.

Amy and Beth felt that when they were apart, they developed different sets of friends. Boyfriends, referred to as "best friends," are now an issue. Beth says, "A major difference in us now is that since college we developed different sets of friends. She can't stand my best friend. We've had our times because she always thought that my best friend, Tony, was taking me away from her and I felt her best friend, Josh, was taking her away from me. So, of course, we've had out-and-out go-rounds. But Tony is very nice to Amy, even though Amy's not nice to him all the time." Amy responds, "Sometimes he's nice to me." Amy and Beth always assumed that their careers would lead them in different life directions. Yet it appears to be relationships, especially Beth's, that are pulling them apart.

> Amy: She [Beth] actually changed our twindom. He [Beth's boyfriend] did. It was sort of like wait a second here. He's not both our friends. He's just Beth's friend, and he is pulling her away from me. I think it was at that point I realized that, yes, my sister is going in a different direction than I am and she's not always around like she used to be. I was so sad. So upset because it was just like she was gone. It was crazy for a couple of months. I needed to find another best friend, and luckily about six months later was when I met my best friend.

Later in the conversation, Amy credits her boyfriend, Tony, as a turning point in her and Beth's relationship. Tony, according to Amy, is "the one big thing that really changes us and that's how we really became different people." This, however, will not change Amy and Beth's relationship. Amy has this to say about her relationship with Tony:

> Amy: He's an only child. He does not understand what it's like to have a brother or a sister, and he really doesn't understand what it's like to have a twin. He doesn't understand the connection that she and I have. We've been friends for a year now and over the year he's gotten a little better about it because he realizes. Our relationship [Beth and Amy] is very special. I think it will remain constant through the changes. I don't plan on ever changing. She is going to remain my sister whether I like it or not.

Amy adds, "Things may change slightly. We'll remain very close. I moved back from Florida to be with my family. I couldn't be away from my family for that long. So I think it's going to stay the same."

Having already dealt with a number of romantic relationship issues, Gina and Ginger and Jeana and Dina are adjusting to the marriage of one twin.

Gina and Ginger

Both Gina and Ginger, twenty-five, have a high school education and work in retail sales. They work in the same department but in different stores. Gina and Ginger lived together until they were twenty-one, and then Ginger moved out to get married. They currently live about five miles away from each other and continue to see each other a lot. Ginger has been married for three years and has a two-year-old son. Ginger remarks that the use of *we* has now become problematic since "a lot of people think I'm talking about me and my husband and not me and my sister." Gina characterizes herself as the quiet twin and Ginger as the more talkative and dominant twin. Yet she also characterizes herself as the more independent twin. Gina says, "I can't imagine not being a twin. I couldn't imagine being like an individual, you know. Although I'm a little more independent than she is, she's always the one who depended on me. She has always had someone around her—me or her husband. You know, she's never really been by herself."

As to the expanding kin associations in their lives, Gina clearly dotes on Ginger's son but states that she does not want children at this stage of her life. Her sister finds this hard to understand since Gina is so good with her nephew. Early on, the baby confused his mother and her sister. Gina and Ginger describe this as "cute" and Ginger describes her twin as a kind of built-in babysitter. He now calls his aunt "mommy Gina." Gina also feels pressure from her sister to get married but is in no rush to do so. As to Gina's husband, this exchange is interesting as it shows the enhanced self and a co-contemporarity being negotiated across new kin ties. Ginger says, "Sometimes my husband gets jealous and he'll blow up. Usually when I want to go out, it is with my sister. It's not always with him. I think he gets kind of jealous with the relationship we have together. He didn't really know when he married me that he kind of married Gina too." Ginger responds, "Yes, he does get very jealous. When we plan a road trip— we plan one every year. This year it is coming here to Twinsburg. So I think he thinks this is kind of crazy. He thinks we are children."

Jeana and Dina

Jeana and Dina, twenty-four, also reflect on the complexities of the process of splitting. Jeana's and Dina's comments on marriage and careers eloquently express their dilemma. Jeana and Dina are both registered nurses. They lived together until they completed nursing school and Jeana got married. In fact, Jeana's husband had casually dated Dina for a while and Jeana did not like him at that time. Jeana told her sister, "I don't know why you keep hanging out with him." A year later he called to wish them a happy birthday and started dating Jeana. Dina says, "That was our first true division. It was like a drastic thing for me when she moved out." Jeana's take on the marriage follows.

> Jeana: [Marriage is] kind of like a culture shock, because you're not used to living with another, well, a male to begin with. I changed jobs. I felt that I had lost my best friend, even though she was only one hour away. Then having to adjust to getting married at the same time made the first six months [of marriage] very

hard. My job was stressful too. I felt like I lost my best friend. Marriage has led to differences between us [Jeana and Dina]. Since I've gotten married, we've kind of gone into separate little worlds, because she is still a single and in the single life. She lives a little bit on the wilder side. I'm settled down more. We [Jeana and husband] have couple friends and she has single friends. Adjusting to the whole married thing, all the responsibilities of marriage and everything, was a big culture shock.

Dina also states that she does not have the financial obligations of her sister, who is paying a mortgage and putting her husband through nursing school. Living in a bigger city with more free time, Dina says she goes out more and takes more vacations than her sister. Moreover, she adds that "when Jeana does have free time, she wants to be with her husband. She doesn't want to go out on the town with me." None-theless, they call each other every day. Jeana and Dina do say that mar-riage has brought out the differences between them. Jeana's husband had said that they are lucky because they will always be each other's best friend. Jeana does remark that her husband also experienced some jealously over her relationship with her twin. This stemmed from the fact that Jeana wanted to spend "sister time" together that excluded him at least once a week. Dina, who is also in a serious relationship, is quite explicit about how marriage does and does not enter the twin relationship as a matter of connection and relationality.

Dina: Just as you mature in any relationship, you mature in your twinship. It's like when you are young, it's like, "Cool, we look alike." We have a full-time playmate. This is great. Then you get a little bit older and you realize how important it is and value more what you have because you realize that, hey, there's not really a lot of twins around here. You value that more as you get older; you tend to appreciate having someone there because you take it for granted. Singletons tell us, "You are so lucky; you have no idea what you have." And that's true. I never realized how close we were and how much I valued it until she did get married. While

Jeana was dating, we never had issues with it because she still lived at home. She lived with me. We always talked. We were study buddies because we were going to school at the same time. But then when she moved out, I felt bad because at the beginning I resented her husband. Because it was like "you took my twin away." And I would have never admitted that when I was going through that stage. I mean, it's taken me awhile to say, "Yes, I guess I was mean to him." I guess I wasn't nice. I can remember her saying, "OK, Tom is coming with us and please be civil to him." It's taken a while and it only happened when they got married, not when they were dating. Then I didn't really see any issue of it. And then they got married and it was like "oh my gosh." You know, she doesn't live with me anymore and I've really felt that.

Currently, Dina feels that adjustments have been made. Dina has this to say about twinship.

Dina: It's not just a sister; it's not just your best friend. It's something you are born into. You can't pay to be in it. You can't be invited into it. It's a bond that will never break. We've had our differences. When she got married, we had our rocky time, but we made it through.

REMEMBERING THE SPLIT

Jeana and Dina, Lucy and Linda, and Mary and Martha also talk about a presplit. They recount this not as current events but as memories. While they argue about whether it was during eighth grade or before, Jeana and Dina report having an early adolescent rebellion in their twinship when they reacted against what they perceived as parent and school forcing their togetherness. Jeana says they were so much together in school that it created "some kind of aggression."

Jeana: There was a time when I hated being a twin, hating the attention, hating the pointing, hating everything about it. We didn't want to be together after eighth grade. We wanted to start having our own friends, to be our own individuals. We didn't dress alike for like a two- [to] three-year period. We would go a week or two without having a close conversation. We went in total opposite directions. Then we realized that we just liked being together. Is it not weird?

Similarly, Lucy and Linda talk about their very early teens as a period when they rebelled against dressing alike and being made each other's chaperones.

Linda: Lucy wanted to go on this date. But Mother said she was too young to date so I had to go with her. We're in this pickup [that] her boyfriend's driving, and I'm sitting next to this door. We go around a corner and, well, the door flies open and she pushes me out. And off they go. I figure that when she's through with her date, she'll just come back and pick me up.

Although the split is an important life and relationship marker in the memories of older twins, they report their splits much more matter-of-factly than do their younger cohorts. Pete and Emil, age seventy-seven, depict their split as drama-free. It dates back to the pre–World War II period.

Pete: Well, we both went to join the service, but I failed on account of my hearing problems.

Emil: I was drafted.

Pete: He went to the service.

Emil: That's when we split up. Back at the age of eighteen.

Pete: And I stayed with the railroad, and then waited for him to come out. He was my best man at my wedding. There was no job for him around, so he reenlisted.

Emil: And I stayed in the military and made a career out of it. And he made a career out of the railroad.

But like their younger counterparts, older twins can also reflect on the split in terms of what it meant in terms of new relationships, different life trajectories, and identities. Relationships are discussed in the following exchange between Tim and Tom, age forty-five.

Tim: I've never been married.

Tom: In fact, my wedding anniversary is tomorrow at eighteen years. So that's been another, I guess, something that is very different. Otherwise, I could have said, "Well, I can't get married until he gets married." I mean, I could have done that. But I got married anyway. So I would say in one respect we are still very similar, but in another fashion we are very different because of our personal relationships with other people.

It is important to note at this juncture that although there is a generic element to the split stories, they are also individualized and context specific. For example, Steph and Jenna, forty-one, had very bad memories of an abusive mother. They were put in an orphanage, and the split came when Steph ran away and joined the navy. Mary and Martha, forty-five, split over an argument they had in midlife that kept them distant from each other for years.

As in the case of Pete and Emil, there was a serendipitous quality to our split. Dorothy and I, compared to the Twinsburg twins, made the split relatively late in life. We both went to the same college and both majored in anthropology. We lived in separate dorms but took all but one of our classes together. We went into the same graduate program. As we completed our MAs in anthropology, one of our professors took Dorothy aside and another one took me aside and had a little split chat. We were both urged to go to different graduate schools in order to pursue our PhDs. The reason put forth was that we looked so much alike that our professors could not tell one of us from the other. To us, this seemed very unfair because we felt our written work and talent in the field were very different. We also felt one of us was being asked to take a second choice in life just because our professors were overwhelmed by our physical similarities. We did take their point that it was about time we were going our separate ways in life. Although we doubt it seemed so at the time, we were the subjects of a hegemonic Western bias toward autonomous individualism. Actually, the split was no big deal. After we received our MAs, we were offered a job at a small college. The college did not care which one of us accepted the job (poor Dorothy: all her As, compared to my Bs, did not help her get the job). We flipped a coin and I got the job. That was the split. It was time to do it and, for us, it was no big deal. That flip of the coin did, however, have a profound impact on our subsequent lives (Davis 2008).[3] Through our twenties and thirties I would become more career-oriented and Dorothy more family-oriented.

STAGE 2: NEGOTIATING OTHER RELATIONSHIPS

The next stage includes twins in their thirties and forties who have negotiated the split and are established in intimate relationships that transcend the twin bond. Karan is married with two children, and Kim, who has one child, is currently divorced. Tina and Ginuh and Karen and Kristy are married with children still at home. For Mary and Martha, Tim and Tom, and Jenna and Steph, one twin is married with children and the other is not. Sandy and Cindy are both currently single and have no children, although Cindy is divorced.

Karan and Kim

Karan and Kim, thirty-nine, are the older of two sets of twins in their family. They characterize themselves as traditional women who like being twins. In contrast, their twin sisters, Sandy and Cindy, are more ambivalent about their twinship. Karan and Kim both have some college training but did not graduate. Karan works in sales while Kim works in accounting. They grew up in a family of eight children. Karan and Kim split when Kim got married at age eighteen and Karan went to college. Eventually Kim got divorced and moved back in for a short while with Karan, who was by then married. Currently, Karan and Kim live about forty-five miles apart. Karan describes herself and her sister as hard workers whose families and kids come first. Karan and Kim have come to terms with their separate lives but still see their relationship as strong. They call each other frequently, even if what they have to say is as simple as, "Hi, I'm going to bed now." Karan and Kim state that they have had their arguments and differences but they always keep the lines of communication open. They have always been able to successfully work their arguments out.

> Karan: I have two children so I'm sympathetic about anything. Kim and I are the same type. If she calls me I'm going

to let her unload, get it off her chest, and try to make her feel better. If she needs me there to lean on or if we are both having a bad day, we'll meet somewhere halfway between our two homes and have dinner.

Tina and Ginuh

Tina and Ginuh, thirty-six, are also both married with children. They are both college instructors in business schools, but Ginuh has her PhD and Tina is working on her master's degree. They were separated after their second year of college when they got married "and went in different directions temporarily." For about three years, Ginuh lived in a different state and "that was as far as we could handle it." They now live, as Tina says, "point zero six miles from each other." They continue to see each other daily and have keys to each other's homes. Both have two children, a boy and a girl each, all of whom Tina says resemble each other. They say that their children are equally comfortable in each other's households. Tina and Ginuh readily care for each other's children and feel free to punish them, noting that they would be uncomfortable disciplining their other siblings' children.

Ginuh has been married to the same man for eleven years and has lived in the same house. Tina has been married three times and has lived in several different houses. They have a lot to say about their respective marriages.

> Ginuh: We married definitely different people . . . and that includes all three of Tina's husbands. Being married at age eighteen meant that for half of my life I was being raised by my husband.

> Tina: Being a single parent changes your whole outlook on life. Also, being married to a man who has also been divorced means that you know when it's not worth a fight.

> Ginuh: She [Tina] and her husband are good at bickering.

They also feel that their current husbands get along really well and are accepting of their twinship.

> Ginuh: It's not double dating; you have kids. It's that we like hanging out together.

Tina: We are able to camp in a camper together. Our
          husbands are not intimidated by our relationship.

Ginuh: Not at all. I think I would say our husbands are pretty
          cool. They like it. They think it is pretty cool. I mean,
          they've been talking about this twin thing [Twinsburg
          festival] longer than we have. I think they are pretty
          proud of it.

Tina: I don't know how to say it. They are proud of us. They
          think we are the prettiest set of twins. They really
          think it's all neat.

When Tina was first married, she took time off to stay home with
her children. Then, becoming a single mom, Tina learned to juggle
work, school, and children. Ginuh characterizes herself as a corporate woman the entire way. Ginuh's education was paid for by her
employer and she delayed having her first child until she had finished
her master's degree. Ginuh says this of her sister:

Ginuh: She doesn't rely on me for her personal life, but we
          do a lot of together things. We go to church together.
          We are involved in the same things together in the
          community. I've been elected to every kind of office
          you can imagine in different community things. She's
          always there working, but I'm there leading.

Tina says that, in general, "Ginuh is always slightly ahead of me
in life; it's comfortable for me because I know that is where I will go
too. I have my own life and my own decisions. I am in control of my
own life, but still there is a lot that involves both of us." Talking about
conversations with surviving twins, Ginuh remarks, "I could lose my
husband and recover. I would be heartbroken. But if it were her, there
would be a permanent hole there."

Karen and Kristy

Karen and Kristy (the self-described "good and evil" twins), forty-six,
are both married and live in the same town. Karen has a high school
education and works in a pharmaceutical factory. Kristy, who has some
college, is an insurance adjuster. Initially Karen and Kristy were in the
same classes at school but because their father moved around a lot,

they were separated at bigger schools. Kristy characterizes the split as when she got married, which was about one week out of school. Yet at this time their parents moved away, and Karen stayed with an older sister through the week and spent weekends with her newly married twin. Kristy says, "We were kind of back and forth. It wasn't a traumatic split." Later in the interview Kristy is asked about how she felt getting married and leaving her sister. She responds, "Good riddance!" To which Karen adds, "Actually, I didn't care. I was staying weekends with her so it was kind of nice. When she got married, we only lived a quarter mile from each other. Now we live like three miles from each other. All our life we have been near each other, so we never had the trauma of separating." Karen and Kristy freely go into each other's houses without knocking. Kristy says, "We're both very close with each other's kids. So that is really nice. It's like everything's hers and mine." Karen adds, "Her daughter always said, 'I have two moms; I can't get away with anything.'" Karen and Kristy each have two children (Karen has two boys and Kristy has a boy and a girl). They had their first child about a year apart; Karen had a son a year before Kristy had a daughter. Although their children do not look alike, they are very close.

> Karen: We raised our kids like brothers and sisters. They saw
> each other every day. And a lot of times I babysat her
> daughter when she was at work, and when she came
> home from work, she would take my son to her house
> and leave her daughter with me. We'd swap them
> in the morning or whatever at night. Sometimes we
> never swapped them back.

> Kristy: It was a kind of an all-around thing, a joint effort.

> Karen: It worked because they are fine young men and women.

Kristy has also raised three foster children who had lost their parents.

When asked to tell a favorite twin story, Kristy relates an incident in which she left her twin at the Twinsburg twins festival. This is their seventeenth time at Twins Days. She tells the story to show that Kristy has a temper but also to illustrate the relational pulls adult twins experience. It is important to note that this conversation is punctuated with laughter. Kristy tells how the twins were sitting in

Karen's car, off a predetermined highway exit, waiting for Kristy's husband (a truck driver) to stop off his route for a brief visit. It was a rainy weekend and Karen was saying that she did not want to go back to the festival the next day. A lively exchange follows that balances twin work versus kin work.

Kristy: It was a muddy and rainy weekend. She [Karen] says, "I'm not going back [to the festival] tomorrow."

Karen: It was my foster son's birthday that morning. My husband was coming through with a load. He was driving a truck. He stopped by to meet us at the exit. It was raining and muddy. And I said, "Well, if it's rainy and muddy and you're not going there, I'm leaving. It's Carl's birthday and I'm going back home for it."

Kristy: I said, "Would you miss it [the next day at Twinsburg]?"

Karen: I said yes. It was his birthday and he had not had too many [birthday parties]. I raised three children who lost their parents and he didn't have a lot of good birthdays. I just didn't want him not to have his birthday celebrated on that day. I had made his birthday cake and everything, stuck it in the freezer before I left. Everything was ready. But I hadn't planned to go back for it. But since it was raining and she threw such a fit . . . she didn't get our button. We always get a button—always. Well, she couldn't get a button the day before because she was too fat [a big bone of contention throughout the interview]. So she said, "Aren't you even going to go over and get a button with me?" and I got nasty and I said, "Why? Did you lose weight since yesterday? 'Cause you were too fat yesterday for a button."

Kristy: And it just escalated. It was bad. She left me.

Karen: I left her. I left with my husband in the truck and left her in the car. I left her.

Karen and Kristy also have an interesting philosophy about mid-life and being together. Although they admit that husbands, careers, and life experiences can shape and change people, they feel that in their case the fact they do live close to each other and see or talk to each other every day means that their differences will less pronounced. Karen says, "When you're away from each other, you learn to live separately; you're going to learn to live separate lives. That's just the way it is. We never did that." Kristy adds, "We've had very different experiences, but because we've shared them with each other, it hasn't made a difference in our lives."

In the cases of Tim and Tom, forty-nine, Mary and Martha, forty-five, and Jenna and Steph, forty-one, one twin is married while the other is not. All three pairs of twins note the continued importance of their twinship after the marriage of one twin.

Tim and Tom

Tim and Tom both have university educations. Tim is in technical sales and Tom is an engineer. Tom is married with no children. Like Karan and Kim and Tina and Ginuh, they grew up in a large family. Tim and Tom say that their oldest brother, who was seventeen years their senior, was often confused for their father. He was also their primary caretaker. Tim and Tom went from grade school to university together. At university, they attended the same classes and had the same major in business. Once graduated, they accommodated to a poor job market by getting real estate licenses and working together. They did everything together until Tom (the engineer) got a job in Sri Lanka that split them up for two years. Tom met his Australian-born wife in Sri Lanka. Tom travels a lot; Tim does not. Currently they live about two blocks away from each other. Although they do not see each other every day, they see each other often because of similar hobbies. They e-mail each other every couple of days. Their hobbies include playing the trombone in several different groups. (All their brothers and sisters show musical talent and two elder brothers also played the trombone.) Tom says, "We play somewhat professionally but don't make a living out of it." When asked how they are same or similar, Tom immediately responds that they share their interest in music but adds, "But, like, I'm married and he's single." Tim adds, "I didn't have a wife. I didn't have a girlfriend. So I focused my relationships into the business. I was pretty successful at doing that." Throughout the interview, Tom asserts his career dedication and success. Moreover, during most of his life, his facial birthmark has resulted in his having a shy personality. He describes himself as "a person who likes to work behind the scenes." The successful surgeries on his birthmark, he feels, has allowed him to build more self-confidence and improve his interpersonal interaction and speaking skills, thus enhancing his career. Tim and Tom characterize themselves as close, always offering each other advice (solicited and unsolicited) and remaining the best of friends. Tom's interview comes toward its end with a comment about his wife.

> Tom: I would have liked my wife to come with me but she chose not to come with me. She chose not to come with me five years ago because she said, "I am not a twin; why should I come?" So on the negative side of it, I left my wife out of something that I'm part of. It's like I am what I am, but she can never become a part of what I am in that regard. And I would have liked her to come because I think that when we were here for the first time five years ago, it blew my mind to see so many people looking alike. But would my wife be seeing the same things? I don't understand that dynamic, what a nontwin thinks of a twin. I don't understand that yet.

Mary and Martha

Mary and Martha, forty-five, have university degrees, are graphic designers, and sell T-shirts at Twinsburg. Although they live in different states, they run an online business together. They grew up together, but Mary got married to a military man when she was nineteen. Since he was in the service for twenty years, the twins lived apart from each other for most of their adult lives. Martha has never been married but refers to Mary's child as her "half daughter." Mary responds that her daughter says she has two moms; she refers to Martha as her "other mom." Although they currently live long distances apart, they get together to sell souvenirs in the Twins Days market. They may get together only two or three times a year, yet they call each other frequently. Martha says, "We got AT&T unlimited." In discussing their differences, Mary notes that she has become less religious than her regular church-going sister. She attributes this to the influence of her husband, who thinks "organized religion is a little wacky." Mary says that her husband led the twins to become different. Mary begins, "I'm the one who is married." Martha adds, "Over the years I thought I would get married at some point too and I just never did." Mary reflects on her marriage.

> Mary: The fact that I got married so young, moved away and developed new circles and new independence means I had to change in a lot of ways. Not just being married but being a military wife. You're sort of a single married person a lot of times when you have to take care of everything yourself and have to take care of a small child and having all those ties that bind. It changed me a lot. I think in some ways I developed certain responsibilities that I felt were strong. At the same time she [Martha] developed certain responsibilities because she had to care of herself financially and all that. Our priorities shifted in those kinds of terms, where my priorities were holding the family together and hers were, "Oh, I have to have enough money to keep the car running" and all that.

At their present age, Mary and Martha continue to feel a sense of closeness that transcends their differences. They feel they can tell their twin everything, even though they know their twin will disapprove. Martha says, "I can look at Mary and her life and what's going on with her and say, 'You know, I could have been that. You know, if I had gone in that direction.' And she could have been where I am. It's like the possibilities are there because we are still basically being the same person." Mary adds, "I've developed over the years and she's developed over the years. It balances out." Like some of the twins at stage 4, Mary and Martha speculate about retiring together, but Martha adds that the husband would have to be out of the picture. For the time being, their sense of mutuality and connection, and the online business, keep them close enough. Mary and Martha do say that they had a three-year tiff, based on lies from a third person, during which they did not speak to each other. Aside from the friendly banter of

Karen and Kristy, this is the only account of not getting along and cutting off contact that Dorothy and I encountered in the Twinsburg narratives. As we will see shortly, Cindy and Sandy comprise a case to themselves, but first the dramatic stories of Jenna and Steph, who are trying to reconnect and set up a relationship together.

Jenna and Steph

Jenna and Steph, forty-one, are both currently unemployed. Both have had some technical school training, but Steph is on disability and Jenna is a stay-at-home mom. Jenna is on her second marriage. She has three grown children from her first marriage and now has a young daughter. Jenna left home at age fifteen and had a baby at age sixteen. At eighteen, Steph left home to become a mechanic in the navy. Steph is very open about being a lesbian and having been diagnosed with schizophrenia. They currently live within a twenty-minute drive of each other but still find it hard to get together because Steph cannot drive at night and Jenna has a young daughter with various extracurricular activities. They do call each other once or twice a day and get together to see a movie at least once a month. Jenna and Steph lost touch for an important segment of their lives, while Jenna was struggling with her first marriage and Steph was in the navy and not coping well with her mental health issues. Steph tells us that she has been a recovering alcoholic for seventeen years. When I asked Jenna if she helped Steph in her recovery, Jenna says, "No, I didn't know her at that time."

Jenna and Steph report that they came from a dysfunctional family. They have an older sister who is forty-two, a brother who died when he was hit by a car at age ten, a brother with Down syndrome who is somewhere (place unknown) with their mother, and a brother, Billy, whom they know nothing about because he left with their father when he was six or seven. Their parents got divorced when they were about sixteen years old. That is when Jenna ran away from home to get married. Steph started drinking when she was six. Their mother was a schizophrenic and "an abusive person," according to Jenna. Steph adds, "She used to lock us up for days, sometimes with our older sister, in the closet." Jenna says, "Or she'd lock us out in the snow, so she wouldn't have to deal with us. Or we'd be locked out of the house when it was hot and stuff. We were lucky to get water from the outside spigot." According to Steph, "If I got too rowdy, Mom would give me valium." They both feel their mother's abuse did not stem from her mental illness or alcohol abuse but from her envy of them as twins.

Jenna has three children from her first marriage—two boys and a girl who are now grown with children of their own. Jenna and her oldest daughter were pregnant at the same time. Jenna says, "I knew this would be my last child. I asked Steph to be there if she wanted to because I know she is never going to have any children. I wanted to share the experience with her." The baby apparently calls Steph "Stuffy." "Recently she started to call me Aunt Steph," Steph says. "It broke my heart. I wasn't going to be 'Stuffy' anymore. Now I'm just Steph." Yet, according to both of them, the daughter does not see any similarities in them and does not know they are twins. This, according to Jenna, is because her four-year-old daughter knows them both quite well.

Jenna's husband does not figure in this narrative. She has told him that she will not move until her child finishes school. Her daughter, rather than Steph, is what will keep Jenna close to Steph. Jenna says, "Since I'm here anyways, we'll probably be in contact with each other." She adds, "She couldn't do anything that I wouldn't stay in contact with her . . . I can call on her [not like the other sister]. It's just that way. I love her different than I love other people, and we treat each other different than other people." For example, they affectionately call each other "bitch." Yet, Jenna and Steph are ambivalent about how much they understand each other. They feel they are not a lot alike; nor do they think alike. Steph says she cannot understand how Jenna likes men and can just take one drink. Jenna says she cannot understand Steph sleeping with women and why she cannot say no after just one drink.

Cindy and Sandy

Cindy and Sandy, thirty-six, are the highly opinionated "anti-twins" from our conversation with two sets of twins from the same family. Both are university educated. Cindy is an army ROTC recruiter, and Sandy is a manager at a retail store. Posing their narratives as the *untwins,* they contrast themselves to their older twin sisters, Karan and Kim, who happily accept their twinship. Cindy and Sandy make a lively contribution to this corpus of twins talk. Karan says of them, "They never liked it from the beginning that they were twins." When Karan says, "Having a twin means never being alone," Cindy interjects, "Having 'friends' means never being alone." Cindy and Sandy went to college together and then Cindy dropped out to get married. They did spend a year together sometime after Cindy's marriage but have resided in different states for the last six years. Cindy and Sandy see each other about once a year but call each other three or four times a week (at one point, it was every six months). Kim adds, "As long as they're not fighting." Sandy remembers resenting being twins and "being forced" to dress alike in well-worn (another item of contention) hand-me-downs from their older twin sisters. They say they were much alike until they broke off in high school and Sandy "did what she wanted and I did what I wanted. But now that we're getting older, I think we are more alike."

According to Kim and Karan, Cindy and Sandy cannot accept each other for who they are. They always need to be competing. They fight and hold grudges and will not work it out or speak to each other for weeks. Sandy says that careers have changed them. She is in the corporate world and Cindy is in the military. The following exchange ensues:

Cindy: Growing up, Sandy's always been the dominant one. She told me what to do, how to dress, how to do everything. I was always in her shadow. Then in high school I got tired of it. I got mad. I decided I wanted to be me. I went my own way. Sandy says I'm not outgoing. That I can't make up my mind. No one I work with thinks that Sandy is right. She doesn't know me. We don't know each other. We kind of let the family see what we want them to see and that's all.

Sandy: Well, all I can say is I'm not going to sit here and wait and ask what you want, what you want, what you want. Time is important. I just make decisions. I do it now.

Karan then offers that Sandy is more self-oriented because she is the only twin among them who has not had to put others before her—either husband or children.

With two sets of twins in the same family, some interesting dynamics emerge. Cindy and Sandy always had to dress in hand-me-downs from their older sisters, but when they were all teenagers together, all four shared the same clothes. All four twins were referred to in high school as the [insert family surname] twins. Born three years apart, they were not distinguished as the older or younger ones; they were just all lumped together. Karan and Kim submit that this may be the origin of Sandy and Cindy's anti-twin notions. Sandy says, "I look at her [Cindy who is dressed in the exact same outfit] and I don't see identical twins; like, I don't see it." Cindy and Sandy, however, move on to remark that "the more similar you are, the harder it is to get along, because you have to fight so hard to be different."

Despite the oppositional nature of their talk, as Cindy and Sandy contrast themselves to Kim and Karan and then to each other, Dorothy and I got the sense that this was a well-honed presentation of self for the younger sisters. They had all come to Twinsburg to celebrate Karan's recovery from a serious disease. Otherwise, Cindy and Sandy told us, they "would not be caught dead at a twins festival." Sandy and Cindy attended the festival only to show love and support for their older sisters and to acknowledge the difficult time that they had recently been through. It was also interesting that Karan said she felt closest to her twin sister, Kim, and also close to Cindy, but not close to Sandy. In this hectic and fascinating talking session involving the excited interchanges and high spirits of three sets of twins (including Dorothy and me), different styles of relatedness emerge. Dorothy and I did wonder how assertively Cindy and Sandy's anti-twin rhetoric would be had their older twin sisters not been present.

STAGE 3: TWIN KIN WORK

Di Leonardo (2008, 109) describes "kin work" as a matter of special effort. As examples, she mentions planning family celebrations, such as Thanksgiving, which bring nonresident kin into the home, and sending greeting cards to extended family members. According to di Leonardo, Hallmark cards exist off kin work. AT&T and the Internet are most commonly referred to by the talking partners as ways of staying in touch with each other. Once the split has occurred and the twins establish other close relationships, a number of strategies for staying in touch are activated, one of which is attendance and shared participation at Twins Days and other festivals.

There is a great deal of overlap between stages and they may be viewed as rather arbitrary. Yet I am also rather amazed at how well these stages become demarcated in the twins' narratives. As a twin in one of the interviews, I am especially cognizant of how the talking partners only present a fraction of their lives, lived both together and apart. Of course, being interviewed as twins at twins festivals features their twin relationship and decenters the "others" in their lives. Given the narratives, however, stage 3 seems to represent a stage where the work of twinship takes on a new aspect. I am especially aware of it because it also characterizes Dorothy and me. As twins' children leave home, the collateral ties of twinship reemerge. Twins at stage 3 are well established in their careers and are content and secure in their work and family situations. With families mostly grown, these twins are looking toward each other and resituating or renegotiating their twinship as mature adults. Dorothy and I were commonly told at the ITAs, "Now our families are grown and the kids have moved out, so we are looking at ways to spend more time together." This is particularly notable at the ITAs, where participants are middle-aged or older. Twins in this stage include Lucy and Linda, Mabel and Bertha, Dona and Dorothy, Jean and Carol, and Annette and Arnette. The fact that some twins had a great deal more to say about themselves and their lives than other sets of twins is reflected in the length of text about them.

Lucy and Linda

Lucy and Linda, fifty-four, are both high school graduates who have some technical school training. Lucy works as a security guard and Linda is a housewife. This is their first time at Twinsburg. Lucy and Linda are a set of "boomerang twins," because they have lived together and apart at various junctures of their adult lives. Two years ago they moved in with each other. They rationalize this move by stating that it is cheaper to live this way and, since neither of them anticipates getting married again, they plan to live together for the rest of their lives.

Lucy and Linda seem to embody one of the country-and-western songs of which they are so fond. Remember, Lucy goes for "them auto freaks [race car mechanics]" and Linda for "the cowboys." Lucy and Linda came from a large family of ten brothers and sisters. Lucy says, "We were born in the middle." They lived together until they were fourteen years old. At age thirteen, they were put in an orphanage. Their brothers and sisters were sent to different orphanages. They report that their mother and father were both chronic alcoholics. After six months, Linda left the orphanage, leaving Lucy behind. Linda explains, "The main reason I left is because I'm a coffee drinker and Linda is not. I drank coffee since I was twelve. Of course, at the orphanage, they don't give you coffee and that's the main reason I told them I wanted to leave. I wanted my coffee. When we were in the orphanage, we shared a room. I tried to smuggle in a coffee maker and it didn't work." Lucy responds, "My sister left me for a cup of coffee." Linda, however, adds, "Well, not really. We talked about it and she said if you must go, go. I wasn't like I just up and said 'I'm leaving.'"

Linda was eventually apprehended and sent to a foster home. Lucy then ran away from the orphanage twice. Lucy states, "I kept saying, 'Send me where she is.' But they never did. They kept sending me someplace else." Lucy and Linda, although constantly on the move, always kept in touch with each other. This ability, Lucy notes, came from their older brother "who was kind of the one who raised us and always knew where we was." At age seventeen, Lucy was sent to live with one married sister while Linda lived with another. They lived in the same town and saw a lot of each other. At eighteen, Lucy says she "ran off and got married." Shortly after her marriage, Lucy and her new husband came to visit Linda, and Linda moved with them to Florida. Linda met her husband when the threesome were driving from Florida to Texas.

Linda: We stayed in Florida for a while. We were going to New Orleans and I met my first husband.

Lucy: We met him on the way to Texas.

Linda: We picked him up hitchhiking outside a motel. And by the time we got to Texas I was married. We were married twenty-seven years and had three kids.

Lucy: We've had an interesting life.

Both Lucy and Linda have lived very mobile, nomadic lives. Linda says, "For seven years she was in Arizona and I was in Florida. Then she moved to Kentucky. Then I got divorced and moved in with her. So for the last two years, we have been living together." Lucy and Linda love cats. They are wearing identical T-shirts with pictures of their three cats on them. Lucy and Linda also brought photos of themselves as young women. Like Karen and Kristy, they are a set of twins who displayed a great deal of interactive and personal charisma. Their lively conversation overflowed from the talking partners' booth to the booths of nearby researchers, who joined in on the conversation. As they passed these photos around to us and researchers in neighboring booths, we all remarked on how attractive these two currently gray-haired, full-figured women were in their younger years.

Their current household includes Lucy's "little boy," who is twenty-seven years old and, Linda inserts, "six feet one with a fifty-four inch waist." Lucy says, "Every time we go somewhere, we drag him off with us. If he had his way about it, he'd stay in his room and be a hermit the rest of his life. And we drag him off to places to get him out." Linda says, "Our constant teasing of each other embarrasses him." Lucy responds, "He always says, 'I can't take you two anywhere.'"

Reflecting on their lives together and apart, Lucy and Linda do feel that their husbands—who figure prominently in their talk—made a difference in their lives. Here is what they have to say about their husbands.

> Linda: My first husband was like a farmer and cowboy type. [He was] always out there working and stuff. My second husband was a cowboy. I mean, he was a bull rider and he worked stockyards. I worked the stockyards with him sometimes. But Lucy and her husband lived more in the city where I lived in the country.

On being asked if their husbands got along with each other, Linda offers, "Our husbands never knew each other." Lucy corrects, "Our first husbands did." Linda amends and Lucy adds in the exchange that follows.

> Linda: Yeah, but not very much because my first husband was always gone. He would say, "I'm going down for a loaf

of bread" and be gone three days, or he might be back in three weeks. I guess that's why our marriage lasted twenty-seven years.

Lucy: My first one lasted nine years. We had an argument and he dropped me off in California. He drove off and said he'd meet me at the bus stop in a couple of hours. I waited all day and he never came back. I called his mother. She wired me some money so I got a place to stay. I called her back every day but she hadn't heard from him. Then after a week she says, "He called me. He said he don't remember. He left you at a corner, but he can't remember which corner. He's been driving all over Texas looking for you." I said, "Ha, he left me in California!"

Linda: We've had hard lives. Really weird lives, but we've enjoyed them. We never get down in the dumps about anything. We learned to take care of ourselves and survive.

Lucy and Linda have entered a postmarriage era of their lives. Lucy and Linda like living together and, because they do not expect to remarry, plan to spend the rest of their lives together. They tell about their brother, the one who kept track of them. He is married to a twin, and his wife's twin sister has just lost her husband and has come to live with him. He is still close to his twin sisters, who live only three blocks away. According to Lucy, he says, "You find any stray twins around, you just tell 'em to come on over."

Mabel and Bertha

Mabel and Bertha, fifty-eight, are college graduates. They are currently both preschool day care directors, yet they are adamant that they did not follow each other into the field. Bertha says her interest in day care was an outgrowth of her experience working as a Sunday school teacher. Mabel states that her interest in the field was a result of feeling discouraged after years of working as a social worker. Mabel and Bertha lived together through junior college but then went to different colleges, one in New Hampshire and the other in Maine. They mention that their parents "brought them up to be individuals" and fought school policy to get them separated into different classes in elementary school. That was their first separation, and they recount it as "the end of living together." Nevertheless, they remark on being very close when they were younger. While Mabel recounts that as a child she was the more outgoing and Bertha was a bit dependent on her, but when they got married and had kids, they both "evolved." When queried about the term *evolved*, they explain that they both became more outgoing and social. This was especially true for Bertha. Bertha says that she had a very hard time separating from Mabel to go to college. "It was really a culture shock for me. I was so homesick; I didn't finish [college]. I moved in with relatives for a while and worked until I got married." They currently live an hour's drive from each other and see each other about six times a year. They talk a lot on the phone. Being able to count on each other has been a constant in their lives. Even after being apart a long time, Mabel says, "It's like picking up where you left off."

With their families grown, Mabel and Bertha have just begun to spend more time together, like their visit to Twinsburg. This is their first time at Twins Days, and they are having a very good time together. Mabel explains.

> Mabel: We haven't done a lot of getting together. We've been
> so busy with our own lives. She got married almost
> right out of college. I got married five years later.
> Then she had her kids and I had my kids later. We'd
> see each other but with our kids, with our families,
> holidays, birthdays, things like that. It wasn't till about
> our fiftieth birthday that we even thought about it like,
> "Let's go out to lunch together" occasionally. I mean,
> we just didn't. It was always with family. Even on the
> plane. This is the first time we have flown together all
> by ourselves without our husbands and children.

Mabel and Bertha say their husbands are very much alike, although Mabel's husband is more outgoing and Bertha's, like Bertha, is "more not a joiner." Both are described as "laid back, mild men." The husbands look so much alike that they are often mistaken for brothers. The husbands (who remain unnamed in this narrative) share a variety of interests and a camaraderie. Bertha describes her life as having gone from family to career, and Mabel describes hers as going from career, to family, to career. Both women stress that their early days of marriage and having children gave them a sense of being out of control. Bertha has this to say.

> Bertha: It wasn't until I was in my early thirties [that I] started to make decisions. It took me longer to grow into an adult. You come out of school, get married, have kids, life moves along, and you have so little control. I felt that life was making choices for me. It wasn't until I was in my midthirties, I knew what I wanted. I went back to school and finished my degree and started making my own choices. That's when I said, "This is what I want; I'll do this," work with kids.

Mabel responds that she had the same feeling of being lost in the flow of children and family and characterizes herself as more career oriented than her twin. She was a social worker but not a very happy one. Marrying later than her sister did, she feels that marriage "regressed" her.

> Mabel: In my twenties I was OK. I liked school and I liked working. But when I got married in my thirties, I felt like I was in limbo. I didn't like staying at home. I felt I had to do something. I went back to school. I got a real job and then I got back on track. Maybe it's just a selfish thing. You know, as a person I had to feel I was accomplishing something. Even though being a mother was the most important thing for me, I still needed a part of me to say I was successful.

Mabel and Bertha feel that their now grown children are very similar and look enough alike to be brothers and sisters. They remark that they have learned to bite their tongues, when they feel the urge to say, "You're just like your cousin." They also feel their children are closer than those of their other siblings.

Dorothy and Dona

Dorothy and I, fifty-five, are both anthropologists. Dorothy has an MA and Dona a PhD in anthropology. Dorothy is divorced with two grown children. Dona is married with no children. We were interviewed by Kristi Cody (Cody 2005). Dorothy and I went to the same college but were not roommates. We both graduated with anthropology degrees and then went to graduate school for our MAs. As mentioned previously in this chapter, I got my first real academic job by flipping a coin with Dorothy. We lived apart for about nine months and then Dorothy moved in with me. We lived together for two years. The final split came when Dorothy got married and I went to work overseas and we set up our separate lives. Today we keep in touch by telephone and try to get together about once every year and a half.

When Dorothy's children were young and I was developing my career, we saw each other less than once every three years. We got together at professional conferences and tried to schedule visits to our mother together. Today, we both describe ourselves as "female jocks," very active but in different sports. We travel a lot, professionally and recreationally, but for different reasons. Dorothy travels to the tropics and I to the Arctic. In our interview, I state that "Dorothy has children and so her life, when they were younger, was much, much different than mine. Now her children are grown, [and] she has this whole relation of people down from her that I don't have." Dorothy says, "I'll get to be a grandmother," and I pipe in, "But her kids are genetically as much mine as they are hers."

We go on to debate whether it was Dorothy's marriage or my PhD that really changed us. Dorothy contends that it was her marriage because it put us in different geographical places: "She was in Newfoundland and I was in Miami and that was the furthest away we have ever been, and we weren't in contact with each other a whole lot." I respond, "When she had her young family, my major effort was investing in my career, so it was like I was the workaholic achiever and she was the workaholic mom. Those differences in our midtwenties to our early thirties made us really different." We agree that we married "two very different men." While I am happily married, Dorothy is divorced. Dorothy defines herself as the "wounded twin, the twin who had the hard life." Dorothy does all the family kin work. I am by far the more private twin. Reflecting on our lives, Dorothy and I feel we were different from the start. As children we had ponies and horses (Davis and Davis 2010) that nurtured those differences. Those differences are reflected in different career routes and partner choices.

Dorothy and I describe our twinship as an enduring sense of connectedness. Dorothy says, "When we did separate, it was like the physical separation was not that big a deal because that part of the person is with you all the time, so it's not the same as physical separation from someone else. She is my alter ego and I am her alter ego, and we never get to the point that we feel like strangers to each other." I respond, "There is an intimacy to it. It is the ultimate familiarity. There are things she does or situations she gets herself into or responses she makes that I can't believe that she does it because I think that I wouldn't, if I was in the same situation myself. But there is a link. It's not psychic or anything like that. It comes from having grown up the same, having so many of our formative years and experiences shared."

Jean and Carol

Jean and Carol, fifty-four, also spend more time together now that their respective families are "pretty much grown and gone." They did not make any special effort to get back together. Carol remarks, "We just slid back into it more than anything else." Carol is a medical assistant with some college training. Jean graduated from high school and is a teacher's aide. Jean and Carol were separated when Jean got married after high school. Carol moved away from their hometown for a couple of years and then returned. Carol says, "We always lived maybe a half an hour apart." Jean responds that even though they were nearby geographically, they did not see much of each other in those early days because neither of them had a driver's license. Jean says, "Then we really got to see more of each other because I got a driver's license. I got divorced. I got a driver's license. That's the first thing I did. Then I got remarried and she comes to my house, what, five times a week."

Carol and Jean remark that they have gone their own ways professionally. While Carol works with young children, Jean works in a neurologist's office, mainly with older people. Their work lives give them more confidence, different sets of skills, different friendship groups, and different kinds of challenges. Yet they also state that nothing truly basic has changed, and spending so much time together has kept them alike in many ways. Carol remarks that when they were younger they tried different things, "but you're not really comfortable with them so you go back to what you know and who you are." Other than references to husbands as driving teachers, the only other mention of husbands comes when Jean and Carol speak of not having to say you're sorry. Carol says, "For me, being a twin means I've got somebody that if I do something wrong, I don't say 'I'm sorry.' It feels like saying I'm sorry to myself." Carol adds, "Early in my last marriage—it was for fifteen years—he didn't quite understand. It was hard to communicate with him because I just assumed he'd know, know what I was saying, what I didn't say." Currently, Jean and Carol get together to work on each other's houses since they each have different skills in this arena. The reason that they always prefer to meet at Jean's house is because Jean lives out in the country. They both love dogs and Carol comes over to let her dogs run through the countryside.

Annette and Arnette

The rich interview of Arnette and Annette, fifty-six, has been the source of a lot of the narrative cited in previous chapters. The account of Arnette and Annette is extensive and reflects the long and dramatic conversation that we had with them. They are the only African Americans in our talking partners sample. During our lengthy conversation a small group of their grandchildren were patiently playing just outside the Research Pavilion. Arnette and Annette refer to their relational styles as "their twindom." They feel that this characterizes not only themselves but also twins in general. Both Annette and Arnette are social workers (in separate settings) and both have master's degrees in social work. Annette is more the professional manager type, while Arnette describes herself as more of a therapist and counselor. They talk about their jobs a great deal throughout our conversation.

Arnette describes their early family history, saying, "Our parents separated. They divorced because my father had a gambling problem." Annette adds, "What happened was our dear father gambled away our house, our crib, everything. We were about three months old. My mother had a job teaching and she couldn't take care of us. So that's why she brought us home to her mother." Arnette says, "Until we were four, I think, we thought our grandparents were our parents. So Christmas before she [their mother] came, my grandmother said, 'Don't forget to call your mother, 'Mother.' And I said, 'Who? What do you mean she is our mother?'" As we have seen, Arnette and Annette have a great deal of affection and respect for the grandparents who reared them, as well as admiration for their mother and her professional accomplishments. Annette says, "We had three parents; our grandparents were two wise people. They had a second- and third-grade education, but they were two of the smartest people I've ever seen. Daddy [Grandfather] learned to read by reading the scriptures and then he taught Grandmother." They are also very proud of their mother, who was a college graduate. Annette says, "We grew up knowing Mother was smart, so therefore we had to be smart because Mother was smart."

Elementary school officials tried to separate the twins in school because Annette was doing all of Arnette's schoolwork for her. Arnette cried and cried for three weeks until school officials gave up and rejoined the twins. They were together through most of graduate school but then, says Annette, "She got ahead of me because I had a baby in graduate school." When Annette got married at around twenty-two, her husband moved into the apartment that the twins shared. Arnette moved home briefly and then got married at twenty-four and moved into her new husband's apartment. When they lost the apartment, she and her husband moved in with Annette and her husband. Annette remarks, "It was right at the time my second baby was due and her first baby was due. They were only two or three weeks apart. Our mother came to stay for two months."

Over the years they have lived together and apart. Their adult times of living together come through far more as a safety net for each other, rather than as a regressive pull toward each other. They currently work in cities that are three hundred miles apart, but they call each other at least twice a month. Although they describe their careers as "the same," they have each developed on "a different plane." While Arnette has become active in national social work associations, Annette stays active closer to home. Annette explains that she has raised four children, six stepchildren, and their younger sister. Three of these stepchildren were diagnosed with schizophrenia, and Annette relates how it made her life hell and sometimes she even feared that one of her stepchildren would kill her. Arnette has five children, two stepdaughters, and two stepsons. Although they both married men they characterize as abusive, Annette says that she stood up to hers. Both sisters feel that their social work skills helped them deal with difficult marriages. Annette, who refers to herself in first person as well as third person, describes her husband and her marriage in the following laughter-punctuated narrative.

Annette: I won't say my husband wasn't abusive. I would say he tried, but Annette wasn't going to give up to that position. Right from the kick, I told him, I said, "First of all, if you hit me it's all over that second, so don't even come that way." And I told him too, "If you hurt one of my children, then we've got problems." My husband is a very bossy person. He has to understand I am who I am. I am a person in my own right. We had to come to a compromise. I have to give it to him, He grew as a person. We worked it out. Part of it's because he's a seven-time loser. Three marriages and the rest of them live together, but still a seven-time loser by the time I got to them. He was like seventeen to twenty years older than I was, so consequently he was more willing to compromise. When you marry someone who had been through the mill, they understand now, they've got to back up. I think knowing therapy helped me to talk with him to get him to figure out why he was acting so aggressive.

Arnette describes her husband and family life, despite its drama, in a very matter-of-fact tone.

Arnette: My husband was also an alcohol and drug addict. That meant I had to take a lot of responsibility. I knew how to take it because I knew what Annette would do. And I figured Annette wouldn't take certain things and neither would I, but I'm more passive-aggressive. So when I got ready to get out of my marriage, I did it in a very passive-aggressive way. A few years before the divorce, I'd already planned what I was going to do. I set up my own credit. I changed bank accounts. I started controlling the children's education and activities so they weren't around him as much. He was so deep in his drugs he couldn't see the changes I was making. This way worked for me. I got out. We gave him an intervention and a chance to change. I gave him a timetable.

Referring to her passive-aggressive style, Arnette says she gave in and met his request for counseling to save their marriage. But she also adds the following:

Arnette: Being my passive-aggressive self, I was going along, but just for the show. I was figuring how to get out of it. So we did all that, and he had one of his big blowups and hit me for the last time. I took all the kids and went to a shelter because I knew where to go and how to get in there and how to get out of my house without being hurt. So it worked out for me, my passive-aggressive ways; I don't think being aggressive with him would have worked out at all. I think I would have got killed. They tell you not to therapize with your family, but if they are about to kill you, you better do something.

Given the nature of their marital relationships, it is not much of a surprise that the sisters feel a strong lifelong connection to each other, as the following exchange illustrates:

Arnette: Being twins means having your best friend with you all the time. It means having emotional support, which is more important to me. It means having psychological support for some reason 'cause I think when bad times happened to me and I thought I was going to pieces. I would think, "Well, you know, Annette would not go to pieces like this." When we was in college, I became pregnant and I had an abortion and I had contemplated suicide because it was quite traumatic for me. And the only reason I stayed alive was that I knew Annette would not want me to die. That was it. That was the only reason. I had no other choice. So to me, it was everything. And I couldn't go crazy because Annette wouldn't let me. At least that's how I thought it.

Annette: That's exactly what happened 'cause when she went through that abortion, I was trying to say those words to her that she just said, that I would not allow her to die and that she couldn't be depressed like that because she had to stay here, if for nothing else for me. I can remember dreaming that to her but I wasn't sure she was getting it. That's a similarity I think we never lost is this closeness that we have together with each other. You know when you go through these bad sorts of things when you get married. But are you going to put down your husband? I say no. But I'll also say, "The closest person I'm to is my twin sister." My husband is next, but no, he has learned to accept that role.

Arnette adds that her husband "never got it." She does not like Annette's husband but does say he understands his wife's relation with her twin sister.

Yet happy times are also shared. Annette says, "The happiest times of my life have always been something I did with Arnette. If something good happened to me when we were separated, I'd save it up to share with her. If Arnette wasn't feeling so good, I'd use my happiness spots to help pull her up on things."

STAGE 4: RETIREMENT AND RENEWAL

Mabel and Bertha are the oldest twins in stage 3. They, along with stage 4 twins, present a "life as twins option" that Dorothy and I had not previously considered, although we joked about it with Mary and Martha. When asked if they want to retire and move in with each other, Mary says, "We have talked about that." Although cited previously, I repeat their exchange here.

Mary: I say, if I ever go old and senile and they have to put me in a nursing home, Martha: . . . They'd have to put us in the same one.

Mary: Ha ha. And we'd sit there and just giggle at each other. And then if one of us was ever gone, we wouldn't have to tell the other. We'd just put a mirror there.

Although Mary and Martha joke about senility and being placed in the "home," twins at stage 3, whose careers are established and children are leaving home, are often looking forward to spending more time together. The majority of twins at stage 4 have realized this ambition. More than 30 percent of the participants at Twinsburg are over forty. At the International Twins Association meetings, more than 50 percent of the participants are over fifty, and the largest cohort of attendees is between sixty and eighty. Retired with fully grown children, stage 4 twins Jenny and Julie, Helen and June, Donna and Dianne, Pat and Phyllis, Pete and Emil, and Janet and Judy are far from senility. They are renegotiating their twinship as a relationship, or point of connection, to be redeveloped or reinvigorated in their older years. They are all vital and active as they engage in the Twins Days festivities. Two things tend to draw our talking partners together at this time of life. The first is the increase in their spare time, and the second is the needs of one of the twins. The following accounts show how kin work is done as older twins navigate a process of reinvesting in their twin relationship.

Jenny and Julie

Jenny and Julie, sixty-nine, born in Malaysia, are the only talking partners who were separated as babies. They are both college-educated, retired accountants. Jenny and Julie were raised in separate households until kindergarten. Julie explains, "Because our parents were too old to take care of us, we were separated." They report that each stayed with a series of unmemorable relatives. Once reunited at boarding school, they stayed together through college. Jenny describes herself as the obedient, fussy twin who liked to dress up and her sister as the rough, rebellious twin who got into fights and played in the mud. They attribute this difference to the families who reared them in early childhood. Although their memories of early childhood appear confused and vague, Jenny recalls that when she and her sister were very young children, the family that she lived with had more resources than her sister's family. Nevertheless, once united at boarding school, they got along very well. Common interests and talents made twinship work out well. Unlike their relationships with other family members, Julie states that "when it came to her sister, sharing seems the natural thing to do." Their split came when they graduated from college and started working. Jenny says, "We wanted to separate, we decided, because we were too much together." Yet their life histories also describe being laid off and changing careers. At various junctures in their working lives, they moved apart and then reunited. Julie says that during their separations, as in their early years, they may have grown in different ways but they also had similarities because they stayed the same, since when together, they "pick up each other's differences." Jenny responds that time spent together makes them "more like Siamese twins."

Neither twin married or had children. At some point late in their careers, Julie quit work and moved into their ailing mother's house to take care her. It was too much work for Julie, so Jenny moved in to help her out. While Jenny kept her job, they split the work hours between them and nobody at work knew what was happening. The twins state that it has been a long time since their mother died, but they have stayed together living in her house because it is more economical. Jenny and Julie are the only twins in the sample who currently dress alike every day. They say they do so because they are both petite and there is no selection in their size, so they end up buying the same things. As they reflect on their lives, they see, unlike the other twins, a sense of sameness emerging. They say they are more the same now than ever before.

Helen and June

Helen and June, seventy-four, are high school graduates. Helen was an office manager in a doctor's office, and June was a housewife married to a dairy farmer. They are both widowed. They were at Twinsburg with their husbands in 1992 and said, "Let's go back and do this again." Helen and June grew up together on a dairy farm. They split when Helen ran away to get married. June remarks, "It was hard for me to have her move away because I depended on her so much." When June got married, they saw each other maybe once a month. Helen adds, "I'd moved away but then I'd come back [to visit June] every week until my third child was born. Then I stayed home."

When they lost their husbands, they spent a lot more time traveling and vacationing together. Helen says, "We live about sixty miles apart right now. Right now we see a lot of each other because after her [June's] husband died, we have been together a lot." When asked about any desire to move in with each other, June replies, "We could live together, except that she lives in one place with all her family and children and I live in another place and there's no way that we're going to leave our families. So otherwise, we might—maybe when we get real old."

They call each other several times a day. Despite the continued importance of their respective families, June and Helen feel they have "lived the same kind of lives and can't see that we have changed much over the years." June has one son and four daughters, and Helen has one daughter and three sons. They say that their husbands were good friends and they traveled together as families; their families remain close. Helen says, "I send all her children and grandchildren a card on their birthdays and she sends cards to all my children. We don't do that for our other brothers and sister or for their children. We're very close." Helen says that although they are both family oriented, June is more so. This is largely because June has more of her children living close to home. They each have their families over for dinner every Sunday. For June, that amounts to about twenty-five family members for dinner; Helen feeds five to ten every Sunday.

Helen and June remark that their father was also an identical twin, but "he never made anything of it." As a man, he was not expected to do any kin work. Helen describes the meaning of twinship thus: "I'm thankful for your [June] unconditional love. I've never had anyone more than God give this unconditional love that we have for each other. That's the way I have felt for all my life."

Donna and Dianne

Donna and Dianne, sixty-four, like Helen and June, are making an effort to spend more time together. Dianne has a high school education and works as a bookkeeper. Donna went to college and is a registered nurse. They report that their mother left their father when they were six years old and express a very special love for their stepfather, who legally adopted them when they were forty. Donna reports that before they were eleven years old, they had moved eleven times in eight years. Their mother was fanatical about dressing them alike. Dianne says, "We made friends easily, but it didn't matter if we didn't because we had each other. I would feel sorry for a single child who has to make friends all on his or her own. We saw it as an adventure.

Every time we came to a new place, as identical twins dressed alike, we were a spectacle."

They split when Dianne got married as a senior in high school. Dianne was engaged to a man who was far away in the navy, but she eloped with another man. Donna helped finance the elopement and was the only one who knew about it. But she also says she had from March to September to get used to living without her sister. Donna graduated from high school and left home to go to nursing school. Since each has moved around a lot there have been times in their lives when they were as close as two hours from each other and other times when they were much farther apart. Donna remembers these separations.

> Donna: We were like two hours apart from, well, I guess
> from 1957 until 1970 or 1971. And then we moved
> to Cincinnati, so then we were four hours apart.
> We saw each other a lot because Charlie [Donna's
> husband] had to come [to Cincinnati] for his medical
> appointments. And then, in '86 we moved to New
> Jersey, and that was horrible because prior to that
> we were able to visit each other fairly often. So then
> we [Donna and her husband] lived in New Jersey for
> two years, and then my husband died, and so then
> I brought my kids and came back to Cincinnati, so
> again we were four hours apart.

Today, Donna says, "Because we are both widows, we try to get together every six or eight weeks. I guess our husbands would be supportive of us getting together. My husband was an only child and here I was with this twin sister. It was a little strange for him, but he was great about it." Donna and Dianne feel they have become closer and more alike as they have aged. Donna says, "I guess to me the similarities have been more obvious the last fifteen years, since we were widowed. And maybe part of it was because until that time, although we spent time together, it was never to the extent or the depth that we do now, because our families were growing up. We had our spouses. We weren't together in the same way."

Unlike some of the other twins, Donna and Dianne say their children are not all that close. This is partly because Dianne had her children much earlier than Donna and her children have long ago moved away from home. As they reminisce about their first Twins Days, Donna states, "We talked the first year we came [to Twinsburg], and we wondered how that would be, if our spouses were alive, and if they came, if they would enjoy it or if we would be so selfish that we would want to just come alone." When asked about their relationship, Dianne replies, "I think being a twin is one of the most wonderful things that God could do to a person. I can't imagine not having her in my life." In response, Donna adds the following:

> Donna: I feel the same way. As upset as we get with each other sometimes, I wouldn't even want to think about what I would do without her. We just have this closeness. I think it's even more so in the last couple of years. I think partly because of coming here. It has helped put a perspective as a twin on how other people, when you're looking at us identical twins here, how other people see us. It's a love and a feeling that no one else can share, that no one else can have.

Pat and Phyllis

Pat and Phyllis, sixty-two, are college educated. Both are retired. Pat was a bus driver and Phyllis was an accounting clerk. During the winter Pat and Phyllis live about thirty miles from each other, but for five months of the year, they live next to each other in adjacent summer camps. They feel they are more alike today and more comfortable with their similarities than they have ever been.

Pat says that she and Phyllis were separated in school in the fourth grade, when they found Pat to be falling behind Phyllis. Pat had her friends and Phyllis had hers. There was no problem with it.

> Pat: I found new friends and everything else, so I didn't have to have Phyllis. I had to be myself. Then I wanted to be myself, but at home I was still Phyllis's twin. Now as adults, now that we have our own lifestyles and stuff, it is really fun. We think it is really great that we can get back together and enjoy our retirement and enjoy [Phyllis inserts "being twins"] being twins and stuff again. For thirty years we were having our

families and doing our jobs and being married and all
that stuff. Now we can just enjoy each other again. It's
lots more fun now because it isn't like your parents
throw you together. It's a matter of choice.

Toward the end of the interview, they reflect that their shared
home environment was very different for each twin. Although in
some ways they report they had a good life, the home environment
was one in which the mother blatantly favored Phyllis (the firstborn)
over Pat. This environment was so painful to Pat that she characterizes Phyllis as the good twin and herself as the twin's twin. Pat
and Phyllis go on to explain that their mother was and is very proud
of having twins. Their mother, at age eighty-two, still wants them
to dress alike. Pat has a really ambivalent feeling about her mother.
Today it is Phyllis who does all the kin work involving their mother.
Pat will have nothing to do with her mother.

Living next to each other over the summer, Pat and Phyllis keep
their houses open to each other and share everything.

Pat: We have keys to each other's camps. We share
        each other's grandkids. She has a paddleboat and
        a rowboat. I have all kinds of tubes and floats and
        stuff—all our grandchildren, no matter which ones,
        use them. Actually she has two grandchildren and I
        have thirty-five. I can share with two more kids. What
        difference does it make?

They see the fact that Pat had five sons and then remarried and
acquired seven additional stepchildren, while Phyllis had a son and
a daughter (much later in life), as a big difference in their respective
family histories. Pat and Phyllis went to college together and lived
together as young working women. They separated when Pat got
married. Pat describes it as an act of rebellion, not against her sister but against her overly strict mother. Pat had five children in six
years. Phyllis got married six years later. She says that her first pregnancy and Pat's last [her sixth son] came at the same time (within two
weeks). They joke about Pat having really wanted a daughter after
five sons. Yet Pat had another son and Phyllis got the daughter. A
reflection on gray hairs leads Pat and Phyllis to recall their hardships.
It was Pat who had the harder time of it. She raised the six children

alone from the time her youngest was six months old until she met her current husband. Pat says that her first husband wasn't jealous, but he did not understand them being twins and did not want them doing things together. Pat's second husband had two sets of twins in his family. He understands twins, so after Pat's second marriage Pat and Phyllis started getting together again.

Aside from problematic mother-twin relationships, Pat and Phyllis report being brought up in some unusual family circumstances. First, their mother ran a foster home when the twins were ages five to fourteen. Their mother always had six babies in the house, and she kept the babies until they were four years old. At one time, Pat and Phyllis recall having six babies less than six months old in the house. Each twin was assigned a different child to take care of. They also report they were very close to their cousins, who were always around. They say, "We were brought up with our cousins like brothers and sisters." In this large and close family, Pat and Phyllis emphasize that as close as they were to other family members, it was nothing like being with their twin.

> Phyllis: But even with our cousins and stuff, they still don't know. Well, you guys [Dorothy and Dona] know; you're twins. But there's a bond that's there and it's a close bond, even when you don't want it to be. You don't have that same bond with your mother. You don't have it with your husband or your children, but you have it with your identical twin. It's a really marvelous thing. It's too bad everyone can't experience it.

Yet twinship was more difficult for Pat.

> Pat: I feel the same way, but not always. Before, it wasn't so much that I didn't like being with her, but I didn't like the fact that Phyllis always came first and Mother wouldn't recognize me as an individual. I'm sixty-two years old and she's eighty-two and Mother still sees me in the light of Phyllis. So you can't change things, and now it's not important. When you're in high school, you really want to be known for yourself. Well, I got married and got away. I lived in different places, had

friends who didn't know her. I'm Pat, then and now. For nineteen years I'd tell people I had a brother and a sister. I'd never say I am a twin. [Phyllis says, "Me too."] Then in 1985, I asked my sister to go to this retreat with me. It was on love. This friend says, "I've known you for nineteen and a half years and I never knew you were a twin." Everyone was saying that. We were so conditioned in the family as twins; it was important to say just "sister."

Pat and Phyllis also associate their closeness with being opposites. One is like their mother; the other like their father. Ironically, Pat is like the disparaged mother. Otherwise, Phyllis says, "Let's face it, it would be boring." Phyllis also says that they had eight sets of twins in their graduating class from high school. At the time, all these twins considered themselves to be special friends. Today Phyllis and Pat both feel an instant bond with other sets of twins and will always mention that they are twins themselves.

Caretaker Twins

In our conversation with Pat and Phyllis, Phyllis reports that she had a heart attack at age fifty. She tells us this almost in passing as an explanation for her gray hair. Many twins told us that being a twin meant that there was always someone there for you. Yet, in the conversations with Pete and Emil and Janet and Judy, a theme emerges in which much more is made of the health problems of one twin and the role of caretaker that emerges in the other. A caretaker twin exemplifies the meaning of "always [being] there for you." This is not unique to the older age groups. Steph and Jenna faced lifelong challenges because Steph, diagnosed with schizophrenia, often needed Jenna's helping hand. Today, Jenna, afflicted with crippling arthritis, turns to Steph for help and support in carrying out her everyday tasks. They help each other out. Annette and Arnette would "flip-flop" between caretaker and cared-for twin throughout their lives as circumstances required. Twins like Sandy and Cindy and Karan and Kim come to Twins Days to celebrate one twin's recovery from a serious illness. Pete and Emil matter-of-factly describe helping each other out, whereas Janet and Judy's kin work is in the form of caring and sharing.

Pete and Emil, seventy-seven, are the oldest of our talking partners and have been retired for some time. Pete worked on the railroad, Emil in the air force. They both have a high school education. Pete and Emil grew up together in a large Italian American family. They were born ninth and tenth out of eleven children. Although they say it is hard to remember way back then, Emil says that he "saw Pete as just another brother." In their large family, there were different groups of the brothers who played together. Their house had three bedrooms, and the six boys shared a room, sleeping three to a bed. Emil states, "I'd say Pete and my brother that was two years older were in a category." Their father worked nights and left all the caretaking to their mother, for whom they both express a special feeling of closeness and appreciation. An older sister also helped take care of them.

Pete and Emil went all the way through high school together in the same class. When they were eighteen years old, the World War II draft in 1944 split them up. Pete failed his hearing test and Emil was drafted into the army. Pete went to work on the railroad and says, "Then I waited for him to come out." Dorothy and I found it ironic that when they reflected on their careers, Emil said he had the easier job. Although he saw action in World War II, reflecting on events that happened over fifty years ago, he remarks that it "was just a job, a duty you performed." Emil sees Pete with the more difficult career since there were periods when Pete would get laid off and times would be tough for him; Emil's military career meant a steady job. Emil says the war did not "make him and Pete any different." According to Emil, "During the war, you don't have time to think." The three years when Emil was in Europe was the longest separation the two ever experienced. Emil says it was not hard splitting up because "we had lots of brothers and sisters." Emil goes on to explain that there were "six boys and five of them went into the service and they all came home." Pete stayed home with their mother. Emil came home to be the best man at Pete's wedding, but since he could not find a job, he reenlisted and pursued a career in the military. Pete continued to work with the railroad.

Pete and Emil are now both widowers.

> Pete: But we both had good marriages. I had fifty-two years with her.

Emil: I was shy three weeks of fifty, through illness and because of circumstances. Since 1950, no, 1970, no, I'm sorry, we're in the '90s now. My wife passed away in 1998, and his wife passed away in 1999. And we've been more or less together, I'd say, every other month. Even though we're ninety miles apart, we see each other; he comes down or I come up. From Midsville is ninety miles from Pittsburgh. It's an hour and a half [drive] to visit each other.

Pete: If there's some family goings-on, we'll get together and meet that way.

Emil: Like Pete was saying, we just picked up about when our wives passed away. We had all this free time. So we picked up naturally to help other people because in our lives, other people helped our wives. So Pete did what he did up in the Midsville, helping the assisted living and nursing home, and I do the same thing down in Pittsburgh. We both did this sort of thing automatically.

Sometimes they meet at a friend's house halfway between them. They also get together for ball games and trips like Twinsburg. Even when they are apart, they independently engage in the same range of activities. They are very proud of the volunteer work they do at nursing homes. They also take delight in telling tales of pulling identity switches at the homes. Pete has three children and Emil has two. They keep up with their children and surviving brothers and sisters through family gatherings and such.

Emil and Pete talk about a health challenge that brought them closer together.

Emil: Ten months after my wife died, I had a routine physical exam. They found out I had heart problems. Doctor asks, "How you feeling?" I said, "Once in a while I get a pain down my right arm but not my left arm." I took the stress test. I failed it. Then they did the heart catheterization. I failed that too. They wouldn't let me come home from the hospital because it was too dangerous, they said. I never knew I had heart problems. But it runs in the family, because the history, I'm telling you, is in the family. Pete here will follow-up, tell you his story. Well, I had the bypass surgery, a triple, and everything worked out fine. Everything's still working out fine five and one half years later. Pete will pick up now and tell ya.

Pete: Like he said, the family history. I told my doctor that I had a family history. I had one brother that did die.

Emil: A heart attack.

Pete: And so the doctor says, "Why don't you have a stress test?" And that didn't work out. And I had a catheterization, and that didn't work out, and then he [the doctor] said maybe it's better off for me [then was the case Emil]. I had no pain, no discomfort, no nothing. But I had it [heart surgery].

Emil: We had our surgeries done in different cities ten months apart. It was about ten months after our wives died.

Pete and Emil said that they really never expected that they would end up back together. For years they were busy with their respective families and hardly saw each other. Pete says, "Now we're making up for lost time." They expected to get back together at family reunions every couple of years but had not anticipated seeing so much of each other at this time of life. Part of their kin work today includes bridging each other's friend and family networks. Nowadays, when they visit their respective children who live far away, both brothers usually take the trip together. Both brothers state that they feel closer and more the same today than when they were young kids. They also share a mutual group of friends; Pete's longtime friends have become Emil's and vice versa.

To Pete and Emil, being twins means having someone like yourself. It means sharing and taking time to be together. Although they admit to having different lifestyles (one was always financially better off), they say they were never jealous and always ready to share. Emil says that today his brothers are more like dear friends, but Pete is his brother. They talk on the phone almost every other day. Emil sums it all up by saying, "We take care of each other too. We do that."

Janet and Judy

Janet and Judy, sixty-one, are also spending more time together than ever before. Their long narrative is punctuated with shared memories and humorous stories about themselves. It is sickness and recovery that unites them now. Having just won a prize in their look-alike contest, Janet proudly took off her hat to show both her hairless head and the hairs from Judy's head that had been glued to the rim of Janet's hat. Judy had planned and paid for the Twinsburg trip, and it was her reward to Janet for being a breast cancer survivor. They are very jolly and hug and kiss each other throughout the conversation.

Janet and Judy are both high school graduates and worked as secretaries, although Janet has recently retired. This is their first visit to Twinsburg. Janet says that they "grew up together, like Siamese twins." They went to school together and were very unhappy to split up in different classes for two years. They relate that their mother's focused attention on an older, sickly sister left them very much to their own devices and threw them together for emotional support. They had each other. They describe themselves as very shy and having a speech impediment, so they did not make friends in school. After graduation they worked for the government, while still living with their mother. They did not work side by side but on different floors of the same high-rise office building.

Then Judy got a promotion and moved to a new job, but within a year, she returned home. Judy was the first to get married. She married an Amish man, and his Amish identity is a matter of much joking between them as they remember and relate courtship stories. Janet says her husband is OK with it, when asked if their husbands are tolerant of their twinship.

> Janet: They don't understand twins. They don't understand
> the closeness of twins, especially her husband.
> But it used to be it almost wrecked our marriages
> because they don't understand that we think alike,
> do everything alike, and there's a need to talk to each
> other all the time and they don't understand.

Later in the interview, they remark that if they had married twins, their husbands would be more understanding. Judy actually plans her talks to Janet when her husband is not around. They also use e-mail. They joke about these sneaky means of communication (an Amish wife is not supposed to have a computer), and Judy remarks, "Like after thirty years, what is he gonna say?" One mention is made that one husband has lots of money and the other is poor, but aside from having no desire to switch husbands, no more mention is made of this disparity in family incomes. Judy explains, "When we were younger, like working through 1960s and that, working for the government, we were OK with going our own ways. We still lived close and everything. We kept in contact with each other, but not the closeness that we have today." Judy has this to say about when they got married.

> Judy: We kind of went in different directions. I was married first and had the first boy baby. She was married after I had two girls. We were always close, but we really did different things. We really didn't get together that much. Especially before Janet's cancer. That was very meaningful. It really got us closer than we have ever been. And we just decided that nothing's going to separate us. We don't care what it is. So we'd say, as of today, there is no separation and there will never be a separation.

Janet explains, "When I found out I had cancer, she went to the doctors with me and she stayed with me all through my chemotherapy, my radiation, my mastectomy, my surgeries, everything. Or I would never have made it as well as I did without her." Although they lived ninety miles apart, Janet's cancer brought them together again, literally and figuratively. Janet and Judy have already been noted for the sense of embodied closeness they communicate to each other and those around them. When Janet was undergoing the worst of her chemo, Judy took her into her home. Judy set up a bed for them in her living room and left her husband alone upstairs. Each night Judy would spoon herself around Janet's body, not only to comfort Janet and share her suffering but also to pass on the strength of her (Judy's) healthy body. Janet says that their bond is shaped by the good times and laughter they share together. Janet says, "I'd look forward to my chemo just to have her around." Judy says that the drugs Janet was taking made her gain weight and become puffy around the face, as if "she had a goiter." Judy repeatedly told Janet she was beautiful, saying, "I see the inside. I love you. She was so happy to be with me [during chemotherapy] that she was beautiful. She'd hug me all the time."

Later in the conversation, Janet says, "Since the cancer, you realize how important life is. Money doesn't matter. It's things like laughing and getting together that we really appreciate." Judy adds, "We really enjoy life." Judy and Janet say being a twin means never being alone. Judy responds, "You are never alone because of God, but even if you're unsure of God, you do know that, because of your twin, you are never alone." Like other twins who had been at a talk given by lone twins, Judy and Janet reflect on how terrible it would to be left behind. Judy tells Janet, "You're not going anywhere. If you do, I'm going right behind you." Janet adds, "And I'll wait for you."

TWINSHIP AND KINSHIP

In this chapter more than any other, I have tried to give voice to the talking partners in a way that allows for self-presentation and making meaning on their own terms. My sincere hope is that their voices dominate the text. The Twinsburg twins come through as dynamic actors in their own right, yet at the same time—although a strictly voluntary and opportunistic sampling of twins—they represent a fair range of diversity. What I have done, however, in ordering the sections of this chapter is to give their narratives a linear flow that certainly did not occur in the narratives as they unfolded. In part, the discussion points we presented shaped the content and influenced the ordering of information imparted among us. The fact is that no matter what they were talking about, the talking partners freely jumped back and forth in talking about the past, present, and future.

At the beginning of this chapter, I raised a series of issues about kinship in its guises of genetics (Pálsson 2007; Prainsack et al. 2010), collaterality (Hirsch 2003; Thornton 2001), and relations of caring and sharing. Twinship, as kinship, involves effort (Miller 2005; di Leonardo 2008), and choice (Stone 2010; Weston 1991). I have tried to feature twinship as a form of kinship that has ramifications well beyond what tends to be subsumed under a rather essentialized genetic approach or a rather narrow focus on parents of twins. Twinship, as lived in the embodied and relational experiences of the Twinsburg twins, puts emphasis on the dynamics of collateral kin and sibling cohort relationships (as opposed to intergenerational forms of descent and ancestry). A combined cross-sectional and longitudinal perspective also illustrates the lifelong efforts that the Twinsburg twins put into maintaining links between entire households and also the ways their relationships may fluctuate over the different times and circumstances of their lives. For example, the dramatic life narratives of Arnette and Annette, Steph and Jenna, Karen and Kristy, Pat and Phyllis, Emil and Pete, and Lucy and Linda show over and over again how the two twins can choose to move together and apart during their lives, all the while sharing each other's pains and pleasures.

Yet additional kin-related themes emerge when twins talk about their relationships and lives, whether apart or together. These include the remarked importance of nontwin kin in their lives. Among the Twinsburg twins, although the twin bond is featured, other family members are frequently mentioned. The least mention of kin is made in the youngest age group. Amy and Beth and Gina and Ginger mention their fathers as making important choices about how to develop and nurture their individuality. Karen and Kristy used their mother as a foil for Kristy's naughtiness. Although their parents were divorced, Jeana and Dina refer to how they each have a combination of characteristics they inherited from their respective parent. Randi and Dante fail to mention any siblings but represent themselves as coming from an Italian family. In the second grouping, Tina and Ginuh express a great deal of appreciation and admiration for their mother, who divorced when they were very young and struggled to raise them as a single mom. Jenna and Steph relate that they had an abusive mother and were raised or given homes at times by sisters and brothers. Tim and Tom report that they were part of a large family and state that their primary caretaker was an older brother. Karan and Kim and Sandy and Cindy, two sets of twins in the same family, are also embedded in larger family groupings; it is interesting that Karan says that she is closest to her twin and then Sandy. Tim and Tom, Jenna and Steph, Karan and Kim, and Cindy and Sandy characterize their families as poor farm families. For stage 4, Annette and Arnette pay special attention to their grandparents who raised them.

Lucy and Linda talk about their neglectful mother, being orphans, and living with other siblings. They say that it is an older brother who keeps track of the family now. Dorothy and I mention a special sense of closeness with our younger brother. In stage 4, Jenny and Julie also talk about a mother who was absent in their early childhood. They were raised by relatives but became long-term caretakers of their mother when she became infirm. Pat and Phyllis report problematic relations with their mother as well as a mutual appreciation of their father and feeling close to their cousins. Janet and Judy also have a problematic portrayal of their mother and resent the fact that she always showed favoritism to their older sister who was sickly. Donna and Dianne and Helen and June report that they came from large farm families. Pete and Emil are also from a large family that frequently gets together. They also say that when they were younger, they were part of a threesome with a slightly older brother.

The life or twin cycle approach to relationship also features accounts of decisions and accidents of happenstance that part twins or bring twins together. In the case of the talking partners, perhaps the most differentiating life choice was when one twin got married and the other did not. This is the case for Tim and Tom, Mary and Martha, Steph and Jenna, Chris and Carla, Jeana and Dina, and Gina and Ginger. Having children or not (Dorothy and Dona) or at very different stages of their lives (Pat and Phyllis) also made a difference in twins' lives—as does who got married first (Donna and Dianne) and the number of times each twin has been married (Tina and Ginuh). Kinship and kin choices are an important variable in the telling of twins' lives, but so is chance. Ginuh had a stable, loving husband who supported her career, while Tina struggled through a series of failed marriages. Emil was drafted into the army and Pete failed his physical. Tim was born with a facial birthmark, which left him shy and retiring, compared to his brother. Widowhood has brought Donna and Dianne, Helen and June, and Pete and Emil back together. Divorce has reunited Lucy and Linda. Sickness has reunited Janet and Judy, and Karan, Kim, Sandy, and Cindy.

The talking partners show a great deal of flexibility when it comes to negotiating a caring and sharing relationship that can become lifelong. Segalen (1997)—noting that in modern society social ties are largely deterritorialized and a culture of autonomy and self-actualization conspire against the perpetuation of family—calls for more flexible frameworks of modern kinship. Segalen depicts modern kinship in terms of three core themes: sociability, support, and transfer, or inheritance. Although the narratives of the talking partners mention little about transfer of wealth, or inheritance, aside from mentions of what's mine is hers (Pat and Phyllis) or shared wealth (as in Julie and Jenny and Lucy and Linda pooling resources to live more comfortably together), sociability and support are constant themes in their life stories. The talking partners, however, portray support and sociability as a constant that may take different forms and present different options and challenges as it evolves or matures over the life cycle. It is a matter of choice.

TWINDIVIDUALS

Webs of significance I have spun.

—*Jackson 1989*

No two people would list the same traits [when describing themselves], but some people are good prototypes and others more marginal.

—*Neisser 1988*

"Biology," in any case, is far more fleeting and complex than normally imagined. And heredity and generation are biosocial things.

—*Pálsson 2013*

TWINS TALK PRIVILEGES AN INSIDER'S PERSONAL AND INTERPERSONAL perspective. It is unique in the twin literature as it not only gives voice to identical twins but depicts large aggregates of twins, with attitude, in action at twins festivals. The webs of significance I have woven have moved twins and ethnography from the margins to the center of critical analysis. The book is also unique within the cultural psychology literature because *Twins Talk* introduces new dimensions of analysis to the embodiment and practice of identity and relationship. Conversations that my twin sister, Dorothy, and I had over a period of two days with twenty-two sets of twins in the Twins Days Research

Pavilion during the 2003 Twinsburg Twins Days Festival provide the narratives that anchor each chapter. Throughout this volume I utilize these conversations with the Twinsburg talking partners, along with my own twin experience, to present, position, and consider how this opportunistic sampling of identical twins as individuals and cotagonists actively collaborate, coexpress, co-construct, and negotiate self in terms of presentation, practice, and knowledge. I further depict this kind of agency as twins' self working, or self work. I develop the notion of *twinscapes* to engage how the talking partners view themselves and their lives in everyday practice, as twins, vis-à-vis nontwin, or singleton, others. Twinscapes also include the perspectives twins have of themselves as a couple, or dyadic pair, as well as one twin's outlook on the other twin. Twinscapes, however, entail more than just a twin's perspective. In *Twins Talk,* the notion of twinscapes is used to draw together, contextualize, position, and critically assess a multiplicity of ways that twins may be envisioned. These twinscapes may be positive or negative and are hardly politically neutral. Twins embedded in Western cultural traditions both enact and oppose culturally hegemonic constructions of personhood. *Twins Talk* privileges the perspective of the talking partners, but it also includes the perspectives of popular science, academically specialized fields of professional twins researchers, and my own viewpoints. These viewpoints are shaped by my own experiences as an identical twin and, equally important, by my background and training as an anthropologist who recognizes a multiplicity of selfways that may exist across different cultural traditions as well as within a single culture.

Twins present an opportunity to explore large issues in small places (cf. Amit and Mitchell 2012, vi). Whether speaking of the small places of genetics and molecular biology, shared space and place, couples' relationships, or individual psyches, twins and twinship are also embedded in and stand at the juncture of much larger issues that transcend much larger multiple disciplinary concerns in biomedicine, genetics, biology, psychology, sociology, and anthropology. *Twins Talk* has evolved into a far-ranging and eclectic study. Despite the diversity of twinscapes among academic disciplines, a common feature tends to run through all of them. All of these twinscapes, whether positive, negative, or mixed, recognize identical twins as located, in a variety of ways, on the fault lines of identity. *Twins Talk,* as verb and noun, is unique in the twin research literature in two ways. First, throughout the text, the privileged twinscapes are those of twins themselves. Second, the very processes of envisioning twinscapes and the twinscapes themselves are subjected to critical cultural analysis. These two considerations give the book a sustained critical, militant edge that is unique in the twin research literature.

My aim throughout this volume, whether I have envisioned twins in terms of festivals, bodies, or relationships—as bond, memory, or practice—has been to describe, compare, and contrast the experientially based narratives of twins to the scientifically based narratives of those who study twins. This consideration of twins' own twinscapes, in addition to those of twins researchers, leads to an additional culturally informed twinscape that views twins in Western society as both inheritors of and challengers to Western traditions associated with conceptualizations of nature and nurture, sociocultural constructions self-identity and personhood, as well as autonomy and mutuality. As an identical twin, as a twins researcher, and as an anthropologist, I have been particularly interested in capturing the dialectical tensions that exist between, on the one hand, knowledge we construct of others and, on the other hand, the knowledge they construct of themselves (Jackson 1989). Unlike most academic books on twins, this one has consistently privileged the latter. Not only have I sought to capture a twin's behind-the-face practical, episode-by-episode experience of being a twin, my aim has also been to situate twins and twins researchers within a wider sociocultural context that takes note of variation within and between cultural contexts in order to further interrogate the very idea of culture and the nature of human relationships that activate it.

TIMELY REFLECTION

It has been a challenge while writing *Twins Talk* to keep up on the ever-changing literature on genetics. Although the narrative data were collected in 2003, Dorothy and I attended our most recent twins festival in 2007 and the latest ICTS conference I attended was in 2007. I have tried to incorporate more recent discussions of twins and genetics in the text without being overly technical in my use of language. Throughout *Twins Talk*, I have tried to engage biology but not surrender to it. Although genetic discourse continues to dominate the scene in twin research, there has been a major paradigm shift from a simplistic genetic determinism that opposed biology to environment and viewed identical twins as "robot-like carriers of self-replicating genes" (Spector 2012, 291) to a postgenomic era that documents genetic plasticity and seeks to rethink or even dissolve distinctions between genes and environment (Pálsson 2013, Spector 2012). While the determinists posited a world of shared genes, symmetry, stability, order, and predictability as well as a limited number of causal agents, the new age of genetics focuses on variation, change, unpredictability, and the interactions of multiple causes (Charney 2012). As in the science of genetics, we also see new ways to think about the relationship of the organism to the environment with in anthropology (Pálsson 2013).

Even before the new genetics, biocultural anthropology has challenged the notion that humans are scientifically understandable independently of culture. The predominant model is that in our species, biology and culture coproduce one another (Marks 2012a, 2012b). We certainly see this in anthropological studies of human evolution, studies of health, disease, and nutrition, and biological variations within human populations (Lock and Nguyen 2010). Since I had originally completed the manuscript for *Twins Talk*, however, two new academic works have emerged advocating new ways to conceptualize and dissolve distinctions between humans and environment, and nature and culture. A new, or renewed, biocultural anthropology has been recently advocated by Alan Goodman (2013). Goodman challenges anthropologists to move beyond geneticization—the idea that genes are hyperdeterminative—to model interrelations between culture and human biology as dynamic, as including real people in real places, and attending to meanings and political-economic processes. In their proposed agenda for a new biosocial anthropology, Ingold and Pálsson (2013) not only question the validity of Darwinian genetics but posit new ways of looking at the relationships between organisms and organisms and their environment. Ingold (2013, 8) asserts we are prefigured by our life histories, not by our genes. Rather than then being expressions or realizations of nature as *a priori* or ready-made, our identities by "nature" are biosocial—to be understood as relational and historically embedded. Ingold (2013, 8) asserts that we are "not beings but becomings." As biosocial forms of becoming, we are continually produced by our actions and pronouncements.

Pálsson's (2013, 16) depictions of human beings as having fluid, flexible, and porous boundaries—as necessarily embedded in relations, as neither purely biological or purely social, and as not fixed but constantly in the making yet context dependent—goes a long way to theorizing humans in nature as biosocial beings. But this statement also takes on special relevance as it aptly describes themes that I have already presented with a great deal of ethnographic specificity in *Twins Talk*.

While I embrace the new biosocial or biocultural anthropologies and while it may behoove the new genetics and Darwinian critics to advocate new paradigms that dissolve the boundaries between nature and culture, I am somewhat ambivalent about doing so. This is because whether we are referring to twins talk as a verb or noun, it is situated within an ethnographic context in which a series of Western dualisms prevails. Although it may be intellectually or academically prescient to experiment with dissolving them, these dualisms, invested with a kind of biopower, are laden with meaning in multiple ways that disadvantage or disfavor twins. Thus, in substance and in action, a host of dualisms have helped shape twins' lived worlds and the hegemonic singletons' perceptions of them. As a kind of deviant persona or located on the fault lines of identity and personhood, identical twins, as the talking partners have shown (by the real world or *a priori* physical fact that they look alike), if not exactly dissolving the boundaries between nature and culture, challenge, contradict, confuse, or conflate them.

SUMMARY AND OVERVIEW

I use the remainder of this conclusion to summarize the book and readdress but not resolve issues concerning some common Western dualisms, such as self and other, nature and culture, and the artifice of segmenting self experience into commonly employed analytical categories, including performance, body, mind, relationship, and culture. I introduce the notions of the twindividual, twindividuals, and twindividuality.[1] I also reengage Lawrence Wright's (1997, 1) question of what twins, in terms of their own subjective experiences and as objects of research by singleton others, "tell us about who we are."

Twins Talk begins with Lindholm's (2001, 3) tale of Mulla's dilemma, in which Mulla awakes after the first night of his journey to find his name tag on another's chest. A surprised Mulla asks, "If you are me, then who am I?" *Twins Talk*, too, has been an accounting of the dilemmas of identity and relation raised by pairs of identical twins, where each twin wears the embodied label (or identifiers) of the other twin. These dilemmas stem not only from the confusion of each twin's identity but also from the nature of their relationship and the co-contemporarity twins share in early life. Looking alike combined with constantly being together leads to the conflation or collapse of each twin's identity into an overbonded, singular, or unit, identity. As we have seen, twin stereotypes can be negative and/ or positive. In this volume, I draw on modes of narrative analysis as espoused by Naomi Quinn (2005b) to compare and contrast the narratives of twins and those who research them. Twins are negatively stereotyped by researchers as "individuality-burdened freaks of nature" (Maddox 2006, 67); as creatures of genetic destiny (Teplica 2004); as a method (Bouchard and Popling 1993); as pathologically "interdependent", "symbiotic", or "split selves" (Klein 2003, 10); as closed societies of two" (Kamin 1974); or as problematic, "liminal beings," existing in states of betwixt and between (Turner 1969, 48). The latter may have positive as well as negative aspects, as twins may be deities, important mythic symbols, or subjects of some kind of special treatment.

Twins tend to be very positively depicted by the talking partners as friends for life (Pat and Phyllis), an enhanced self (Tim and Tom), or a blessing from God (Tina and Ginuh). Throughout the text, I use twins' own narratives as I relate their behind-the-face, face-to-face, and in-your-face depictions of the pragmatic aspects of the twin experience, paying particular attention to how twins agentively self work, from the ground up, as individuals, as a set of twins, and as twins en masse to actively reverse, challenge, accommodate, conform to, or reaffirm societal stereotypes of twins.

A strong reflexive tone runs through this volume. I am an identical twin and I conducted the first Twins Days phase of this study with my twin sister, Dorothy, who later participated in two more festivals with me. Like Quinn (2005a), I fully intended to find culture in talk as I designed the Twins Talk Study and the Twins Days interviews.

What I had not anticipated is how the venue I chose to begin my study would lead to additional research and come to shape the tone of my later efforts. Initially, my sole reason for obtaining a booth in the Research Pavilion was to reach a large number of twins over a short period of time. This certainly turned out to be true. Yet I had failed to take into account (and as an experienced ethnographer, I should have known better) how much the surrounding context of the study—the festival itself—would affect not only the narratives I collected but the direction my study would come to take. As an identical twin and, for the first time in my anthropological career, a native, I thought I knew pretty much all there was to know about being a twin. I also thought I had a background of academic knowledge sufficient for a quick and focused study on the embodiment of identity. What I had not expected was how much the festival experience and festival setting, where twins revel in and perform their twinship, would come to influence the writing of *Twins Talk*.

My long-term, firsthand familiarity with being and having a twin hardly prepared me for the shock of seeing thousands of twins together at Twinsburg. Being a twin is not the same as seeing twinship celebrated by a massive collectivity of twins of all types and ages. Being a twin at a twins festival heightens awareness of twinship not only as a relationship and type of identity but also in terms of twins and twinship as a sociocultural category of a particular kind of self. One does not have to be a trained anthropologist to realize this, as the chapter 3 narratives—whether from participating twins, conference organizers, researchers, or media—show.

The talking partners came to our sessions dressed identically. They were hyper-stimulated over being twins. As we saw in chapter 3, for two or three days, twins position themselves as the norm and singletons as the exotic other. For twins, the festival twinscapes are permeated with notions of rebellion and actions as rites of reversal. In addition, my choice to bring my own twin sister, Dorothy, into the study, and to talk with twins as twins, positioned our talk as four-way conversations in which the conversationally negotiated, collective aspects of being twins emerged in ways that may not have surfaced had I chosen to talk with each twin separately or even interview pairs of twins by myself. The extent to which I had absorbed "us" (as twins) as opposed to "them" (as singletons, media, and researchers) would become even more apparent as I attended and participated in my first twin research conference—the ICTS in Denmark.

As I attended more twins festivals and participated in more twin research conferences, my interest moved beyond those of the twins' own strategies for dealing with Mulla's dilemma expressed as the embodiment of identity among twins to encompass a range of dilemmas raised by twins researchers within the multiple fields of twin research. Although, as we have seen, there is considerable controversy within the field of twin research, one emergent dilemma I began to appreciate—whether in reference to biologies, psychologies, or sociologies of twins and twinship—was the prevalence of unrecognized or unexamined culture-bound, Western-based assumptions that predominated among researchers. My revelry in being "the native" for once and my nascent militancy began to develop beyond an opposition to the largely reductionist and negative characterizations of twins and twinship. By reductionist I mean twins as method, twins as population, or twins as DNA/clones. By negative I refer to twinship as a psychological handicap (twins as impaired selves, twins as overly connected or too close). As an anthropologist attending research conferences, I began to appreciate that the view from the ground up and practical experiences of twinship, as related by twins, ran counter to what many researchers concluded about them; I also appreciated the degree to which the perspectives of the researchers were culturally bound and determined. Certainly, there is a good deal that is helpful and positive in twin research and the twin method. I have chosen to weave my critique of selected twins researchers around their rather naive notions of what constitutes culture and ethnography, as well as the idea that objectivity of science exists above and beyond culture. In what follows, I proceed to combine my conclusion and summary in ways that bridge, blend, or integrate the artificial topical divisions imposed by segmenting the twin experience to a chapter-by-chapter presentation and analysis. In so doing, I will revisit the dualisms it has also been my intention to bridge, if not dissolve or collapse.

THINKING WITH TWINS

When Dorothy and I asked Tim and Tom what it meant to be twins, Tom responded that if he knew the answer to that question, he would "write it down in an equation and not worry about it." Yet, Tim and

Tom, in their enthusiastic, philosophical, and extremely informative talking session, certainly eschewed the notion of formulas or equations, preferring instead to "worry" the question. Tim and Tom even employed new terms, like the *twin dynamic,* to put into play their own experience-based notions of twinship. Thinking about twins through use of formulas or equations, however, is exactly what most of the ICTS twins researchers do. As we have seen throughout *Twins Talk,* and especially in chapters 4 and 5, twins and their twinship do tend to be formulaically reduced to numbers. In this sense, twins never get to participate in acts of becoming (cf. Ingold 2013). This is definitely the case when referring to biocomputing or the use of huge data sets collected from twins, dead and alive, who represent a particular "research population." It is also the case when twins become reduced to a method, as in the twin method in which data from samples of identical twins, nonidentical twins, and their singleton siblings are conceptualized through a series of dependent and independent variables and are statistically compared and contrasted to each other. Lykken's dictum "anecdote is not data" (McGue and Jacono 2007) sums it up well. Also formulaic are the extremely essentializing or nomothetic theories that can be associated with genetic determinism and objects relation psychology or even the notion that all exotic attitudes and practices toward twins, as exhibited cross-culturally, can be explained by a single factor—the shock of a twin birth. In addition, at twin research conferences, disciplinary boundaries remain largely intact, with geneticists, obstetricians, and psychologists allotted their own coterminous sessions. Aside from the shared venue and social events, there is little attempt to cross disciplinary boundaries to either engage the discordance or bring it all together.

The "data" in *Twins Talk* are hardly formulaic. The sense of order created through ethnographic writing and interpretation belies the oftentimes chaotic delivery of the data. Twins talk is a messy form of data that transgresses the rather rigid boundaries that characterize the academic or disciplinary specialties of twins researchers. The twins' narratives come from free-ranging, largely spontaneous conversations between four and even six talking partners. The level of enthusiasm and engagement the partners brought to our talking sessions was high; as Tom said during his talking session, "How are we doing? I've only been rehearsing for this for forty-nine years." The festival experience itself contributed to the high levels of passion and urgency that the talking partners brought to our conversations. The equalizing, shared twin status of all the partners provided them with the ability to take the conversation in any direction they desired. The partners freely talked over each other or finished each other's sentences. They abruptly changed the subject, argued, and agreed, and skipped from one life cycle stage to another. They mixed specifics and generalities, contradicted themselves, and fluctuated between states of high humor, extreme silliness, tears, and profound revelations. Moreover, they did so sitting side by side in look-alike, acting, and interacting bodies.

When twins enact, describe, and reflect on their twinship, much more than Lykken's despised anecdotes becomes evident. *Twins Talk* is far more than tales being told; it is twinship in action. Rather than being rooted in the quest for significant statistical relationships between a limited range of predetermined variables, *Twins Talk* works from the ground up, focusing on both the performance of twinship and the lived and practical experiences of being twins. When identical twins talk about, perform, and make sense of their own lived experiences of twinship, they do so in ways that pay little attention to the requisites of statistical measurement, to the search for underlying genetic codes, or to explications of the psychopathologies of the twin bond that so capture the attentions of twins researchers. Moreover, festival twins articulate a sense of self-determination and self-awareness, which are both singular and paired and sometimes in agreement with—but also often counterhegemonic to—the largely unexamined Western cultural ideals of individualism that are tacitly assumed or espoused by researchers. The Twins Talk Study demands a bio-psycho-socio-cultural–informed analytic approach that can deal with the lifelong practice, experience, and performance of twinship as well as the inherent contradictions and messiness of qualitative data.

In the process of developing this manuscript, I encountered the cultural psychology approach as so succinctly developed in Neisser and Jopling's book *The Conceptual Self in Context* (1997). This comprehensive and culturally sensitive paradigm allowed me to focus and fine-tune my wide-ranging anthropological perspectives and interests in twins.[2] Adopting the perspectives that narrative or talk (Quinn 2005b, 2) reflects, produces, and enacts culture and that culture exists in performance (Hastrup 1995a, 78), I have employed the cultural psychology approach, with its emphasis on language and interaction, to bring the diverse subject matters and perspectives of this book into a singular conceptual framework. As we have seen, cultural psychology draws from an amalgam of perspectives that cross disciplinary boundaries and recognize the interactive impacts of biology, psychology, and culture. In every chapter of *Twins Talk*, I have addressed twins and twinship in terms of cultural psychology's concept of selfways. Selfways are characteristic patterns of sociocultural participation or characteristic ways of being a person in the world. Whether the subject is the collective performance of twinship at festivals, twins' bodies, their relationships, or their life stages, these selfways encode key cultural ideals and values. Among these is what makes a good, appropriate, moral person. Located on the fault lines, twins certainly evidence that multiple constructions of self can coexist within a particular society and that multiple layers of self can coexist within a particular individual. Twins in talk and action show how self in practice is situated, contextualized, and negotiated. Twins talk dynamically combines high humor with utter seriousness. Twins agree both to disagree and to agree. Twinsburg twins' selfways, whether embedded in narrative or practice, illustrate a kind of creative engagement with the sociocultural environment that experientially grounds, coalesces, or transcends traditional disciplinary or academic boundaries. In chapter 6 and in most other chapters, twins' selfways are reflected in the wider schema of power relations, histories, and societal structures. The militant oppositional ethos that flows through *Twins Talk*, variously expressed as enhanced selves and a less constrained mutuality or as things only a twin can know, shows a twinned persona that not only acts within a cultural context but acts to challenge, change, or alter that context (cf. Markus et al. 1997; Neisser and Jopling 1997; Shweder 1991).

I have presented twins existing, in their various guises of self, identity, and relationship, both as an exceptional or deviant kind of walking and talking personification of a culturally imagined type and as evidence of the fact that there is room for multiple selfways and self stylings within Western society. Twin selves and a twin's self as embodied, active, agentive, performing, relational, and remembering entities flow through the chapters of this book. Located on the fault lines of identity in Western culture, identical twins both challenge and confirm hegemonic notions of self.

Throughout *Twins Talk*, I have employed and developed a number of terms in addition to *selfways* to help explicate the performance and practice of identity, as well as the biopsychosocial politics of identity making as they relate to twins and twinship. Concepts like *self stylings, self work, the twin game, intercorporeality, co-contemporarity, inter-est, the split, embodiment, enskilment, minimalist ethnography, embodiment of identity, performance of identity, enhanced self, rites of reversal, insider-outsider, couple effect, collateral kin, sociocentric-egocentric, cultural persona, deviance as positive and negative,* and *the twin dynamic* have been embraced, invented or redeveloped to analyze twins talk and the practice of twinship. The cultural psychology umbrella or multifaceted and dynamic approach has opened up some new perspectives with which to consider twins' perspectives on Mulla's "Who am I?" question, but in the case of identical twins it also opens some new perspectives on the "Who are we?" question. The latter question has a double meaning in that the "we" relates to the dyadic qualities of twinship as well as the collectively identified societal "we." What do twins tell us about ourselves? In *Twins Talk*, the concept of *our selves* (a term largely unexamined by twins researchers and popular science writers) is hardly taken for granted. Instead, *our selves* gets depicted in detail as the historically based sociocultural and largely hegemonic constructions of self and identity particular to a kind of self that is normative in Western contexts.

TWINDIVIDUALS: CROSSING DIVIDES

Although I have readily engaged a critique of traditional twins studies, I would like to reengage two key conceptual issues that I have critiqued but also reified in this book. These include segmenting the twin experience into analytic categories, such as separate chapters on festival, body, bond, culture, and kin. Although *Twins Talk* purports that these distinctions are quite artificial when it comes to actual lived, practical experiences of twins (whether observed, enacted, or remembered), I have structured my text in a way that replicates the long-standing disciplinary boundaries or fissures that I critique twin research conferences for perpetuating. Second, in my attempts to identify, challenge, collapse, or bridge the numerous dualisms associated with thinking with or through twins, I have not only created dualisms of my own—most prominently perhaps that of twin versus researcher—but also, much to my chagrin, apparently reified the very dualisms I have sought to collapse. In what follows, I seek to reengage these two issues by placing parts or aspects of self and dualisms in the contexts of ethnography and reflexive anthropology. I do so by developing the bridging notions of the twindividual as one of a twin pair, twindividuals as a twin pair or dyad, and twindividuality as the practice of twinship as well as a socioculturally shaped and constructed phenomenon. By using the terms *twin, twin pair,* and *twinship,* the talking partners embody and enact coexisting relational and individual selfways.

A culturally informed ethnography of twins and twinship provides descriptive and analytic depth to the concept of a biosocial self, advocated by Ingold and Pálsson (2013). As we have seen, bridging the realms of biology and culture, cultural psychology takes the body into account as a biological domain of self. Locating self within the body, Ulric Neisser (1988) identifies multiple kinds of information that constitute self-knowledge, as well as self/other knowledge. He is especially concerned with how the body self both perceives and acts on the world around him or her and is also the object of perception and cognition. Neisser (1988), whose work is rooted in neurology and cognitive and perceptual psychology, elaborates on his notion of the perceiving, acting, conceived body self by identifying five interrelated and interactive features of self: the ecological self, the interpersonal self, the extended self, the private self, and the conceptual self. Each self is marked by its own version of an answer to the "Who am I?" question. Neisser (1988) offers two caveats to his multidimensional model of self that relates to the issues raised in the preceding paragraph. First, these five kinds of self-knowledge, although useful for analytic purposes, are actually rarely experienced as distinct. And second, they are riddled with contradictions. Neisser (1988, 58) goes on to conclude his discussion of self theories with the addendum that he hopes that his five features of self "will turn out to be correct in outline if not in detail." It is Neisser's outline I draw upon here in the discussion of twindividuality as a concept that both distinguishes and unifies twins' selves.[3]

Neisser's notion of the *ecological self*—as in "'I' am the person here, engaged in this place and this particular activity" (Neisser 1988,

36)—connotes an experiential, physical, bounded body that is embedded in a physical environment. The *interpersonal self*—as in "I am the person who is engaged here in this particular human interchange" (Neisser 1988, 36)—involves a concept of self and a concept of other. This interpersonal self also involves intersubjectivity (as attributing thoughts and feelings to other people) and mutuality (as intimacy) and comes into existence when two people interact (Neisser 1988, 41). The *extended self*—as in "I am the person who regularly engages in certain specific and familiar routines" (Neisser 1988, 36)—refers to memories of a unique past that confirms identity. This extended self is thus cumulative and autobiographical. The *private self*—as in " I am in principle the only person who can feel this unique and particular pain" (Neisser 1988, 36)—refers to private, internal self-consciousness and personal thoughts, beliefs, and ideas that are exclusively our own and not available to anyone else. The *conceptual self* describes conceptual or cultural models of self, as in "I am what I am, what I notice and what I have been told" (Neisser 1988, 53). The conceptual self includes dominant and alternative theories of how we fit into society, what we should do, and how we should be treated. Identical twins and twins talk certainly confirm the existence of these overlapping or interrelated categories or features of self, but they also give play to their contradictions. This is particularly true when it comes to the problematic details of self and self/other relations as expressed in my outline of the various chapters of *Twins Talk*, in which evolving, interpersonal, intersubjective, and twin-twin dyadic relationships play a central role in forming an individual sense of self as well as a sense of having a paired identity. Considering what we have seen about twins, it would be fairly easy to amend each one of Neisser's five "Who am I?" questions with "Who are we?" versions that refer to the twin couple. This facility with *I-ing* and *we-ing*, as demonstrated throughout *Twins Talk*, is a core characteristic of the twindividual or twins' own self theories. In what follows, I situate Neisser's (1988) discussion of the five selves in twins talk in order to create a brief review and to bridge the boundaries I have created in the structure of my text.

Ecological Self

Identical twins offer interesting conundrums when it comes to notions of embodied self and embodied sensibilities. The talking partners make much of their physical bodies as compromising key definitions of embodied identity, such as the idea that each individual is physically unique in the world and that face and body are key identifiers and authenticators of an individual self. Despite the tendency of outsiders to conflate or confuse their resembling physical identities, twins talk demonstrates how twins play the twin game as they mine the surfaces of their bodies for traits of same and different and act together to take on the role of educating the observer by providing clues to their twinned and individual identities. Using data from twins talk, I have argued that biologically identical twins actually have a more refined and detailed body image or sense of embodied self-awareness than singletons. At the same time, however, identical twins enact a strong sense of embodied sensibility that includes a highly developed, hypercognized, or even intercorporeal "we." Twins must act and react in an environment where others constantly confuse their identities. Twins, as we have seen, bring an embodied enskilment to identity negotiation. Twindividuals negotiate a sense of each twin as physically distinct or distinguishable from the other twin, yet at the same time hold that they are unique because they are twins. Moreover, in the depictions of the Twins Days twins through childhood to at least early adolescence, one's body was ecologically located alongside one's constant companion, or twin. This also has important implications for the interpersonal self.

Neisser (1988) integrates, or brings a unity to, his five features of self in two ways. First, he orders them as sequential stages of child development. Second, he uses the category of the conceptual self to assert that "self-concepts do not stand alone," and "each one of the other four kinds of self-knowledge is represented in the conceptual self" (Neisser 1988, 52). By unifying or transcending the categories of self, which are artificially segmented or distinguished for purposes of analysis, self-concepts originate in social life and include ideas about the physical body, interpersonal communication, autobiographical memories, as well as how thoughts and feelings take on meaning. When it comes to the Western theories of self, Neisser (1988) recognizes the conceptual self as sociocultural and rooted in theories of the mind as expressed through psychology, philosophy, religion, and—most importantly for Neisser when it comes to the body self—biology and medicine.

Interpersonal Self

The interpersonal self describes the development of self-awareness and self-knowledge in terms of self/other relations. This certainly relates to the physical resemblance of twins as Karen and Kristy raise the issue that being a twin means that there is someone else walking around with your face and body. But the slash in *self/other* also evokes the notion of self-knowledge among twindividuals not only as an indicator of division or boundaries, as in "I am me and not you," but also in terms of the twin bond as a self/other awareness coexisting with a well-developed shared sense of connection as well as separation. The talking partners can clearly communicate a concept of self and a concept of other, as when Jeana states, "Make no mistake, we are two distinct individuals." Yet, when it comes to the interpersonal self, the twins also express a sense of fluidity or openness in their self/other boundaries, as when Pete and Emil collaborate in the production of a single sentence or when Mary and Martha state that they hold each other to account for being the same ethical person. Neisser (1988) describes intersubjectivity as how accurately we attribute thoughts and feeling to other people. Not only does this sample of twins feel that they are best friends for life, but they feel that they know each other better than would be possible for any pair of singletons. Although Neisser holds that mutuality (1988) comes into existence when two people are engaged in personal interaction, my analysis of the twins talk leads me to a more practical view of mutuality as a tool or strategy for negotiating relationships rather than a state of being or abstraction of self/other relationships. Also, when it comes to interpersonal relationships as a form of self/other awareness among the Twins Days twins, the festival experience itself documents a strongly developed sense of self/selves as a kind of twin enhanced self or twinned pair (as in self plus other) as opposed to the inferior and pitied singleton (self versus other) self. The co-contemporarity and dyadic identities of the talking partners not only influence the physical body self and interpersonal self but affect an extended self who exists in a dynamic state of twindividuality.

Extended Self

The extended self is cumulative and autobiographical. It is a self-knowledge, where identity is constituted and confirmed through personal and shared memories of a unique past (Neisser 1988). For Neisser, although memories can be shared, memory records many more of one's own actions than of anybody else's. All of the talking partners who were reared together (except Jenny and Julie) report a sense of intensely shared space and place, especially in childhood. Annette and Arnette recount memories of earliest childhood as an unbounded extended self or as a single left- and right-sided, shared being. Tina states, "I can't remember a moment in my childhood when she [Ginuh] wasn't there." In the case of all the talking partners, shared memories are of extreme importance. Festival twins dress alike to relive their childhoods. They talk to other twins about their shared pasts. Twins' pasts are also unique in that the shared memories are also positioned. As twindividuals, the Twinsburg twins' memories confirm their "unique" identities both as individuals and as a twin pair. For example, many of the talking partners can recall vivid and elaborate memories of being separated for the first time from their twin. When it comes to self-knowledge as an extended self, identical twins constitute notable exceptions to the extent that their lives are shared and unique because they are twins. Throughout *Twins Talk*, I have made much of the co-contemporarity of twins. Complaints, such as Karen and Kristy's grievance of being treated as a unit, exemplify autobiographical memories of a unique twinned past. We have certainly seen how when sets of twins talk to sets of twins, biographies are co-constructed through discourse. In mutually recounting their memories, twins will argue about which event affected which twin. For example, one twin will recount a personal memory and the other will assert it actually happened to her. Moreover, chapter 7 shows how when twins in different friend groups recollect their lives, their twinned memories encode similar stages of self-development as they reflect on twin cycles that involve an original state of being together, splitting up, going their separate ways in life, and in the case of the Twins Days and festival twins, coming back together. From a life cycle perspective, twins talk shows twins' autobiographies of extended selves have an elastic quality that shifts back and forth between closeness and distance and between autobiographies and co-constructed biographies. Twindividuality is a lifelong process of becoming. The closeness, intimacy, and importance of co-presence as expressed in twins talk and action (as in Amy and

Beth's mutual grooming, and Janet and Judy's hugging and kissing) also raise a host of issues related to privacy.

Private Self

The private self refers to a private, internal self-consciousness. It includes personal thoughts, beliefs, and ideas that are exclusively one's own and not available to anyone else (Neisser 1988). According to Neisser, "We typically have less information about other individuals than about ourselves and our private experience is exclusively our own" (1988, 55). Although our talking partners, as twindividuals, show a highly developed private sense of self, albeit shaped in comparison and contrast with one's twin's self (as in Pat being like their mother and Phyllis being like their father; Tom emphatically stating I'm married, he [Tim] is not; or split stories). Some would also assert that their bonded intimacy is such that they cannot keep secrets from each other and that they can wordlessly share thoughts, or even enter into each other's bodily or mindful experiences (as in the ESP stories of Lucy and Linda, Pat and Phyllis, and Donna and Dianne). Certainly this sample of twins has a named, self-acknowledged identity, but it can be compromised when their named singular identities are accompanied by acknowledged and named pair identities, as in "the Davis twins," or by rhyming or alliterating pairing monikers like "Twin and Twain," "Tina and Gina," or "Lucy and Linda," or simply by being referred to as "the twins." As we have seen, identical twins have to assert their private selves and individuality in the face of those who see their twinship and the private nature of their shared bond as undermining their own boundaries of self-consciousness. According to Neisser (1988, 51), "Philosophers in the Western tradition such as Descartes have described this private self as the only self worth knowing." This leads us to the final facet of self and self-knowledge.

Conceptual Self

Neisser's (1988, 35) last feature of self, the conceptual self, refers to a "self-concept" as drawn from networks of socially based meaning, assumptions, and theories about human nature. It is what people believe about themselves in the sense that "each of us has a concept of himself as a particular person in a familiar world" (Neisser 1988, 52). While there is a single predominant cognitive model, Neisser also recognizes that the hegemonic cultural model (in this case, I would argue, twindividuality) can be accompanied by several more or less distinct subtheories of self. Clearly, although chapter 7 shows that the talking partners live or have lived fairly conventional lives, their festival participation heightens their sense of being, as twins, a kind of deviant persona. When it comes to cultural models of self, festival twins have an acute sense of being a case apart or on the fault lines of identity in Western culture. As many of them state, only a twin can know what it means to be a twin. Thoroughly aware of the negative popular stereotypes of twins as freaks, the festival twins develop a counterrhetoric that celebrates their twinship as the closest of human bonds. In chapter 6, we saw how twins talk encoded basic Western values, such as equal opportunity, fairness, freedom of choice, and self-development. Throughout the text I have tried to document how twindividuals act collectively, individually, and as pairs to situate and position knowledge about their selves through a multiple series of insider and outsider views. These include twins' perspectives on themselves, others' views of them, and how they, as twins, view others' views of them.

CONCEIVING THE BODY SELF: CULTURES OF SCIENCE

Neisser's (1988) five kinds of self-knowledge also flow through the work of twins researchers. Among researchers, however, twins are positioned as the objects or tools in the study of self-knowledge. The "Who am I?" questions become replaced by "What are they?" questions. In this usage, twins exist mainly as suppliers of a kind of informational crop to be planted and harvested by nontwin others. The emphasis is placed not on twins' subjective knowledge as twins, but on what they reveal about the nature of identity, self, and personhood in general or in terms of some predefined hypothesis or purposes of a particular study. When subjective or intersubjective kinds of self-knowledge among twins emerge as topics of consideration, authoritative knowledge rests securely in domains of the researchers' expertise, operating from the top down rather than the ground up. Also, when experts in the psychology of twins and twinship grapple with topics of self-knowledge, self-development, and intersubjectivity, as in the twin bond, the view of twins that emerges gets positioned in a largely negative fashion. Unlike the experiential case for twins, twins researchers would view twindividuals not in terms of a flexible or fluid and situated sense of self as identity and relationship; instead, they would view the notion as a kind of oxymoron in that being paired and being individual are either mutually exclusive or somehow self-impairing. In *Twins Talk*, I have tried to show how twin research, although multi-themed, tends to reflect and reify disciplinary divisions rather than integrate or unite them. But when twins become concept or method rather than actors, dualisms of self and other and twin versus individual remain largely unchallenged. There is little space for the acting, practicing, self work, and intercorporeal-identified, same and different, twindividual to emerge. Throughout *Twins Talk* I have argued that these scientifically, hegemonic, singleton-dominated kinds of self-knowledge can also be located within particular sociocultural and historical frameworks.

While it was relatively easy to integrate twins' own experientially based kinds of self-knowledge into Neisser's (1988) five-feature framework, it was more difficult to do the same with the works of twins researchers unless I focused on psychological and neurological studies of cognitive and perceptual development among twins in ways that directly parallel Neisser's. As I have chosen (following Lindholm 2001) to utilize Neisser's theory in outline, rather than detail, I find it necessary to collapse some of his features or categories. While the ecological, physical, embodied twin self or twin selves continue to stand out at both twin research conferences I attended, as well as in the twin research literature, the interpersonal, extended, and private self categories can be easily collapsed, and the conceptual self remains relatively underdeveloped.[4]

Ecological Self

Among twins researchers, we find the physical, ecologically located body to be the subject of a variety of veins of research that tends to view twins (in "What are they?" terms) as a kind of special condition, whether it be shared genes, medical issues concerning maternal and child health, or the nature/nurture debates. The most essential of the essentialists view twins as clones, as products of their genes or hidden biological and biochemical codes of self, as contemporary clones, as 100 percent genetically identical twins who are as close to being the same biological person as possible. Collectively, because of the high degree of genetic resemblance, identical twins' MZ bodies—as compared with each other and the bodies of DZ fraternal twins and/or singleton siblings—become a resource population with which to investigate potential interactions between body and the wider physical environment. Research interests may range from the subcellular environment (as in epigenetic) to environment as lifestyle choices (as in diet and exercise) or exposure to environmental toxins. Twins' bodies become medicalized to the extent that the larger the sample, the more likely researchers will be to find twins who are discordant for a host of diseases such as diabetes, heart disease, or specific categories of mental disorder. Twin bodies also become medicalized as a risk category in terms of potential hazards regarding in utero development, birth, and early childhood development. Not only do twins pose a risk for each other, but the developing fetuses pose risks for the mother. Identified as the Rosetta Stone of behavioral genetics (Bouchard and Popling 1993), twins' bodies have also dominated the nature/nurture debates. The indirect genetics pits genes against environment, or the immediate social environment as in the twins' own nuclear family.

Interpersonal, Extended, and Private Self

I bring these categories together—as theories of mind and interpersonal interaction, as opposed to theories of bodies—not only because they reflect a mind/body dualism that characterizes twin research but because twins and twinship are commonly portrayed as of interest only to the extent that they are deficient or wanting in each of these attributes of self-knowledge. Despite statements to the effect that most twins develop normally and are psychologically healthy, the interpersonal twinned self that is of interest to researchers is the impaired or unhealthy one. The "What are they?" question becomes the "What is wrong with them?" question. Researchers may fault the interpersonal twin self in terms of an inadequate differentiation of self and other. When it comes to the extended self, twins are seen as too close or governed by a strongly bonded sense of mutuality that is seen to compromise each twin's independence. This closeness and inadequate differentiation of self from other, along with looking the same, also compromises the private self in the sense that twins' unit identity may override their individual ones and close them off from developing relationships with nontwin others. Because, in part, independence is favored over mutuality, and twins as pairs tend to be compared with singletons rather than with other types of coupled or paired relationships, the twin condition becomes pathological and twinship impedes normal psychosocial development.

Conceptual Self

As Neisser (1988, 51, 56) notes, "Philosophers of the Western tradition have treated the private self as the only self worth knowing." Neisser's notion of the conceptual self entails various versions (true or untrue) of what people believe about themselves. Although, in their own introductions or in review articles or books, twins researchers pay lip service to some notion of culture, in terms of variation in twin beliefs and practices, these seldom take the form of any serious examination of alternative (to Western) conceptions of self. When social factors are taken into account, they focus on environment as family, class, or lifestyle choice. What remain unexamined are conceptual theories of self as documented or described across the cultural spectrum. Most importantly, researchers who query "what twins tell us about ourselves" seem to overlook that we too have a culture and that more open, fluid, or processual, relational constructions of self may predominate in cultures less dominated by a Western historical tradition where individual persons are viewed as distinct from the relationships that bring them together and produce them (Strathern 1988, 13). Twindividuality, as a kind of self plus or self enhanced by relationship, fails to emerge as a topic of interest among twins researchers largely because researchers reflect a Western cultural bias of opposing individual to relationship. For researchers, the twindividual is problematic; for a talking partner twin, it is a real-life state of practice and lifelong shared being.[5] If Neisser's conceptual self is useful in bringing together that which has been made artificially distinct by textual format, one more "divisive" issue begs additional consideration. This is the notion of dualism or tendency and habits for dualistic thinking. Dualism has special resonance for twins and the twindividual.

ENGAGING DUALISMS

As already stated, the venue I chose to initiate the Twins Talk Study had a marked effect on the direction of the study. Our location in the Twins Days Research Pavilion brought us face to face with groups of twins researchers as well as twins. As I listened to what twins had to say, I also became increasingly interested in what was said about them. In a discussion of the ethnographic process, Jackson (1989, x) refers to the "dialectic between knowledge we construct of others and knowledge they construct of others and of us." Ironically, while becoming a twins researcher, I was coming to position myself as a militant twin in order to more critically appraise (if not actually oppose) what researchers had to say about twins and twinship. To paraphrase Jackson, I myself have created a dialectic between the knowledge that twins construct of others (as singletons and researchers) and the knowledge that researchers directly construct of twins and, thus, indirectly of themselves. For purposes of analysis, therefore, I have introduced a new dialectic into a field already riddled with them. It is important to note, however, that although there are areas of agreement as well as disagreement among the talking partners and twins researchers, I may be legitimately faulted for skewing the twins' perspectives as against that of researchers when in fact twins talk in practice enacts a more positioned or refined rather than dialectic standpoint.[6] In the section that follows, I use twindividuality, as concept and practice, to bridge some key dualisms inherent in twin research and popular notions of twinship.

Also a twin, Penelope Farmer (1996, 10), in her own combination of autobiography and anthology of literary and scientific texts on twins, has made much of the dialectical and dualistic characteristics of twins. She refers to twins as the "objects of fascination compounded by fear," or what she calls the "simple freakdom of mere doubleness." According to Farmer (1996, 6), "What began as a book on twins, pure and simple, turned itself increasingly into a book on doubles, alter egos, generally, and so digresses into one on the number two generally, on duality, dichotomy, and division." Farmer (1996, 10, 6) notes the negative and positive features of twins and twinship, stating that while identical twins confound the notion that each person must be and is unique, both identical and fraternal twins embody the myth of perfect companionship. Tensions between alike and unalike stand at the heart of many of the dichotomies, ambiguities, paradoxes, or dualities of twins. As with any doubled image of anything that is and is not what it relates to (Farmer 1996, 370), twins evoke and challenge many of the dualisms intrinsic to Western thought and philosophical traditions.

A number of these dualisms flow through twins talk, both in terms of the voices of twins and the text itself. Prominent among these are nature/culture, self/other, single/dual, same/different, individual/collective, close/distant, autonomy/mutuality, separate/merge, informant/researcher, and action/abstraction.[7] Certainly a postmodernist feminist agenda in anthropology in particular has criticized the dualistic thinking of Western traditions (Mascia-Lees and Johnson Black 1999) and has offered strategies to challenge, reconceptualize, bridge, deconstruct, or eschew these dualisms. Recognizing that culture is a system of contested meanings, I have tried to approach these dualisms as flexible, far from mutually exclusive, in that one does not negate or deplete the other. Rather than relegate twins to some kind of rarified realm of meaning or symbolic state of being liminal or the betwixt and between (as does Turner 1984), I have sought to present a kind of middle ground where dualisms are experienced, negotiated, repositioned, contested, collapsed, or ignored.

Just as I find the concept of twindividual useful for transcending, integrating, or collapsing what Neisser (1988) holds to be five distinct kinds of self-knowledge, I find the notion of the twindividual as useful in the sense that it joins person to relationship. A twin may be construed both as an individual person and as a relational being. Twins, whether they are speaking of themselves or whether others are speaking about them, exemplify what Strathern (1988, 12)—although speaking of constructions of personhood in Melanesia—describes as a person who is "construed from the vantage point of the relations that constitute him or her." In *Twins Talk*, I have depicted twinship as a kind of enhanced self, self plus, or self plus other, where a less constrained mutuality or a sense of connectedness operates in the negotiation of both individual and collective identities. Twindividuals produce and are produced by their dyadic relationship. The physical embodied likeness of identical twins, along with the intense and positioned co-contemporarity of childhood and adolescence, both produces and eliminates differences. A defining feature of twinship is the lifelong negotiation of same and different, both within the twin dyad and as twins in a singleton-dominated world. Twinship is plural and singular at the same time. Strathern (1988, 348) writes of the Melanesian "dividual" as having partible or divisible aspects of self. She contrasts this construction of self with the Western notions of the individual as an indivisible, bounded unit. Identical twins originate from the same fertilized egg. Conceived, gestated, and born together, their relationship, not their singleness or individuality, is the *a priori* fact of their shared existence.[8] Despite the new emphasis on genetic variation, identical twins are more genetically similar than artificially created clones. They also, in their formative years, share space and place in a social as well as physical sense. The twindividual and twindividuals are relationally constructed. Yet they exist in and express Western sociocultural constructions of self and identity and mutuality and autonomy at the same time that they refine and challenge them. Cross-cultural comparisons of twins and their identities and mutualities with exotic others are certainly informative as they help mark our own cultural biases of what is held (by twins researchers) to be natural in the human condition. But the talking partners are not Wari, Nyaka, or Melanesians; they are Westerners and demonstrate the notions that contingent elements of the egocentric and sociocentric exist in us all. *Twins Talk* shows how adult twins in action, interaction, and reflection readily and enthusiastically engage the "Who am I?" and "Who are we?" questions of identity posed by their existence as a "special condition or deviant persona.

A twindividual as a type of personal identity is conterminously at the same time an individual, a particular kind of self/other, and a "we" relationship. If the cultural fit of comparative frameworks like the Wari or Melanesians as processual or divisible identities seems strained and may well baffle our talking partners, let me choose a different metaphor they would agree with. Just as their homes are unlocked to each other, the Twinsburg life histories show that within the edifice of each twindividual's self there is always a place or a room for her or his twin.

ACTING THROUGH CATEGORIES AND CONTRADICTIONS

Analysis of concepts and ideas (whether in categories such as body or bond) or attempts to recharacterize dualisms, as discussed above, tend to remove twins and twinship from the realms of immediate experience. Like many twins researchers, I see twins are indeed good to think with. In *Twins Talk*, I have taken an ethnographic approach that captures twins in action and interaction, performing their twinship at festivals through embodied self styling, conversational interactions, mutual reflections on commonplace and exceptional activities, and experiences and interpretations of their wider world of meaning. Self work among twins takes place from the ground up. *Twins Talk*, as a study of identical twins, captures what Prainsack et al. (2007, 5) term twins' "practical experience of being genetically identical." *Twins Talk* reveals in situated detail how identical twins agentively pose alternative selfways or self stylings wherein twins are enhanced selves and the intimate mutualities of twinship, forged in shared childhood, can develop to become lifelong, uniquely kinned bonds.

Most twins researchers, certainly those who eschew anecdotal data, work in the Western intellectual tradition of proceeding deductively from the top down (cf. Cohen 1994, 276). In contrast, I have positioned my study from the ground up. As Westbrook (2008, 85) states, "Why bother with the cumbersome apparatus of ethnography if there is nothing to discover or if the 'native' is operating in the domain of the already known?" To paraphrase Westbrook (2008, 23), who refers to the process of ethnography not twins, if you want to know the world of twins, then why not ask the people who live there and have conversations with them? When analysis becomes grounded, in part, in the actual experiential worlds of adult twins, it provides them a forum to co-communicate and construct their selves from a lifetime perspective. Although the talking partners may state that only a twin knows what it means to be a twin, they are very adept at expressing through performance, practice, and talk how their twin bodies, in likeness and shared space and place, act and interact as (to borrow from Csordas 1994, 1) sites of "representation and being in the world." When twins talk and experience becomes a baseline for analysis, we begin to understand how twins, as named individuals and oftentimes as named pairs, act to negotiate both a public and private sense of self. Twins talk demonstrates how it all hangs together. It illustrates how self and nonself can get sorted out differently in different contexts and places.

If working from the ground up and giving voice to twins helps to situate twinship beyond categories and helps to bridge, challenge, or even dissolve dualisms, so does the use of the ethnographic method and the holistic perspective of anthropology. *Twins Talk* is a cross-culturally informed study of talk in action and action in talk. The kind of bricolage generated by research venues and discordant voices (messy stuff) replaces order with disorder as it undermines and destabilizes top-down, one-dimensional forms of ordering that characterize more deductive models. In this sense, ethnography exists, not on Kaprio's (2007) margins of twin research, but in center field. Ethnography thrives on the margins (Westbrook 2008) and twins are good to think with ethnographically because by investigating the margins, we learn more about how the mainstream works.

As Holland and Leander (2004, 219) state, "Subjectivities, sense of self, self worth, social relations and embodied sensibilities are created by experiences of being positioned." Identical twins may well embody negative cultural traits, as in a compromised individuality, but they also embody positive attributes of self, as in equality, fairness, and choice. Whether located on the fault lines as deviant personae or in some kind of liminal betwixt or between states of embodied identity and affinity, identical twins both destabilize and confirm the dualisms, paradoxes, and ambiguities concerning the self as constructed within the history and traditions of Western society. Twins provide a unique perspective from which to view the biological, cultural, and relational working of a strongly defined collateral connection. Twins in practice display an embodied self-image or terrain that is quite flexible (cf. Napier 2005, who doesn't study twins), operate with and against stereotype, embody positive and negative dimensions, and transcend yet confirms categories and dualism. Twins are unique and yet like everyone else.

The talking partners of *Twins Talk*, however, are not questionable beings or co-beings, to be relegated to vaguely defined categories of meaning and who namelessly and passively float around in some sort of rarified, hapless state of liminality. Whether as individuals or as a pair, they exemplify tensions between wider meaning systems and norms associated with key notions, such as the collective and individual, and mutuality and independence. The talking partners played a major role in setting the agenda as they acted and interacted to take over the talking sessions. Through the collaboration of presenting their own narratives, they act to assert, situate, contextualize, and normalize a hypercognitized insider's view. Whether based in narrative, practical experience, observation, or interaction, the talking partners orient themselves within the wider frameworks of society. Reveling in the rebelliousness of the festival itself, the talking partners, who are keenly aware of doing so, make the more hegemonic cultural models of self more visible. Ironically, it is twins who do this, much more so than twins researchers with their avowed interest in "environment."

As twindividuals, they enact a keen self-conscious awareness of dominant, hegemonic construction of self and copresent alternative or reprioritized theories of self (Neisser [1988] calls these subtheories). Festival twins bring their own experientially based and uniquely enskiled practices to identity management. Throughout this book, I have documented the levels of enskilment and kinds of self work that twins must take on as they express, create, and negotiate their identity and relationships. Positioning is important; twins do not just reflect or react to the wider society in which they live, through their own imagination and agency, by posing their twin selves in familiar worlds, but they also challenge existing hegemonies of self by creating or positioning themselves as normative models for all others.

A final way of bringing this together, of incorporating the critical, analytical, and practical aspects of twinship, rests in the fact that I am an anthropologist but, more importantly for this effort, a twin and a rather old one at that. Although I wrote my master's thesis on twins, amazingly I never considered the potential for doing further kinds of twin research.[9] Twins and twinship were interesting, yes, but not enough to do any serious research. Then one day I found myself around age fifty working with one of my graduate students in anthropology at the University of Tromsø in northern Norway. I was in Norway for her thesis defense but also to teach a short course titled Body, Culture, and Society. Early in our acquaintance I had learned that she was a twin. We had a very interesting conversation about each of us being a twin and what the relationship has meant to us. There were certainly some interesting generational differences and probably some cultural ones too, but what came out of our fascinating conversation was how different her experience had been because she was not identical to and was always clearly distinguishable from her sister. It became the practical experience with sameness that interested me.[10] Stimulated by the differences in our experiences, I began to rethink twins both as the familiar and the faraway. Twins Talk has focused on identical twins, reflecting my own twin experience but also my interest in embodiment and identity. There certainly exists an opportunity for a practice approach to other kinds of twinship and other kinds of socio-bio-psycho-cultural analysis.

By being both one of the twins studied as well as one of the people who studies twins, I bring multiple positioned and experientially integrated perspectives to the study of twins and twinship in particular and distinctiveness and diversity on the more general level. *Twins Talk* has been an experiment in both short- and long-term ethnography. The data from Twinsburg were collected in three days; when the conferences and festivals are combined, the total comes to twenty days.[11] Yet, as one of the "natives," I have felt free to bring my own reflexive, autoethnographic accounts into *Twins Talk*. Before this project began, like many of the twins researchers I have admired and criticized, I saw culture largely in terms of beliefs, attitudes, and practices accorded to twins in exotic other cultures. My twinship was relatively unproblematic to me because it was my firsthand, normal, practical experiential world.[12] Being a twin was part of my private life. For the past nine years it has become an important component of my academic life. Being an individual who has a twin sister and being a twin pair is still central to my personal and relational concept of self, even as I begin my sixth decade of life. The Twins Talk Study, whether through participation in festivals or research conferences, introduced me to a shared sense of commonality with other twins and sets of twins where twindom itself has become an aspect of my own special or cultural identity.

NOTES

CHAPTER 1: TWINSCAPES

1. In this sense, DZ or fraternal twins (where twins result from two eggs being fertilized separately by two sperm and whose relationship, genetically speaking, is the same as ordinary brothers and sisters) who look identical would have the same kinds of experiences. MZ or identical twins (where twins result from a single fertilized egg) who were clearly discernable would not. Triplets who all look alike would certainly add another dimension but are not considered here.

2. Holland and Leander (2004, 129) and Conklin and Morgan (1996) are anthropologists who do not study twins, but I find their terms useful. Holland and Leander use the term *deviant persona* to refer to individuals who mold themselves into "walking, talking, feeling, thinking personifications of a culturally imagined type," like "bad girls" or Appalachian "hicks." Conklin and Morgan, paying attention to debates over when life begins, place the human fetus on the fault lines of personhood. The corporeal resemblance of identical twins, however, is a far less common aspect of human experience. Thus, perhaps twins exist on a double fault line.

3. The term *cultural psychology* was coined by the anthropologist Richard Shweder. He defines cultural psychology as "the study of ways subject and object, self and other, psyche and culture, person and contexts, figure and ground, practitioner and practice, live together, require each other, and dynamically, dialectally and jointly make each other up" (Shweder 1991, 73). Although Lindholm (2001) critiques this theory as having limited applicability cross-culturally because it is overly based on Western notions of freedom and personal agency, as *Twins Talk* involves a Western population, this bias is not all that limiting for the analysis that follows.

4. The notions of *selfways, self work,* and *process of selving* entail the active negotiation of identities and interpersonal relations (later referred to as the *twin dynamic*) within the twin dyad. The concepts of *selfways* and *selving processes* have been developed by cultural psychologists (Markus, Mullally, and Kitayama

1997; and Neisser 1997). Selfways refer to characteristic ways of being a person in the world. Selfways include key cultural ideals, values, and actions, such as how to be a good, appropriate, or moral person. When cultural selfways are activated in practice, this is called *selving* or the *process of selving* (Markus, Mullally, and Kitayama 1997, 14). *Self work* refers to the pragmatic ways selves are performed and worked out within a social field; emphasizes action, rather than meaning and thought; and privileges the subjects' (twins') perspectives and experiential worlds (Goodman 2008). By using these concepts to engage, describe, and analyze identical twins within the frameworks of Western culture, I may go well beyond the original intent of those who have put forth these concepts.

CHAPTER 2: TALK

1. As a feminist anthropologist, I have always approached knowledge as positioned and situated, often being critical of the positivist claims of science. My own anthropologically informed critiques of, for example, menopausal syndrome and psychiatric diagnosis, challenge Western medicine and psychiatry for both their cultural biases and androcentrism.

2. While twins talk normalizes twinship by focusing on twin perspectives and self stylings, researchers, as my participation in twin research conferences shows, tend to medicalize or pathologize twinship. While twins see themselves as both exceptional and normal, others, including so-called objective researchers, may portray them as "scary" (Teplica 2004) or as an unsettling presence. As identical twin anthropologists who have shared one research project and more than sixty years of twinship, Dorothy and I challenge this portrayal of "scary." Scary, as we have seen for those who do not have an everyday familiarity or firsthand association with twins. Being a twin implies the greatest firsthand familiarity, a daily lived experience of being a twin. Dorothy (Davis and Davis 2004) wrote this statement about being in the contact zone for a paper we delivered together:

> We are a pair of identical twin anthropologists who do not see
> ourselves as scary, frightening, eerie or as four-legged freaks. One
> of us is left-handed, the other right-handed. When we look at
> each other, we do not see double. We are comfortable with being
> somewhat clone-like, with having palates that are mirror images
> of each other's and with having hair curls and cowlicks in the same
> place that go in opposite directions. Having phantom itches on
> the same place of opposite side shoulders is just a fact of our lives
> and hardly appears as "incredible" to us. (We know whose legs are
> whose.) Despite an embodied similarity that seems to wax and wane
> over our life cycles, we feel that we have separate identities, and
> despite predictable physical similarities in our physical patterns of
> aging, on reflection, we know we lead distinct and different lives.
> Although we are by no means two halves of the same self, what we
> do have is a sense of mutuality, a sense of being connected, that is

not necessarily salient in Western styles of selfhood, but that has been well depicted in other cultural or social settings. Additionally, we feel that our shared births, embodied similarities, the almost constant togetherness and shared experiences that characterized our first 18 years of life, shaped the points of connection between us—the interfaces of self and other or intersubjectivities—across the twin dyad in ways that are different from (but not distinct from) the experiences of most singletons.

3. Each chapter stands by itself so that the chapters may be read in any order. When twins talk about their biologies, psychologies, or their sociocultural circumstances, they not only freely jump from one topic to another but also conflate these artificial academic disciplinary distinctions.

CHAPTER 3: PERFORMANCE

1. Klein (2003) medicalizes this kind of event (which she refers to as twins sharing center stage in the compare and contrast game) as a potentially emotionally crippling experience one twin is doomed to lose.

2. Of course, a twin pair are not strangers to each other. Another exception here would be the twin pairs who have attended Twins Days since they were children and have, over the years, formed friendships that are renewed each year with other sets of twins.

CHAPTER 4: BODY

1. When I was growing up, Dorothy and I were always asked if we were identical or fraternal twins. I certainly am amused by Charlemaine's (2002, 18) use of the term "outbred individuals" to refer to singletons.

2. Jay Joseph (2004, 342), a critic of the genetic essentialism that dominates twin research, states that genetic researchers often portray dissenters as "armchair critics" who have little right to tear down the work of "scientists" and offer alternative explanations.

3. An SNP, or single-nucleotide polymorphism, is a site on a single DNA base where people's genetics differ. Sets of SNPs on the same chromosome are inherited in chunks called *haplotype blocks* or *DNA neighborhoods* (Pálsson 2008). While the indirect hereditarians focus on the inheritance of same traits and what Goodman (2013, 360) refers to as "hyperdeterminitive genes uninfluenced by environment," the direct hereditarians focus on genetic bases of difference among identical twins. Neogenetics focuses on variation between a set of identical twins. Environmental and genetic factors are modeled as interactive. Besides epigenetics and SNPs (or copy number variations), neogenetic phenomena affecting twin differences further include retrotransposons, mitochrondrial DNA, and aneuploidy (Charney 2012).

4. At the 2007 ICTS, there was an entire session focused on the research of David Lykken, one of the Minnesota twins researchers. At the 2007 ICTS, three out of twenty-seven sessions were dedicated to genetics and behavioral issues.

5. See www.davidteplica.com for examples of Teplica's artful photographs of twins. These photos are not all used in his ICTS presentation. For more Teplica photos, see Keith et al. (1995).

6. Tucker (2002) notes that not only was Bouchard a student of Arthur Jensen, but he was the largest single grantee of money from the Pioneer Foundation. Jensen and the Pioneer Foundation are both associated with what is commonly called "scientific racism" (Charlemaine 2002, 12; Tucker 2002). In response to this critique, Bouchard said he would take money from anyone who would support his research (Tucker 2002).

7. When the twins researcher Jay Joseph (2002, 2) states that MZ twins share 100 percent of the same genes, and DZ twins share 50 percent of the same genes on average, he is referring to the fact that identical twins develop from the fertilization of one egg by one sperm. DZ twins result when two different eggs are fertilized by two different sperm. This comparison of two individual humans should not be confused with gene-based comparisons of species—for example, humans may share over 98 percent of their DNA with chimpanzees—or with genomic studies of human variation in which any two humans may differ on the average of 0.1 percent of nucleotide sites.

8. Devereux's (1978, 64) original statement is "If two people do the same thing, then it's not the same thing."

9. Pálsson (2008) notes that genetic researchers interested in population genetics show a tendency to distance themselves from the populations they study. Bouchard (Segal 1999) employed a number of means for distancing researchers from subjects for the purpose of eliminating researcher bias. (An extreme example of distance would be the Scandinavian twin registries where dead twins from hundreds of years ago generate "data" from their birth and death records.)

10. Body pragmatic should be distinguished from Pálsson's term bodily pragmatics which is used to describe include a wide range of scientific skills (explicit) and sociocultural assumptions (implicit) utilized in the hunt for genes by human genome researchers. While Pálsson uses the word bodily, I prefer the word body. This is more than a semantic quibble. Whereas as *bodily* is defined as "of or pertaining to the body," the term *body* is colloquially associated with the person, the physical person, and the individual (American Collegiate Dictionary).

11. On being described as "peas in a pod," Dorothy asks, "How would you like to be compared to a vegetable—a particularly unpopular one at that?"

12. I have been tempted to capitalize the twin *We*, to give it importance equal to the *I* of English grammar, but it would be too confusing.

13. This was a kind of an embarrassing moment for me and shows biases I had developed by immersing myself in the twin literature.

CHAPTER 5: BOND

1. TAMBA and ICOMBO sessions at the ICTS cover issues concerning early child development and debates over the best parenting and childrearing practices and policies for different types (fraternal, identical, same sex, different sex,

twins with different personalities, talents and abilities etc.) of twins. These include practical issues such as securing resources for financially strapped families, appreciating the labor involved in parenting young twins, and learning about birth and early infant care issues.

2. Although I am critical of some examples of the psychological literature, I would not deny its relevance to studies of child and personality development and development of agendas for parenting or educational policies toward twins; nor would I take issue with the fact that some twins do have problems when it comes to the practice of normative selfways. What I do take issue with, however, is the overweening assertion that the twin condition itself is somehow pathological.

3. At the 2007 ICTS, I heard social scientists complain about how they were beginning to feel like second-class citizens at the conference. Complaints were numerous. For example, it was felt that the big plenary sessions tended to feature the research of geneticists, while the social sciences had little meaningful overall representation or input into the ICTS organizational hierarchy. In addition, the timing of the congress had been changed to suit the schedules of geneticists, and future congress venues favored those with generous travel budgets.

CHAPTER 6: CULTURE

1. Quetzalcoatl's twin brother, Xotil, was god of the moon. Clytemnestra was the wife of Agamemnon in Homer's *Iliad*. Clytemnestra and Helen of Troy were actually half sisters. Coming from one egg, Clytemnestra and her twin, Castor, were fathered by Leda's husband, Tyndareus. Also originating in one egg were Helen and her twin, Polydeuces, the result of the rape of their human mother, Leda, by Zeus in the form of a swan.

2. In Norway during this time (2007), women who had worked for six of the last ten months before having a baby would get 56 weeks of maternal leave at 80 percent of their salary or else 46 weeks at 100 percent of their salary. Fathers were required to take a minimum leave of 6 weeks or they lost the benefit. Fathers were also permitted to take 45 weeks' leave at 80 percent of salary or 35 weeks at 100 percent salary. Nonworking women received a lump-sum payment at the birth of a child. Currently, mother-leave is the same and fathers can take up to 14 weeks of leave.

3. In this academic example of the twin trickster tale, Mahmoud Sadri sent his identical twin brother, Ahmad, to lecture in Mahmoud's sociology class. They then interview the students about the switch to sociologically "examine assumptions of the constancy and uniqueness of self in social life" (Sadri and Sadri 1994, 215).

4. Before the development of the new reproductive technologies (such as use of fertility drugs, egg harvesting, in vitro fertilization and embryo transfer) and the explosion of twins' births in natural populations, DZ twinning rates were held to be variable, while MZ rates appeared constant across different populations (Segal 1999).

5. StoryCorps is an oral history project at the American Folklife Center of the U.S. Library of Congress. Excerpted or short broadcasts of the conversations,

originally forty minutes or more, are a regular feature on National Public Radio. Conversations occur between two people who are usually related, such as child and parent or child and grandparent. This twin segment can be accessed at the National Public Radio StoryCorps website, http://storycorps.org.listen /caroline-satcholl-and-janice-morris/.

6. The egocentric self is also known as the Western, capitalist, Protestant, male and/or referential self, as contrasted to the Mediterranean, Asian, indexical, sociocentric self. There is a large and lively literature on this topic (Gaines 1992; Gjerde and Onishi 2000; Holland and Kipnis (1992;) Landrine 1995; Lutz 1990; Kitayama and Markus 1995).

7. Because of the limited number of males who participated in the Twins Talk Study and because neither our informed consent statements nor our questions led the talking partners to anticipate that class would be a topic of study, I save considerations of class and gender for future projects. I have sensed empathetically, or perhaps intuitively, that the talking partners would be offended if their narratives were used in this manner.

8. For example, see Davis (1998, 1997, 1995, 1983a) and Davis and Joakimsen (1997).

9. For example, Japanese twins researchers at the ICTS (Kamakura, Ando, and Ono 2004; Hayakawa, Onoi, and Katoka 2007) fail to mention any differences in typologies of self when comparing Japanese twin data to data collected by Europeans and Americans. To have data that is comparable, they employ the same methods and research instruments in all studies. Twins researchers from Sri Lanka informed me that the major cultural issue that emerged in their twin studies concerned issues of obtaining informed consent with nonliterate populations.

CHAPTER 7: KIN

1. To give my students credit for their creativity, the stories also include fantastical tales of twins as space aliens, princesses, and agents of good and evil. The Arbus twins, in particular, led students to recall the twin in the movie *The Shining*. These were elaborated into some very weird tales.

2. When the life-cycle approach is taken in twin research, it usually focuses on risk factors for adult onset diseases, such as diabetes, multiple sclerosis, Alzheimer's, and degenerative diseases of old age. The data for such studies come from huge, internationally shared twin databases that do not include data on twins' subjective experiences of their twinship (for example, Whitfield et al. [2003]). Farmer's (1996) anthology draws on excerpts from twins in literature. She features literary works in which twins have experienced some sort of dramatic effect as a result their twinship. Piontelli (2008, 9) describes the dark side of an African twinship in Benin, where twins represent closeness and union, but if they are irritated or angered in later life, their bond could turn to a malignant alliance that brings death and misfortune. I particularly like the Benin saying "Never irritate a twin."

3. One of my editors mentioned that readers may be interested in Dorothy's response to the coin flip and asked if she was bitter about losing. I asked Dorothy by e-mail; her response follows. The first part I found predictable; the second after forty-one years clearly surprised me. Dorothy responded, "Not really, I think that is part of the twin thing. We both agreed that it was fair. Although I do think about the fact that since I answered the phone [Dorothy always did] I could have told you that they wanted me."

CHAPTER 8: TWINDIVIDUALS

1. I cannot claim to have coined these terms. Throughout this text I have had grammatical problems with attempting to refer to a twin as part of a *dyad*, two twins as a *dyadic pair*, and twins (singular and plural) in general.

2. Anthropologists have certainly been active in the field of cultural psychology. The anthropologist Richard Shweder (1991 is a pioneer in the field. I have chosen to feature Neisser (1997, 1988), a psychologist, since his take on cultural psychology has more resonance with twin research.

3. In doing so, I also somewhat loosely adapt the outline of Neisser's model, keeping in mind Lindholm's (2001) more culturally informed adaptation of Neisser's categories of self. In Neisser's (1988) discussion, the first two of these categories describe earliest infancy; the latter emerge around age five but develop through life. While overlooking the neurological and developmental details of Neisser's first three categories—describing the emergence of self-knowledge in infancy and early childhood—I still find the foci on interpersonal relationships they enjoin warrant this continued inclusion as categories. Although Lindholm (2001) is an anthropologist, I find that his remodeling of Neisser's five categories of self pays short shrift analytically to intersubjective self/other relationships and the notion of mutuality. Reduced to a list that summarized his own book *Culture and Identity* (Lindholm 2001, 208), these include (1) the experiential, physical, ecologically located body; (2) identity-confirming memories of a unique past; (3) a private, internal self-consciousness composed of personal thoughts, beliefs and ideas; (4) a named personal self, acknowledged, remembered, and confirmed by others; and (5) conceptual or cultural models of self. Kihlstrom, Marchese-Foster, and Klein (1997, 154–56) note six similar features of self. These include representations of self as (1) mental representation or the mind; (2) self-awareness as knowing who we are and what we are like and also as idiographic and contextual; (3) body as the idea of what we look like and as a primitive boundary of self as me and not me; (4) episodic, subjective autobiographical knowledge; (5) social interaction where it is impossible to separate the intrapsychic from the interpersonal; and (6) organized knowledge about beliefs of selves that can be communicated to others.

4. I tried writing this section with both Lindholm's (2001) and Neisser's (1988) categorizations of aspects of self. Neisser's categories seemed to fit better with appreciations of the various aspects of their being that came through as twins talked.

5. Although Neisser (1988) does note that concepts of self vary both within and across different societies and cultures, I would add that the very notion of categories or constructions of self is cultural. What, for example, would the processually selved Amazonian Wari (Conklin and Morgan 1996) have to say?

6. For example, although the talking partners actively opposed twins as a category to singletons as a category, they did not view themselves as twins in opposition to researchers.

7. Other dualisms would include the following: (1) boy/girl, good/evil; (2) single/double, one/two, single/paired, MZ/DZ, singleton/twin; (3) autonomy/mutuality, individual/collective, independent/interdependent, egocentric/sociocentric; (4) open/closed, bounded/unbound, unique/contingent, horizontal/vertical, dominant/subordinate; and (5) concordant/discordant, subject/object, informant/researcher, and us/them.

8. Biersack (1991, 148) comments on relationality as "born of others"; actually, a twin is born with another.

9. My master's thesis, a library thesis, was on the possible effects of culture on the genetics of twinning within a specified population. Dorothy and I both wrote anthropology master's theses on twins. We were both, in different ways, interested in the effects of cultural beliefs and practices on twinning rates. My interest in the thesis was quite accidental. I was walking out of the library and noticed at eye level a book titled *Twins and Super Twins* (Scheinfeld 1967). Wondering if I was a super twin, I briefly looked the book over and discovered the term referred to multiple births of three or more. Intrigued nonetheless, I took the book home and read it with great interest.

10. She also felt that despite shared childhoods and the fact that her sister continued to live nearby, they did not have any kind of special relationship or bond, and even the sister link was quite weak.

11. In the time between the collection of data at Twins Days and the completion of this book, I have been able to use what I have learned or thought about in opportunistic discussions with twins since that time. Unfortunately, most conversations are in the form of me talking to another twin. In addition, however, since our attendance at Twins Days, Dorothy and I have made presentations, separately and together. We also have done media and video interviews. Our own twinship has been kept under the ethnographic lens.

12. This is not the case for other twins researchers who are a twin, as evidenced in the texts of Klein (2003) and Farmer (1996).

REFERENCES

Ainslie, Ricardo. 1985. *The Psychology of Twinship.* Lincoln: University of Nebraska Press.

Amit, Vered, and Jon Mitchell. 2012. Series Preface to *Humans and Other Animals,* by Samatha Hurn, vi. New York: Pluto Press.

Arbus, Diane. 1972. *Diane Arbus: An Arperture Monograph.* Millerton, NY: Rapoport Printing.

Bacon, Kate. 2005. "'It's Good to Be Different': Parent and Child Negotiations of 'Twin' Identity." *Twin Research and Human Genetics* 9 (1): 141–47.

Baete, Frank. 2007. "De Twee Ambachten" [The Twins of Ambatchen]. *Jaargang* 15 (1): 1–171.

Bakhtin, Mikhail. 1994[1965]. "Carnival Ambivalence." Translated by H. Iswolsky, from M. M. Bakhtin, *Rabelais and His World.* In *The Bakhtin Reader,* edited by Pam Morris, 194–255. London: Edward Arnold.

Barrell, Tony. 2003. "Gone with the Twinned." *London Sunday Times Magazine,* November 16.

Barth, Fredrik. 1997. "How Is the Self Conceptualized? Variations among Cultures." In *The Conceptual Self in Context,* edited by Ulric Neisser and David Jopling, 75–91. Cambridge: Cambridge University Press.

Battaglia, Deborah. 1995a. "Fear of Selfing in the American Cultural Imaginary, or 'You Are Never Alone with a Clone.'" *American Anthropologist* 97 (4): 672–82.

———. 1995b. "Problematizing the Self: A Thematic Introduction." In *Rhetorics of Self-Making,* edited by Deborah Battaglia, 1–15. Berkeley: University of California Press.

Beckwith, Jonathan, Lisa Geller, and Sahorta Sakar. 1991. "IQ and Heredity." Letter to Editor. *Science* 12:191.

Behar, Ruth. 1996. *The Vulnerable Observer: Anthropology That Breaks Your Heart.* Boston: Beacon Press.

Benthien, Claudia. 2002. *Skin on the Cultural Border between Self and the World.* New York: Columbia University Press.

Besharat, Mohammad Ali, and Mojataba Habibi. 2004. "A Comparative Study of Interpersonal Problems among Twins and Singletons." Abstract. *Twin Research* 7 (4): 339.

Besnier, Niko. 1994. "The Evidence from Discourse." *Handbook of Psychological Anthropology*, edited by Phillip K. Bock, 197–210. Westport, CT: Greenwood Press.

Biersack, Aletta. 1991. Review of *The Gender of the Gift*, by Marilyn Strathern. *Oceania* 62:147–54.

Bird-David, Nurit. 2004. "Illness-Images and Joined Beings: A Critical Nayaka Perspective on Intercorporeality." *Social Anthropology* 12 (3): 325–40.

Bouchard, Thomas J., Jr. 1984. "Twins Reared Together and Apart: What They Tell Us about Human Diversity." In *Individuality and Determinism: Chemical and Biological Bases*, edited by S. Fox, 147–78. New York: Plenum.

——. 1999. Foreword to *Entwinned Lives: Twins and What They Tell Us about Human Behavior*, by Nancy Segal, ix–x. New York: Dutton.

Bouchard, Thomas, Jr., Matt McGue, Yoon-Mi Hur, and Joseph Horn. 1998. "A Genetic and Environmental Analysis of the California Psychological Inventory Using Adult Twins Reared Apart and Together." *European Journal of Personality* 12:307–20.

Bouchard, Thomas, Jr., and P. Popling. 1993. "Twins: Nature's Twice Told Tale." In *Twins as a Tool of Behavioral Genetics*, edited by T. J. Bouchard Jr. and P. Popling, 1–15. New York: John Wiley and Sons.

Briggs, Charles. 1986. *Learning How to Ask: A Sociolinguistic Appraisal of the Role of the Interview in Social Science Research*. Cambridge: Cambridge University Press.

Brogaard, Berit, and Kristian Marlow. 2012. "Identical Twins Are Not Genetically Identical." *Psychology Today*. http://www.psychologytoday.com/blog/the-superhuman-mind/201211/identical-twins-are-not-identical. Posted November 25.

Bruder, Carl, Arkadiusz Piotrowski, and Antoinet Gijsbers. 2008. "Phenotypically Concordant and Discordant Monozygotic Twins Display Different DNA Copy-Number-Variation Profiles." *American Journal of Human Genetics* 82:763–71.

Bruner, Jerome. 1987. "The Transactional Self." *Making Sense: The Child's Construction of the World*, edited by H. Haste, 81–96. London: Methuen.

——. 1990. *Acts of Meaning*. Cambridge: Harvard University Press.

Burlingham, Dorothy. 1952. *Twins: A Study of Identical Twins with 30 Charts*. London: Imago Publishing Co. Ltd.

Burton, John W. 2001. *Culture and the Human Body*. Long Grove, IL: Waveland Press.

Casey, Conerly, and Robert Edgerton. 2005. Introduction to *A Companion to Psychological Anthropology*, edited by Conerly Casey and Robert Edgerton, 1–14. Malden, MA: Blackwell Publishing.

Casselman, Anne. 2008. "Identical Twins' Genes Are Not Identical." *Scientific American*. http://www.Scientificamerican.com/article.cfm?id=identical-twins-genes-are-not-identical. Posted April 3.

Celtel, Andre. 2005. *Categories of Self: Louis Dumont's Theory of the Individual*. New York: Berghahn Press.

Cerroni-Long, E. L. 2003. "Comparing 'US.'" Paper presented at American Anthropological Association Meeting, Chicago, November 13.

Chakravarty, Sanjib. 1994. "Twinning in Bharmour Teshil (Chambra) of Himachal Pradesh." *Journal of Anthropological Survey of India* 43:179–85.

Charlemaine, Christiane. 2002. "What Might MZ Twin Research Teach Us about Race, Gender and Class Issues?" *Race, Gender and Class* 9 (4): 9–32.

Charney, Evan. 2012. "Behavior Genetics and Postgenomics." *Behavioral and Brain Sciences* 35 (5): 331–410.

Clark, Cindy Dell. 2005. "Tricks of Festival: Children, Enculturation and American Halloween." *Ethos* 33 (2):180–205.

Cody, Kristi. 2005. "Twins Talk: A Set of Twin Anthropologists Conducting Research at the Twins Day Festival in Twinsburg, Ohio." *Society of Anthropology in Community Colleges Newsletter* 12 (2): 3–10.

Cohen, Anthony. 1992. "Self-conscious Anthropology." In *Anthropology and Autobiography*, edited by J. Okely and H. Callaway, 221–41. London: Routledge.

———. 1994. *Self Consciousness: An Alternative Anthropology of Identity.* New York: Routledge.

Colt, George, and Anne Hollister. 1998. "Were You Born That Way?" *Life* 21 (4): 38–47.

Conklin, Beth, and Lynn Morgan. 1996. "Babies, Bodies, and the Production of Personhood in North American and Native Amazonian Society." *Ethos* 24 (4): 557–694.

Conley, Dalton. 2004. *The Pecking Order: Which Siblings Succeed and Why.* New York: Pantheon Books.

Cool, Alison. 2007. "The Secret History of Twin Studies." Unpublished manuscript. New York University.

Csordas, Thomas. 1990. "Embodiment as a Paradigm for Anthropology." *Ethos* 18:5–47.

———. 1994. "The Body as Representation of Being-in-the-World." In *Embodiment and Experience: The Existential Ground of Culture and Self,* edited by Thomas Csordas, 1–24. New York: Cambridge University Press.

———. 1999. "The Body's Career in Anthropology." In *Anthropological Theory Today,* edited by Henrietta Moore, 173–205. Cambridge: Polity Press.

DaMatta, Roberto. 1984. "Carnival in Multiple Planes." In *Rite, Drama, Festival, Spectacle: Rehearsals toward a Theory of Cultural Performance,* edited by J. MacAloon, 208–38. Philadelphia: Institute for Study of Human Issues.

Davis, Dona. 1971. "Biological, Demographic and Cultural Factors in Twinning Frequencies." MA thesis, University of North Carolina at Chapel Hill.

———. 1983a. *Blood and Nerves: An Ethnographic Focus on Menopause.* St. John's, Newfoundland: Memorial University Institute of Social and Economic Research.

———. 1983b. "The Family and Social Change in a Newfoundland Outport." *Culture* 3 (1): 19–32.

———. 1995. "The Cultural Constructions of Menstruation, Menopause and Premenstrual Dysphoric Disorder." In *Gender and Health: An International*

Perspective, edited by Carolyn Sergeant and Caroline Brettell, 57–86. Englewood Cliffs, NJ: Prentice Hall.

———. 1997. "Blood and Nerves Revisited: Menopause and the Privatization of the Body in a Postindustrial Fishery." *Medical Anthropology Quarterly* (1): 3–20.

———. 1998. "The Sexual Disorders of DSM-IV: A Critical Review." *Transcultural Psychiatry* 35 (3): 403–14.

———. 2007. "Same and Different/Fair and Balanced: An Anthropological Analysis of Identical Twins and the Embodiment of Core Cultural Values in North America." Paper presented at the 12th International Congress on Twin Studies, Ghent, Belgium, June 8.

Davis, Dona, and Dorothy Davis. 2004. "Acting the Part: Identity Politics and the Performance of Twinship at Twin Festivals in the USA." Paper presented at the 11th International Congress on Twin Studies, Odense, Denmark, July 2.

———. 2010a. "'I-We, Me-You, Us-Them': Navigating the Hyphens of Intersubjectivity among Sets of Identical Twins." In *Mutuality and Empathy: Self and Other in the Ethnographic Encounter*, edited by Anne Sigfrid Grønseth and Dona Lee Davis, 122–42. Wantage, UK: Sean Kingston Publishing.

———. 2010b. "Dualing Memories: Twinship and the Disembodiment of Identity." In *The Ethnographic Self as Resource: Writing Memory and Experience into Ethnography*, edited by Peter Collins and Anselma Gallinat, 129–49. Oxford: Berghahn.

Davis, Dona, and Lisa Joakimsen. 1997. "Nerves as Status and Nerves as Stigma: Idioms of Distress and Social Action in Newfoundland and Norway." *Qualitative Health Care Research* 7 (3): 370–90.

Davis, Dorothy. 1971. "A Cross-Cultural Study of Beliefs and Practices Surrounding Twin Births Viewed from an Ecological Perspective." Master's thesis, University of North Carolina at Chapel Hill.

de Munck, Victor. 2000. *Culture, Self, and Meaning*. Prospect Heights, IL: Waveland Press.

Devereux, George. 1978. *Ethnopsychoanalysis*. Berkeley: University of California Press.

di Leonardo, Micaela. 2008. "The Female World of Cards and Holidays: Women, Families and the Work of Kinship." In *Reflecting on America: Anthropological Views of U.S. Culture*, edited by Clare Boulanger, 107–18. Boston: Pearson.

Diduk, Susan. 1993. "Twins, Ancestors and Socio-Economic Change in Kedjom Society." *Man* 28:551–71.

Dodd, Evelyn. 2005. "Rupture of Self: What Twins Represent in North American Culture." Paper presented at National College and University Student Research Conference, Lexington, VA, April 22.

Edgerton, Robert. 1985. *Rules, Exceptions and Social Order*. Berkeley: University of California Press.

Ehrenreich, Barbara. 2007. *Dancing in the Streets: A History of Collective Joy*. New York: Metropolitan Books.

Ellis, Carolyn. 2004. *The Ethnographic I: A Methodological Novel about Autoethnography*. Walnut Creek, CA: Alta Mira Press.

Ellis, Carolyn, Tony Adams, and Arthur Bochner. 2011. "Autoethnography: An Overview." *Forum: Qualitative Social Research* 12 (1): 1–14.

Erchak, Gerald. 1992. *The Anthropology of Self and Behavior*. New Brunswick, NJ: Rutgers University Press.

Evans-Pritchard, E. E. 1967. "A Problem of Nuer Religious Thought." In *Myth and Cosmos: Readings in Mythology and Symbolism*, edited by John Middleton, 181–202. Garden City, NJ: Natural History Press.

Ewing, Katherine. 1990. "The Illusion of Wholeness: 'Culture,' 'Self' and the Experience of Inconsistency." *Ethos* 18:251–78.

Fannon, Franz. 1967. *Black Skin, White Mask*. Translated by Charles Lam Markmann. New York: Grove Press.

Farmer, Penelope. 1996. *Two or the Book of Twins and Doubles: An Autobiographical Anthology*. London: Virago.

Featherstone, Mike, with Mike Hepworth and Bryan Turner. 1991. *The Body: Social Process and Culture Theory*. London: Sage Publications.

Finkler, Kaja. 2000. *Experiencing the New Genetics*. Philadelphia: University of Pennsylvania Press.

Fivush, Robyn, and Janine Buckner. 1997. "The Self as Socially Constructed: A Commentary." In *The Conceptual Self in Context*, edited by Ulric Neisser and David Jopling, 176–91. Cambridge: Cambridge University Press.

Ford, Marjorie. 2003. Foreword to *Not All Twins Are Alike: Psychological Profiles of Twinship*, by Barbara Schave Klein, i–ii. Westport, CT: Praeger.

Fowler, Chris. 2004. *The Archaeology of Personhood: An Anthropological Approach*. New York: Routledge.

Fraga, Mario, with Esteban Ballestar, Santiago Ropero, and Fernando Setien. 2005. "Epigenetic Differences Arise during Lifetime of Monozygotic Twins." *Proceedings of the National Academy of Sciences* 102 (30): 10604–9.

Franklin, Sarah, and Helena Ragone. 1998. Introduction to *Reproducing Reproduction: Kinship, Power, and Technological Innovation*, edited by Sarah Franklin and Helena Ragone, 1–15. Philadelphia: University of Pennsylvania Press.

Franklin, Sarah, and Susan McKinnon. 2001. "Relative Values: Reconfiguring Kin and Kinship Studies." In *Relative Values: Reconfiguring Kinship Studies*, edited by Sarah Franklin and Susan McKinnon, 1–25. Durham, NC: Duke University Press.

Frazer, James George. 1900. *The Golden Bough*. London: Macmillan Publishing Company.

Freese, Jeremy, and Brian Powell. 2003. "Tilting at Twindmills: Rethinking Sociological Responses to Behavioral Genetics." *Journal of Health and Social Behavior* 44 (2): 130–35.

Gaines, Atwood. 1992. "From DSM-I to III-R: Voices of Self, Mastery and the Other: A Cultural Constructivist Reading of U.S. Psychiatric Classification." *Social Science and Medicine* 35 (1): 3–24.

Galton, Francis. 1876. "On Twins." *Journal of the Anthropological Institute of Great Britain and Ireland* 5:324–29.

———. " Eugenics: Its Definition, Scope and Aims." *American Journal of Sociology* 10 (1): 1–6.

———. 1975. "The History of Twins, A Criterion of the Relative Powers of Nature and Nurture." *Frazer's* (November): 566–76.

Garro, Linda. 2000. "Remembering What One Knows and the Construction of the Past: A Comparison of Cultural Consensus Theory and Cultural Schema Theory." *Ethos* 3:275– 319.

Gedda, Luigi. 1961. *Twins in History and Science.* Translated by Marco Milani-Comparetti. Springfield, IL: Charles Thomas Publisher.

———. 1995. "The Role of Research in Twin Medicine." In *Multiple Pregnancy: Epidemiology, Gestation and Perinatal Outcome,* edited by Louis Keith, Emile Papiernik, Donald Keith, and Barbara Luke, 3–8. New York: Parthenon Publishing Group.

Geertz, Clifford. 1975. "From the Native's Point of View: On the Nature of Anthropological Understanding." *American Scientist* 63:47–53.

Gergen, David. 1991. *The Saturated Self.* New York: Basic Books.

Gjerde, Per F., and Miyoko Onishi. 2000. "Commentary for Selves, Cultures and Nations: The Psychological Imagination of 'the Japanese' in the Era of Globalization." *Human Development* 43 (4/5): 216–26.

Goffman, Erving. 1959. *The Presentation of Self in Everyday Life.* New York: Doubleday and Company.

Goode, Judith. 2001. "Teaching against Culturalist Essentialism." In *Cultural Diversity in the United States,* edited by Ida Susser and Thomas C. Patterson, 434–56. Malden, MA: Blackwell.

Goodman, Alan. 2013. "Bringing Culture into Human Biology and Biology Back into Anthropology." *American Anthropologist* 115 (3): 359–73.

Goodman, Yehuda. 2008. "Knowledges of the Self and Social Action: A Report from the 2007 AAA Meeting." *Anthropology News* 49 (3): 61.

Granzberg, G. 1973. "Twin Infanticide: A Cross-Cultural Test of Materialistic Explanations." *Ethos* 1 (4): 405–12.

Guarnaccia, Peter. 2001. "Introduction: Contributions of Medical Anthropology to Anthropology and Beyond." *Medical Anthropology Quarterly* 15 (4): 423–27.

Gullestad, Marianne. 1996a. *Everyday Life Philosophers: Modernity, Morality, and Autobiography in Norway.* Oslo: Scandinavian University Press.

———. 1996b. "Modernity, Self and Childhood in the Analysis of Life Stories." In *Self and Society in Autobiographical Accounts,* edited by Marianne Gullestad, 1–40. Oslo: Scandinavian University Press.

———. 1997. "From 'Being of Use' to 'Finding Oneself': Dilemmas of Value Transmission between Generations in Norway." In *Family and Kinship in Europe,* edited by Marianne Gullestad and Martine Segalen, 202–18. London: Pinter.

Gullestad, Marianne, and Martine Segelen, eds. 1997. *Family and Kinship in Europe.* London: Pinter.

Handelman, Don. 1990. *Models and Mirrors: Towards an Anthropology of Public Events*. Cambridge: Cambridge University Press.

Handwerker, W. P. 2002. *Quick Ethnography*. New York: Rowan and Littlefield.

Haraway, Donna. 1991. *Simians, Cyborgs, and Women*. New York: Routledge.

Harden, K. P., E. Turkheimer, and J. C. Loehlin. 2007. "Genotype by Environment Interaction in Adolescents' Cognitive Aptitude." *Behavior Genetics* 33:273–83.

Hardman, Charlotte E. 2000. *Other Worlds: Notions of Self and Emotion among the Lohorung Rai*. New York: Berg.

Harris, Grace. 1981. "Concepts of Individual, Self, and Person in Description and Analysis." *American Anthropologist* 91:599–612.

Harris, Helen. 1995. "Rethinking Heterosexual Relationships in Polynesia." In *Romantic Passion: A Universal Experience?* edited by William Jankowiak, 95–127. New York: Columbia University Press.

Harris, J. R. 1913. *Boanerges*. Cambridge: Cambridge University Press.

Harris, John. 2004. *On Cloning*. New York: Routledge.

Harter, Susan. 1999. *The Construction of the Self: A Developmental Perspective*. New York: Guilford Press.

Hastrup, Kristen. 1995a. *A Passage to Anthropology: Between Experience and Theory*. London: Routledge.

———. 1995b. "The Inarticulate Mind: The Place of Awareness in Social Action." In *Questions of Consciousness*, edited by Anthony P. Cohen and Nigel Rapport, 181–97. London: Routledge.

Hay, David A. 1999. "Adolescent Twins and Secondary Schooling." In *Twin and Triplet Psychology: A Professional Guide to Working with Multiples*, edited by Audrey Sandbank, 121–43. London: Routledge.

Hayakawa, Cai, K. M. Onoi, and K. Katoka. 2007. "Genetic Environmental Factors Affecting Satisfaction Levels of Later Adulthood: A Twin Study from Japan." Paper presented at the 12th International Congress on Twins Studies, Ghent, Belgium, June 10..

Hayden, Corinne. 1998. "A Biodiversity Sampler for the Millennium." In *Reproducing Reproduction: Kinship, Power, and Technological Innovation*, edited by Sarah Franklin and Helena Ragone, 173–205. Philadelphia: University of Pennsylvania Press.

Herdt, Gilbert. 1999. *Sambia Sexual Culture: Essays from the Field*. Chicago: University of Chicago Press.

Hirsch, Jennifer. 2003. *A Courtship after Marriage: Sexuality and Love in Mexican Transnational Families*. Berkeley: University of California Press.

Hollan, Douglas. 2001. "Developments in Person-Centered Ethnography." In *The Psychology of Cultural Experience*, edited by Carmella C. Moore and Holly F. Mathews, 48–67. Cambridge: Cambridge University Press.

Holland, Dorothy and A. Kipnis. 1992. "Metaphors for Embarrassment and Stories of Exposure: The Not-So-Egocentric Self in American Culture." *Ethos* 22:316–42.

Holland, Dorothy, William Lachicotte, Debra Skinner, and Carole Cain. 1998. *Identity and Agency in Cultural Worlds*. Cambridge: Harvard University Press.

Holland, Dorothy, and Kevin Leander. 2004. "Ethnographic Studies of Positioning and Subjectivity: An Introduction." *Ethos* 32 (2):127–29.

Horwitz, Allan, Tami Videon, Mark Schmitz, and Diane Davis. 2003. "Rethinking Twins and Environments: Possible Social Sources for Assumed Genetic
Influences in Twin Research." *Journal of Health and Social Behavior* 44:111–29.

Hubbard, Ruth. 1979. *Women Look at Biology Looking at Women: A Collection of
Feminist Essays*. New York: Pergam Press.

Hubbard, Ruth, and Elijah Wald. 1993. *Exploring the Gene Myth: How Genetic Information Is Produced and Manipulated by Scientists, Physicians, Employers, Insurance Companies and Educators*. Boston: Beacon Press.

Ingham, John M. 1996. *Psychological Anthropology Reconsidered*. Cambridge: Cambridge University Press.

Ingold, Tim. 2004a. "Introduction: Anthropology after Darwin." *Social Anthropology* 12 (2): 177–80.

———. 2004b. "Beyond Biology and Culture: The Meaning of Evolution in a
Relational World." *Social Anthropology* 12 (2): 195–208.

———. 2013. "Prospect: Death of a Paradigm." In *Biosocial Becomings: Integrating
social and Biological Anthropology*, edited by Tim Ingold and Gisli Pálsson,
1–21. Cambridge: Cambridge University Press.

Ingold, Tim, and Gisli Pálsson. 2013. *Biosocial Becomings: Integrating Social and
Biological Anthropology*. Cambridge: Cambridge University Press.

International Twins Association. 2005. *The Stage Is Set for You*. 71st ITA convention announcement flier for Nashville, TN, March 14.

Jackson, Michael. 1989. *Paths Toward a Clearing: Radical Empiricism and Ethnographic Inquiry*. Bloomington: Indiana University Press.

———. 1998. *Minima Ethnographica*. Chicago: University of Chicago Press.

Johnson, Elizabeth. 2005. "Twins Talk: An Anthropological Analysis of ESP Stories." *Society for Anthropology in Community Colleges Newsletter* 12 (2): 10–17.

Johnson, Wendy, Robert Krueger, Thomas Bouchard Jr., and Matt McGrue. 2002.
"The Personality of Twins: Just Ordinary Folks." *Twin Research* 5 (2): 125–31.

Jopling, David A. 1997. "A 'Self of Selves'?" *The Conceptual Self in Context*, edited
by Ulric Neisser and David Jopling, 249–67. Cambridge: Cambridge University Press.

Joseph, Jay. 2002. "Twin Studies in Psychiatry: Science or Pseudoscience?" *Psychiatric Quarterly* 73:71–82.

———. 2004. *The Gene Illusion*. New York: Algora.

Josephides, Lysette. 2010. " Speaking-with and Feeling-with: The Phenomenology of Knowing the Other." In *Mutuality and Empathy: Self and Other in the
Ethnographic Encounter*, edited by Anne Sigfrid Grønseth and Dona Davis,
161–76. Wantage, UK: Sean Kingston Publishers.

Kamakura, Toshimitsu, Juko Ando, and Utaka Ono. 2004. "Genetic and Environmental Factors Shared between Self-Esteem and Temperament Dimensions." Abstract. *Twin Research* 7 (4): 11.

Kamin, L. 1974. *The Science and Politics of IQ*. New York: Halsted Press.

————. 1995. "Behind the Curve." *Scientific American*, February, 99–103.

Kapferer, Bruce. 1984. "The Ritual Process and the Problem of Reflexivity in Sinhalese Demon Exorcisms." In *Rite, Drama, Festival, and Spectacle: Rehearsals Toward a Theory of Cultural Performance*, edited by James MacAloon, 179–207. Philadelphia: Institute for Study of Human Issues. New York: University Press.

Kaprio, Jaakko. 2007. "Twin Studies in the 21st Century." Presidential address at the International Congress on Twin Studies, Ghent, Belgium, June 8.

Keith, Louis, Emile Papiernik, Donald Keith, and Barbara Luke. 1995. *Multiple Pregnancy: Epidemiology, Gestation and Perinatal Outcome*. New York: Parthenon Publishing Group.

Keller, Evelyn. 2000. *The Century of the Gene*. Cambridge: Harvard University Press.

Kihlstrom, John, Lori Marchese-Foster, and Stanley B. Klein. 1997. "Situating Self in Interpersonal Space." In *Conceptual Self in Context*, edited by Ulric Neisser and David Jopling, 154–75. Cambridge: Cambridge University Press.

Kirmayer, Lawrence. 1992. "The Body's Insistence on Meaning: Metaphor as Presentation and Representation in Illness Experience." *Medical Anthropology Quarterly* 6:323–46.

Kitayama, Shinobu, and Hazel Rose Markus. 1995. "Culture and Self: Implications for Internationalizing Psychology." In *The Culture and Psychology Reader*, edited by Nancy Rue Goldberger and Jody Bennet Verdoff, 366–88. New York: New York University Press.

Klein, Barbara Schave. 2003. *Not All Twins Are Alike*. Westport, CT: Praeger.

Koch, Helen. 1966. *Twins and Twin Relations*. Chicago: University of Chicago Press.

Konner, Melvin. 1991. *Why the Reckless Survive*. New York: Penguin Books.

Kusserow, Adrie. 1999. "De-Homogenizing the American Self: Socializing Hard and Soft Individualism in Manhattan and Queens." *Ethos* 27 (2): 210–34.

Laderman, Carol, and Marina Roseman. 1992. Introduction to *The Performance of Healing*, by Laderman and Roseman, 1–16. New York: Routledge.

Landrine, Hope. 1995. "Clinical Implications of Cultural Differences: The Referential vs. Indexical Self." In *The Culture and Psychology Reader*, edited by N. R. Goldberger and Jody B. Veroff, 744–66. New York: New York University Press.

Lebra, Takie. 1992. "Self in Japanese Culture." In *Japanese Sense of Self*, edited by Nancy Rosenberger, 105–20. Cambridge: Cambridge University Press.

LeCompte, Margaret, and Jean Schensul. 1999. *Analyzing and Interpreting Ethnographic Data*. London: Alta Mira Press.

Leonard, M. R. 1961. "Problems in Identification and Ego Development in Twins." *Psychoanalytic Study of the Child* 16:300–320.

Lester, David. 1986. "The Relation of Twin Infanticide to Status of Women, Societal Aggression and Material Well-Being." *Journal of Social Psychology* 126 (1): 57–59.

Levick, Stephen. 2004. *Clone Being: Exploring the Psychological and Social Dimensions*. Boulder: Rowman and Littlefield.

LeVine, Robert A. 1982. *Culture, Behavior, and Personality: An Introduction to the Comparative Study of Psycho-Social Adaptation.* New York: Aldine.

Lévi-Strauss, Claude. 1963. *Structural Anthropology.* New York: Penguin.

———. 1978. *Myth and Meaning: The 1977 Massy Lectures.* London: Rutledge and Kegan Paul.

Lindholm, Charles. 2001. *Culture and Identity.* New York: McGraw-Hill.

Linger, Daniel. 2005. "Identity and Cultural Anthropology." In *A Companion to Psychological Anthropology,* edited by Casey Conerly and Robert Edgerton, 185–200. Malden, MA: Blackwell.

Lock, Margaret. 1993. "Cultivating the Body." *Annual Review of Anthropology* 22:133–55.

———. 2005. "Eclipse of the Gene and Return to Divination." *Current Anthropology* 46:47–70.

———. 2007. "Medical Anthropology: Intimations for the Future." In *Medical Anthropology: Regional Perspectives and Shared Concerns,* edited by Francine Saillant and Serge Genest, 267–88. Malden, MA: Blackwell Publishing.

Lock, Margaret, and Vinh-Kim Nguyen. 2010. *An Anthropology of Biomedicine.* Malden, MA: Wiley-Blackwell.

Lukes, Steven. 1968. "Methodological Individualism Reconsidered." *British Journal of Sociology* 19:19–29.

———. 1973. *Individualism.* Oxford: Basel Blackwell.

Luttrell, Wendy. 1996. *School-Smart and Mother-Wise: Working-Class Women's Identity and Schooling.* New York: Routledge.

Lutz, Catherine. 1990. "Engendered Emotions." In *Language and the Politics of Emotion,* edited by Catherine Lutz and Lila Abu-Lughod, 69–91. Cambridge: Cambridge University Press.

Lykken, David. 1995. *The Antisocial Personalities.* Hilldale, NJ: Lawrence Erlbaum Assoc.

MacAloon, John J. 1984a. Introduction to *Rite, Drama, Festival, Spectacle: Rehearsals toward a Theory of Cultural Performance,* by John MacAloon, 1–18. Philadelphia: Institute for Study of Human Issues.

———. 1984b. "Olympic Games and the Theory of Spectacle in Modern Societies." In *Rite, Drama, Festival, Spectacle: Rehearsals toward a Theory of Cultural Performance,* edited by John MacAloon, 241–80. Philadelphia: Institute for Study of Human Issues.

Maddox, Bruno. 2006. "What a Twins Convention in the Midwest Tells Us about the Future of Humanity." *Discover Magazine,* November, 66–67.

Madrigal, L. 1994. "Twinning Rates in Admixed Costa Rican Populations." *American Journal of Human Biology* 6 (2): 215–18.

Mageo, Jeannette. 2002. Introduction to *Cultural Memory: Reconfiguring History and Identity in the Postcolonial Pacific,* edited by Jeannette Marie Mageo, 1–10. Honolulu: University of Hawaii Press.

———. 2002. "Toward a Multidimensional Model of Self." *Journal of Anthropological Research* 58 (3): 339–65.

Marks, Jonathan. 2001. "'We're Going to Tell These People Who They Really Are': Science and Relatedness." In *Relative Values: Reconfiguring Kinship Studies*, edited by Sarah Franklin and Susan McKinnon, 354–83. Durham, NC: Duke University Press.

———. 2003. "The Profound Relevance in Irrelevance of Biology." Paper presented at the American Anthropological Association Meetings, Chicago, November 21.

———. 2004. "What, If Anything, Is a Darwinian Anthropology?" *Social Anthropology* 12 (2): 181–208.

———. 2012a. "The Biological Myth of Human Evolution." *Contemporary Social Science* 7 (2): 139–65.

———. 2012b. "Recent Advances in Culturonomics." *Evolutionary Anthropology* 21:38–42.

Markus, Hazel Rose, with Patricia Mullally, and Shinobu Kitayama. 1997. "Selfways: Diversity in Modes of Cultural Participation." In *The Conceptual Self in Context*, edited by Ulric Neisser and David Jopling, 13–61. Cambridge: Cambridge University Press.

Marriot, McKim, and Ronald Inden. 1977. "Toward an Ethnosociology of South Asian Caste Systems." In *The New Wind: Changing Identities in South Asia*, edited by K. A. David, 393–416. Chicago: University of Chicago Press.

Mascia-Lees, Frances, and Nancy Johnson Black. 1999. *Gender and Anthropology*. Prospect Heights, IL: Waveland Press.

McCallum, Cecilia. 2000. *Gender and Sociality in Amazonia: How Real People Are Made*. New York: Berg.

McCollum, Chris. 2002. "Relatedness and Self Definition: Two Dominant Themes in Middle-Class Americans' Life Stories." *Ethos* 30 (1/2): 113–39.

McGue, M., and G. Iacono. 2007. "The Minnesota Twin Family Study: David Lykken's Lasting Legacy to Developmental Behavioral Genetics." Abstract. *Twin Research and Human Genetics* 10:42.

M'Charek, Amade. 2005. *The Human Genome Diversity Project: An Ethnography of Scientific Practice*. Cambridge: Cambridge University Press.

Merleau-Ponty, Maurice. 1962. *Phenomenology of Perception*. Translated by James Edie. Evanston, IL: Northwestern University Press.

Meyerhoff, Barbara. 1978. *Number Our Days*. New York: Simon and Schuster.

Middleton, Dwight. 2001. *Exotics and Erotics*. Prospect Heights, IL: Waveland Press.

Miller, Barbara. 2005. *Cultural Anthropology*. Upper Saddle River, NJ: Prentice Hall.

Miller, Peter. 2012. "A Thing or Two about Twins." *National Geographic Magazine*. http://ngm.nationalgeographic.com/2012/01/twins/miller-text. Posted January.

Miller, Shelly. 2003. *Twins Days Festival: Souvenir Program*. Twinsburg, OH: Twinsburg Committee.

Mol, Annemarie. 2003. *The Body Multiple: Ontology in Medical Practice*. Durham, NC: Duke University Press.

Morris, Pam. 1994. "Carnival Ambivalence." In *The Bakhtin Reader*, edited by Pam Morris, 194–255. London: Edward Arnold. [From M.M. Bakhtin, *Rabelais and his World*. 1965. Translated by H. Iswolshy.]

Murray, Dwight. 1993. "What Is the Western Self? On Forgetting David Hume." *Ethos* 21 (1): 3–23.Narayan, Kirin. 1997. "How Native Is the Native Anthropologist?" *American Anthropologist* 95 (3): 671–86.

Neimark, Jill. 1997. "Natures Clones." *Psychology Today*, July/August, 39–69.

Neisser, Ulric. 1988. "Five Kinds of Self Knowledge." *Philosophical Psychology* 1:35–39.

———. 1997. "Concepts and Self-Concepts." In *The Conceptual Self in Context*, edited by Ulric Neisser and David Jopling, 3–12. Cambridge: Cambridge University Press.

Neisser, Ulric, and David Jopling, eds. 1997. *The Conceptual Self in Context*. Cambridge: Cambridge University Press.

Nelkin, Dorothy, and M. Susan Lindee. 2004. *The DNA Mystique: The Gene as Cultural Icon*. Ann Arbor: University of Michigan Press.

Nelson, Christian Kjaer. 1994. "Ethnomethodological Positions on the Use of Ethnographic Data in Conversation Analytic Research." *Journal of Contemporary Ethnography* 23 (3): 307- 329.

Newman, Stuart, and Gerd Muller. 2006. "Genes and Form." In *Genes in Development: A Re- reading of the Molecular Paradigm*, edited by Eva Neumann-Held and Christoph Rehmann-Sutter, 9–73. Durham, NC: Duke University Press.

Ochs, Elinor, and Lisa Capps. 2001. *Living Narrative: Creating Lives in Everyday Storytelling*. Cambridge: Harvard University Press.

Okely, Judith. 1992. "Anthropology and Autobiography: Participatory Experience and Embodied Knowledge." In *Anthropology and Autobiography*, edited by Judith Okely and Helen Callaway, 1–28. London: Routledge.

Ortmeyer, D. H. 1970. "The 'We-Self' of Identical Twins." *Contemporary Psychoanalysis* 6:125–42.

Ortner, Sherry. 2006. *Anthropology and Social Theory: Culture, Power and the Acting Subject*. Durham, NC: Duke University Press.

Overing, Joanna, and Alan Passes. 2000. *The Anthropology of Love and Anger: The Aesthetics of Conviviality in Native Amazonia*. New York: Routledge.

Pálsson, Gisli. 1994. "Enskilment at Sea." *Man* 29 (4): 901–27.

———. 2007. *Anthropology and the New Genetics*. Cambridge: Cambridge University Press.

———. 2013. "Ensembles of Biosocial Relations." In *Biosocial Becomings: Integrating Social and Biological Anthropology*, edited by Tim Ingold and Gisli Pálsson, 22–41. Cambridge: Cambridge University Press.

Parisi, Paolo. 1995. "The Twin Method." In *Multiple Pregnancy: Epidemiology, Gestation and Perinatal Outcome*, edited by Louis Keith, Emile Papiernik, Donald Keith, and Barbara Luke, 9–20. New York: Parthenon Publishing Group.

———. 2003. "Twin Research, and Its Multiple Births and Expressions: A Short, Personal Voyage through Its Scope, History and Organization." *Twin Research* 7 (4): 309–17.

Peltonen, Leena. 2007. "The GenomEUtwin Project." Keynote lecture at the Twelfth International Congress on Twin Studies, Ghent, Belgium, June 9.

Penninkilampi-Kerola, Varpu, Jaako Kaprio, Irma Moilanen, Hanna Ebeling, and Richard Rose. 2004. "Co-Twin Dependence and Twins' Psycho-Emotional Well-Being and Health from Adolescence to Early Adulthood: A Longitudinal Study of Development and Health of Five Consecutive Birth Cohorts of Finnish Twins." Abstract. *Twin Research* 7 (4): 371–72.

Perola, M. S. Sammalisto, J. Kettunen, T. Hiekkalinna, and L. Peltonon. 2007. "Combined Genome Scans for Body Stature in 6602 European Twins." Abstract. *Twin Research and Human Genetics* 10:46.

Piontelli, Alessandra. 1992. *From Fetus to Child: An Observational and Psychoanalytic Study.* London: Travistock and Routledge.

———. 1999. "Twins in Utero: Temperament Development and Intertwin Behavior Before and After Birth." In *Twin and Triplet Psychology: A Professional Guide to Working with Multiples,* edited by Audry Sandbank, 7–18. London: Routledge.

———. 2008. *Twins in the World: The Legends They Inspire and the Lives They Lead.* New York: Palgrave Macmillan.

Plomin, R., J. C. Defries, G. E. McClearn, and R. Rutter. 1997. *Behavioral Genetics.* New York: W. H. Freeman.

Prainsack, Barbara. 2006. "The 'Conflict of Conflicts': Human Reproductive Cloning and the Creation of New Citizens." Paper presented at European Consortium for Political Research Workshop on the Comparative Dynamics of Problem Framing: How Science and Power Speak to Each Other, University of Vienna, Vienna, Austria.

Prainsack, Barbara, L. F. Cherkas, and T. D. Spector. 2006. "Twins: A Cloning Experience." *Social Science and Medicine* 63:2739–52.

———. 2007. "Attitudes towards Human Reproductive Cloning, Assisted Reproduction and Gene Selection: A Survey of 4,600 British Twins." *Human Reproduction* 22 (8): 2302–8.

Prainsack, Barbara, Y. Hashiloni-Dolev, A. Kasher, and J. Prainsack. 2010. "Attitudes of Social Science Students in Israel and Austria towards Belated Twins Scenario: An Exploratory Study." *Public Understanding of Science* 19 (4): 435–51.

Quinn, Naomi. 2005a. *Finding Culture in Talk: A Collection of Methods.* New York: Palgrave.

———. 2005b. Introduction to *Finding Culture in Talk: A Collection of Methods,* edited by Naomi Quinn, 1–34. New York: Palgrave Macmillan.

Rajan, Kaushik. 2005. "Subjects of Speculation: Emergent Life Sciences and Market Logics in the United States and India." *American Anthropologist* 107 (1): 19–31.

Ramirez-Goicoechea, Eugenia. 2013. "Life-in-the-Making: Epigenesis, Biocultural Environments and Human Becomings." In *Biosocial Becomings: Integrating Social and Biological Anthropology*, edited by Tim Ingold and Gisli Pálsson, 60–83. Cambridge: Cambridge University Press.

Rapport, Nigel. 1997. *The Transcendent Individual: Towards a Literary and Liberal Anthropology*. London: Routledge.

Rapport, Nigel, and Joanna Overing. 2000. *Social and Cultural Anthropology: Key Concepts*. London: Routledge.

Reardon, Jenny. 2005. *Race to the Finish: Identity and Governance in the Age of Genomics*. Princeton: Princeton University Press.

Reischer, Erica, and Katheryn Koo. 2004. "The Body Beautiful: Symbolism and Agency in the Social World." *Annual Review of Anthropology* 33:297–317.

Richardson, Laurel. 1990. "Narrative Sociology." *Journal of Contemporary Ethnography* 19 (1): 116–35.

Rogoff, Barbara, and Gilda Morelli. 1994. "Cross-Cultural Perspectives on Children's Development." In *Handbook of Psychological Anthropology*, edited by Philip K. Bock, 231–42. Westport, CT: Greenwood Press.

Rosaldo, Renato.1986. "Ilongot Hunting as Story and Experience." In *The Anthropology of Experience*, edited by Victor W. Turner and Edward M. Bruner, 97–138. Chicago: University of Illinois Press.

Rosambeau, Mary. 1987. *How Twins Grow Up*. London: The Bodley Head.

Rosch, Eleanor. 1997. "Mindfulness Meditation and the Private (?) Self." In *The Conceptual Self in Context*, edited by Ulric Neisser and David Jopling, 185–202. Cambridge: Cambridge University Press.

Sadri, Mahmoud, and Ahmad Sadri. 1994. "Doppelganger: Twins' Disruption of the Assumption of Constancy and Uniqueness of Self in Everyday Life." *Symbolic Interaction* 17 (2): 203–23.

Sahlins, Marshall. 1976. *The Use and Abuse of Biology: An Anthropological Critique of Sociobiology*. Ann Arbor: University of Michigan Press.

Sandbank, Audrey. 1999a. *Twin and Triplet Psychology: A Professional Guide to Working with Multiples*. London: Routledge.

———. 1999b. "Personality, Identity and Family Relationships." In *Twin and Triplet Psychology: A Professional Guide to Working with Multiples*, edited by Audrey Sandbank, 167–85. London: Routledge.

———. 2007. "A Case Study of the Breakdown of an Interpair Relationship." Paper presented at the International Congress on Twin Studies, Ghent, Belgium, June 10.

Schave, Barbara, and Janet Ciriello. 1983. *Identity and Intimacy in Twins*. New York: Praeger.

Scheinfeld, Amran. 1967. *Twins and Super Twins*. London: Chatto and Windus.

Schensul, Stephen, Jean Schensul, and Margaret LeCompte. 1999. *Essential Ethnographic Methods*. London: Alta Mira Press.

Scheper-Hughes, Nancy. 1994. "Embodied Knowledge: Thinking with the Body in Critical Medical Anthropology." In *Assessing Cultural Anthropology*, edited by Robert Borofsky, 229–42. New York: McGraw Hill.

Scheper-Hughes, Nancy, and Margaret Lock. 1986. "The Mindful Body: A Prolegomenon to Future Work in Medical Anthropology." *Medical Anthropology Quarterly* 1 (1): 6–41.

Schildkrout, Enid. 2004. "Inscribing the Body." *Annual Review of Anthropology* 33:319–44.

Segal, Nancy. 1985. "Holocaust Twins: Their Special Bond." *Psychology Today* 19:52–58.

———. 1999. *Twins and What They Tell Us about Human Behavior.* New York: Penguin Putnam.

———. 2005. *Indivisible by Two: Life of Extraordinary Twins.* Cambridge: Harvard University Press.

———. 2006. "Psychological Features of Human Reproductive Cloning: A Twin-Based Perspective." *Psychiatric Times* 23 (14): 1–3.

Segal Nancy, with Scott Hershberger and Sara Arad. 2003. "Meeting One's Twin: Perceived Social Closeness and Familiarity." *Evolutionary Psychology* 1:70–95.

Segalen, Martine. 1995. Introduction to *Family and Kinship in Europe,* edited by Marianne Gullestad and Martine Segalen, 1–13. London: Pinter Press.

Shweder, Richard. 1991. *Thinking through Cultures: Expeditions in Cultural Psychology.* Cambridge: Harvard University Press.

Spector, Tim. 2012. *Identically Different: Why You Can Change Your Genes.* London: Weidenfeld and Nicolson.

Stewart, Elizabeth. 2003. *Exploring Twins: Towards a Social Analysis of Twinship.* New York: Palgrave Macmillan.

———. 2007. "Birth Order: A New Variable?" Abstract. *Twin Research and Human Genetics* 10:53.

Stoeltje, Beverly. 1978. "Cultural Frames and Reflections: Ritual, Drama and Spectacle." *Current Anthropology* 19:450–51.

Stone, Linda. 2010. *Kinship and Gender.* Boulder, CO: Westview.

Strathern, Marilyn. 1987. "The Limits of Auto-Anthropology." In *Anthropology at Home,* edited by Anthony Jackson, 16–37. London: Routledge.

———. 1988. *The Gender of the Gift.* Berkeley: University of California Press.

———. 1992. *After Nature.* Cambridge: Cambridge University Press.

———. 1995. "Nostalgia and the New Genetics." In *Rhetorics of Self-Making,* edited by Deborah Battaglia, 97–120. Berkeley: University of California Press.

Synnott, Anthony. 1993. *The Body Social: Symbolism, Self and Society.* London: Routledge.

Szerzsynski, Bronislaw, Wallace Heim, and Claire Waterton. 2003. Introduction to *Nature Performed: Environment, Culture and Performance,* edited by Bronislaw Szerzsynski, Wallace Heim, and Claire Waterton, 1–14. Oxford: Blackwell.

Tabor, J., and E. Joseph. 1961. "The Simultaneous Analysis of a Pair of Identical Twins and the Twinning Reaction." *Journal of the Psychoanalytic Study of the Child* 16:275–99.

Taylor, Janelle. 2005. "Surfacing the Body Interior." *Annual Review of Anthropology* 34:741–56.

Tellegen, Auke, Thomas Bouchard Jr., Kimberly Wilcox, Nancy Segal, David Lykken, and Stephen Rich. 1987. "Personality Similarity in Twins Reared Apart and Together." *Journal of Personality and Social Psychology* 54 (6): 1031–39.

Teplica, David. 1994. "Special Photography." Photos are unpaged chapter headings. In *Multiple Pregnancy: Epidemiology, Gestation and Perinatal Outcome*, edited by Louis Keith, Emile Papiernik, Donald Keith, and Barbara Luke. New York: Parthenon Publishing Group.

———. 2004. "The Twinsburg Archive." Presidential Speech. 11th International Congress on Twin Studies. Odense, Denmark.

———. 2009. "Plastic Surgery [and] Photography." Accessed July 2009. www.davidteplica.com/mfa.html.

Thornton, A. 2001. "The Developmental Paradigm, Reading History Sideways and Family Change." *Demography* 38 (40): 449–66.

Throop, Jason C. 2003. "Articulating Experience." *Anthropological Theory* 3 (2): 219–41.

Truscott, Barbara, Derek Paulson, and Robin Everall. 1999. "Participants' Experiences Using Concept Mapping." *Alberta Journal of Educational Research* 45 (3): 320–23.

Tucker, William H. 2002. *The Funding of Scientific Racism: Wickliffe Draper and the Pioneer Fund*. Urbana: University of Illinois Press.

Turkheimer, Eric, Andreana Haley, Mary Waldron, Brain D'Onofrio, and Irving Gottesman. 2003. "Socioeconomic Status Modifies Heritability of IQ in Young Children." *American Psychological Society* 14 (6): 623–28.

Turner, Terence. 1994. "Bodies and Anti-Bodies: Flesh and Fetish in Contemporary Social Theory." In *Embodiment and Experience: The Existential Ground of Culture and Self*, edited by Thomas Csordas, 27–47. New York: Cambridge University Press.

Turner, Victor. 1967. *The Forest of Symbols: Aspects of Ndembu Ritual*. London: Cronell University Press.

———. 1969. *The Ritual Process: Structure and Anti-structure*. London: Routledge, Kegan and Paul.

———. 1984. "Liminality and the Performance Genres." In *Rite, Drama, Festival, Spectacle: Rehearsals toward a Theory of Cultural Performance*, edited by James MacAloon, 19–41. Philadelphia: Institute for Study of Human Issues.

Van Wolputte, Steven. 2004. "Hang On to Yourself: Of Bodies, Embodiment and Selves." *Annual Review of Anthropology* 33:251–69.

Visweswaran, Kamala. 1993. *Fictions of Feminist Ethnography*. Minneapolis: University of Minnesota Press.

Wagner, Joseph. 2003. "Thousands Revel in Seeing Double." *Cleveland Plain Dealer*, August 3.

Walby, C. 2002. "Biomedicine, Tissue Transfer and Intercorporeality." *Feminist Theory* 33:239–54.

Waller, Niels, Brian Kojetin, Thomas Bouchard Jr., David Lykken, and Arluke Tellegen. 1990. "Genetic and Environmental Influences in Religious Interests, Attitudes, and Values." *Psychological Science* 1:138–42.

Weiss, Gail. 1999. *Body Images: Embodiment as Intercorporeality.* New York: Routledge.

Weiss, Rick. 2005. "Twin Data Highlight Genetic Changes." *Washington Post,* July 4. http://washingtonpost.com/wp-dyn/content/article2005/07/04AR2005070400845.html.

Westbrook, David. 2008. *Navigators of the Contemporary: Why Ethnography Matters.* Chicago: University of Chicago Press.

Weston, Kath. 1991. *Families We Choose: Lesbians, Gays, and Kinship.* New York: Columbia University Press.

Whitfield, Keith, Dwayne Brandon, Sebrina Wiggins, George Volger, and Gerry McClearn. 2003. "Does Intact Pair Status Matter in the Study of African American Twins? The Carolina African American Twin Study of Aging." *Experimental Aging Research* 29:407–23.

Whittaker, Elvi. 1992. "The Birth of the Anthropological Self and Its Career." *Ethos* 20 (2): 191– 219.

Wierzbicka, Anna. 2005. "Empirical Universal of Language as a Basis for the Study of Other Human Universals and as a Tool for Exploring Cross-Cultural Differences." *Ethos* 33 (2): 256–91.

Wikan, Unni. 1991. "Toward an Experience Near Anthropology." *Cultural Anthropology* 6:288–305.

Wilder, Harris. 1904. "Duplicate Twins and Double Monsters." *American Journal of Anatomy* 3:287–472.

Wright, Lawrence. 1997. *Twins and What They Tell Us about Who We Are.* New York: John Wiley and Sons.

Wright, William. 1998. *Born That Way: Genes/Behavior/Personality.* New York: Routledge.

Zazzo, René. 1976. "The Twin Condition and the Couple Effect on Personality Development." *Acta Geneticae Medicae et Gemellologiae* 25:343–52.

———. 1978. "Genesis and Peculiarities of the Personalities of Twins." *Progress in Clinical and Biological Research* 24:1–11.

INDEX

agency. *See* choices and decision making
Ainslie, Ricardo, 136
anthropology, 170, 174–78, 180, 204, 206;
 biocultural, 266–67
Anthrosource, 177
Arbus, Diane, 85, 208, 298n1
autoethnography, 33, 275, 291

Bakhtin, Mikhail, 57, 67
Barrell, Tony, 66, 68
Battaglia, Deborah, 77, 94, 116, 128, 135,
 164, 187
Benin twins, 298n2
Besnier, Niko, 209
Biersack, Aletta, 300n8
biomedicine, 4–5, 39, 79–80
biosocial theory, 3, 13, 80, 88–89, 94, 96, 98,
 204, 266–67, 275
Bird-David, Nurit, 180, 181–82
body pragmatic, defined, 102, 296n10
Bouchard, Thomas, Jr., 82–83, 84–85, 86–87,
 89, 93, 99, 296n6, 296n9
Bruner, Jerome, 21
Burlingham, Dorothy, 203

Cameroon twins, 178
Charlemaine, Christiane, 295n1
Charney, Evan, 81–82
choices and decision making, 197–203,
 207–8, 262
cloning, 4, 10, 67–68, 77, 81, 93–97, 139
Cody, Kristi, 20, 25–26, 32, 34, 58, 61, 63–64,
 66, 68, 167, 239
Cohen, Anthony, 16, 20, 137, 158, 161, 163
Conklin, Beth, and Lynn Morgan, 180–82,
 293n2
Conley, Dalton, 118, 132
Cool, Allison, 26

cultural psychology, 9–11, 38, 102–3, 172, 175,
 184, 263, 273, 275, 299n2; defined, 293n3
culture, defined, 172, 175

Davis, Dorothy, 10, 11, 16, 18–20 *and passim*,
 294n2, 299n3, 300n9
Devereux, George, 78, 98, 296n8
Diduk, Susan, 178–79
di Leonardo, Micaela, 207, 232
DNA, 4, 79, 83, 90, 94, 106, 295n3
dualisms, 12, 15, 284, 285–86, 300n7
DZ. *See* MZ

Ehrenreich, Barbara, 74
Ellis, Carolyn, 33
enskilment, defined, 102, 109
epigenetics, 4, 90, 92, 124
equality, 191–97
Erchak, Gerald, 189
ethnology and ethnography, 170, 174, 176,
 179, 203, 263, 275, 288–89, 291
Evans-Pritchard, E. E., 177–78
Ewing, Katherine, 34
extrasensory perception, 121–22, 124, 189

fairness, 193–97
Farmer, Penelope, 6, 285, 298n2
fault lines concept, 6–8, 14, 103, 106, 153,
 167, 183, 273–74, 289
Franklin, Sarah, and Susan McKinnon,
 207–8
Frazer, James George, 177

Gedda, Luigi, 132–33, 148, 157, 174–75
Geertz, Clifford, 184
genetics, 3, 4, 10, 79, 80–93, 98–99, 124,
 169–70, 173, 202, 206–7, 260, 265–67,
 295nn2–4, 296n9

319

GenomeEUtwin Project, 83, 91, 92
Goodman, Alan, 94, 266, 295n3
Gullestad, Marianne, 17, 27

Haitian twins, 3
Handelman, Don, 54, 76
Harris, Helen, 161
Harris, John, 88
Harris, J. Rendel, 174–75
Harrison, Angela, 21, 29
Harter, Susan, 154, 162–63, 166, 179, 184
Hastrup, Kristen, 33, 52, 55
Herdt, Gilbert, 1, 6
heredity (and hereditarians), 4, 80–81, 82–83,
    85, 88–89, 91, 93, 100, 101–2, 173, 295n3
Hollan, Douglas, 33
Holland, Dorothy, and Kevin Leander, 289,
    293n2
Hubbard, Ruth, 37
Human Relations Area Files, 177

individualism, 17, 55, 68, 76–77, 94, 98, 103–
    4, 111, 116, 131, 148, 173, 183, 185, 189, 202,
    220, 272, 286–87; "soft," 202; Western
    origins, 188
Ingold, Tim, 14, 99, 166, 266, 275
intercorporeality, defined, 102, 117, 119
International Congress of Twin Studies
    (ICTS), 38–39, 78–80, 84, 91–92, 123, 135,
    146, 169–71, 204, 295n4, 296n1, 297n3
International Council of Multiple Births
    Organization (ICOMBO), 39, 91, 126,
    135, 296n1
International Twins Association (ITA), 19,
    28, 36, 56, 57–59, 73–76, 123, 233
intersubjectivity, 276, 278

Jackson, Michael, 152, 154–55, 157, 160, 162,
    263, 285
Jensen, Arthur, 296n6
Jopling, David A., 14, 272
Joseph, Jay, 191–92, 295n2, 296n7

Kamin, Leon J., 132
Kaprio, Jaakko, 83, 169–70, 174, 203, 289
Kihlstrom, John, et al., 299n3
kinship, 206–9, 259–62
kin work, 232, 246, 253, 256
Klein, Barbara Schave, 134, 174, 295n1
Kusserow, Adrie, 202

Laderman, Carol, and Marina Roseman, 57
Levick, Stephen, 134

Lévi-Strauss, Claude, 176, 177–78
Lindholm, Charles, 1, 11, 13, 183, 186, 188–92
    passim, 197, 202, 268, 293n3, 299nn3–4
Lock, Margaret, and Vinh-Kim Nguyen,
    124
Lukes, Steven, 188, 197
Lykken, David, 20, 101, 271, 272, 295n4

Maddox, Bruno, 16, 67–68, 72, 76
Markus, Hazel Rose, et al., 167, 172
McCollum, Chris, 72
Meyerhoff, Barbara, 156
Miller, Barbara, 207
Miller, Peter, 90
Minnesota Twins Studies, 82–83, 84–85,
    87, 89
Mol, Annemarie, 6
MZ (monozygotic/identical) and DZ
    (dizygotic/fraternal) distinctions
    and terminology, 59, 78–81, 82, 91,
    93, 99, 100, 102, 107, 123–24, 282–83,
    293n1, 296n7, 297n4 {author: delete
    parenthetical explanations if you think
    them unnecessary}

narrative, 10–11, 18, 20–22, 81, 209, 271–73
nature/nurture debates, 13, 80, 85, 87,
    124–25, 265
Ndembu people, 3, 178
Neisser, Ulric, 263, 272, 275–84, 286, 299–
    300nn2–5
Nelkin, Dorothy, and M. Susan Lindee, 88
Nuer people, 178
Nyaka people, 173, 180, 181–83, 186, 204

Okely, Judith, 12, 39
Ortmeyer, D. H., 133–34

Pálsson, Gisli, 1, 82, 102–3, 109, 127, 207, 263,
    266–67, 275, 296n9
Parisi, Paolo, 82, 174
Peltonen, Leena, 83
personhood. See selfhood
Pioneer Foundation, 296n6
Piontelli, Alessandra, 66, 133, 135, 175,
    176–77, 179, 184, 189, 298n2
Plomin, Robert, et al., 186
Prainsack, Barbara, et al., 97–98, 102, 130,
    288
privacy, 189–90
public events, defined, 56–57

Quinn, Naomi, 16, 21–22, 39, 268